The practical Christian

The
practical Christian

The message of James

by

Gordon J. Keddie

 EVANGELICAL PRESS

EVANGELICAL PRESS
12 Wooler Street, Darlington, Co. Durham, DL1 1RQ, England.

© Evangelical Press 1989
First published 1989

British Library Cataloguing in Publication Data

Keddie, Gordon J. The practical Christian.
1. Bible. N. T. James.
Critical Studies.
I. Title.

ISBN 0-85234-261-6

Cover picture reproduced by courtesy of Dave Pepler.

Typeset by Outset Graphics, Hartlepool.
Printed in Great Britain by The Bath Press, Avon.

To
JANE
a truly practical Christian
and a wonderful wife and mother
Proverbs 31:28-29

Contents

Preface

When historians get round to assessing the Christian church in the last few decades of the twentieth century, they will be confronted by a startling paradox. Never before had there been such a pervasive emphasis upon 'practical' Christianity. Never before had there been a comparable torrent of 'how to' books, covering every aspect of life, right down to the finest of details (although from a myriad of conflicting viewpoints). Never had there been such interest in Christian social activism on such a wide range of issues – not even in the days of the anti-slavery and temperance movements. Yet all this coincided with the decline of basic Christian morality within the churches and the most startling advance of biblical and doctrinal illiteracy among church members since that medieval darkness which preceded and precipitated the sixteenth-century European Reformation.

This reflects, no doubt, the emerging tragedy of our computer age; we have marvellous electronic communications technology but, it seems, very little to communicate! We seem to be all journey and no destination: we are all medium and no message. This is perhaps to be expected from a world that has cut itself off from the Word of God as the real revelation of the mind of the living God. But the church ought to know better. Why then are we so much at sea on basic issues of biblical teaching and morality? I believe it is because, in keeping with the spirit of the age, Christians have cut themselves adrift from the anchor of revealed truth, from what the Scriptures actually teach. 'Practical' Christianity has become 'pragmatic Christianity'. The basis for decision-making has owed more to the weighing up of 'strategies' and 'options', with a view to what 'works', than to an unshakeable commitment to the bedrock of biblical principle in the context of a life walked by faith rather than sight. The prevailing trend has been increasingly in the direction of finding ways of explaining why simple and straightforward biblical teachings should be reinterpreted to allow wider latitude in faith and practice. Uncertainty appears to be the universally accepted starting-point for any discussion of the norms of Christian belief and behaviour – even within the churches. Every camp has its 'scholars'. And the more footnotes, the more flexibility. Riding on a veritable tidal wave of contrary plausibilities, a new universalism is sweeping through the evangelical world, in which more and more people are 'right' and fewer 'wrong', even though they all contradict one another.

The epistle of James is perfectly adapted to be an antidote to muddled and latitudinarian thinking. There is an ethical crispness to it that places the issues relentlessly in the foreground of the mind. James gives a definitive prescription for truly practical Christianity. Here is the practical Christian in a nutshell, yet with a fulness that, for the richness of its challenge, will not be exhausted by a lifetime of discipleship.

When Thomas Manton began his epic and incomparable exposition of James, he remarked to his congregation: 'We are all apt to divorce comfort from duty, and to content ourselves with a "barren and unfruitful knowledge" of Jesus Christ (2 Peter 1:8) as if all that he required of the world were only a few naked, cold and inactive apprehensions of his merit, and all things were so done *for us*, that nothing remained to be done *by us*.'[1] Manton says of his own time – the England of the seventeenth century – that it was the 'wretched conceit' of many either to turn the sweetness of God's grace into 'looseness' or the power of his grace into 'laziness'. One says God is too nice to be hard on me for being a less than active Christian, while the other says God is so surely accomplishing his will that he doesn't need me as much as all that! Human nature has not changed much in 300 years! We therefore constantly need a recurrent emphasis upon the practical instructions of God's Word – the words that say, 'Do this' and 'Don't do that', and address the nuts and bolts of daily attitudes and actions. Herein lies the great usefulness of the epistle of James: it assumes the great doctrines of salvation taught elsewhere in the New Testament and proceeds, somewhat like the Proverbs but with a greater evangelical richness, to give detailed practical instruction on basic Christian behaviour. It is a manual for practical godliness, which, when truly written on our hearts with power, will transform us as individual believers and as Christian fellowships. Everything is here: facing trials, blaming God for misfortunes, snobbery, sharp tongues, faith and works, squabbling in churches, worldliness, use of money and so on: there is a word for us all to lay up in our hearts and put into practice in our lives.

As with everything I have written in the past, this book has emerged from the pastoral ministry, the unchanging goal of which is to address the Word of God to the hearts and consciences of men and women, in terms of the claims of Jesus Christ. Jesus does not want us to wallow in a quagmire of doubt and indecision over doctrine or practice. He wants us to change in his very definite direction and become established in the truth. This little volume goes out in the hope that it may help many to be truly 'practical Christians'.

Gordon J. Keddie
State College,
Pennsylvania, USA.
July 1989

Introduction – James and his readers

'James, a servant of God and of the Lord Jesus Christ, to the twelve tribes scattered among the nations: Greetings' (James 1:1).

The most famous comment ever made on the epistle of James surely came from the pen of the sixteenth-century Reformer Martin Luther. He called it 'a right strawy epistle' which, in his view, had 'no evangelical character'. He felt justified in his opinion by the lack of any reference in James to the resurrection of Christ and the excessive attention, as he saw it, to good works in the Christian life, without a similar or greater weight being put on justification by faith alone.[1] This cannot be said to be one of Luther's more discerning observations, but it serves to remind us that even the best of God's servants can have their blind spots! It also reminds us that the epistle of James is a powerful and controversial part of the New Testament. James, as we shall see, assumes the doctrinal framework so carefully enunciated in the Pauline epistles and confines himself to a searching exposition of what it means to *do* the Word, as distinct from merely hearing it and letting it go in one ear and out of the other. This is the gospel as it ought to be lived – the gospel as it is really believed!

Who is James?

James introduces himself as **'a servant of God and the Lord Jesus Christ'**. He makes no attempt to impress us with any additional credentials. He does not 'name drop', for he might have said, 'I am the brother of the Lord Jesus Christ.' He makes no attempt to bask in the reflected glory of his natural relationship to the Lord, but is content with the simple title of 'servant', which in the Greek of the New Testament indicates an absolute, permanent and, not least, loving subjection to his Saviour. But why do we identify this James, who is so sparing in his self-introduction, as the brother of Jesus?

The New Testament mentions four men called James and from what we are able to glean about each of them, we are able to deduce with a fair degree of certainty which is the most probable candidate for the authorship of the epistle of James. Two of these men belonged to the Twelve – the disciples of Jesus – a third was the father of one of the Twelve and the fourth was the Lord's brother.

1. James the son of Zebedee was the brother of the apostle John (Matthew 4:21; Luke 6:14). He was to be the first martyr among the apostles, suffering under Herod Agrippa around A.D. 44 (Acts 12:1-2). His early death rules him out as author of the epistle, which clearly addresses a later and more developed church than we would expect in little over a decade after Pentecost.

2. James the son of Alphaeus (Luke 6:15), also called 'James the younger' (Mark 15:40), was probably the brother of Matthew (cf. Mark 2:14). He is only briefly mentioned in the New Testament and indeed drops from sight before James the son of Zebedee. He has consequently never been regarded as the author of the epistle.

3. James the father of the apostle Judas – not Judas Iscariot but probably the 'Jude' who authored the epistle of Jude – is apparently only mentioned to identify his son (Luke 6:16; Acts 1:13).[2] He is not the author.

4. James the brother of the Lord (Matthew 13:55; Mark 6:33) was not an apostle, but certainly has all the attributes of the writer of the epistle that bears his name. He was converted only after Jesus' death (John 7:5), but went on to lead the Jerusalem Church in the years prior to his martyrdom in A.D. 62 (Galatians 1:19; 2:9; Acts 12:17; 15:13-21; 21:18). His role in the church and the time in which he exercised leadership – the years running up to the cataclysmic destruction of the old Israel in A.D. 70 – as well as the contents of the epistle, all point to him as the author. 'We must realize',

writes the modern commentator James Adamson, 'that this epistle is alive with the personality of its author and other influences of which we here name only these – the Galilean background, the home bond between James and Jesus, the gospel of Jesus, his Christian mandate to the disciples, the pastoral passion of James for the people of Israel (matching that of Paul for the Gentiles), and the essential condition of the gospel as preached by both: "Refuse all substitutes."'[3] This, we believe, is the James who wrote the epistle of James.

Who are James' readers?

James writes to **'the twelve tribes scattered among the nations'**. The general content of his letter indicates that it was written primarily to converted Hebrews outside of Palestine. It parallels Paul's ministry to the Gentiles. It is possible to argue that James was thinking of the whole Christian church and used the term 'twelve tribes' as a synonym for spiritual as well as physical Israel, but this notion seems redundant, since any divinely inspired letter to a segment of the body of Christ could not but spill over, in its application, to the rest of the church. The fact that it was written in a time when the ambiguity of the Jerusalem temple and its sacrifices still cast its shadow across the advance of the gospel of Christ (i.e., prior to A.D. 70) gives added point to the claims of the gospel for Jew and Gentile alike, both for that generation and for all that would follow after. No Gentile believer would see himself outside of the ministry of James' epistle. On the contrary, as a letter written for Hebrew believers, it would confirm to Gentile believers that we are, indeed, all one in Christ Jesus.

What is James' purpose?

The opening word of the letter itself is the one word: **'Greetings.'** This has the root meaning of 'joy' and that is most appropriate to the intent of the epistle and, of course, to the gospel itself. This fundamental perspective ought not to be lost in the detailed moral and behavioural imperatives of the teaching of James. This ties in with the co-ordinate theme of the centrality of Christ in the Christian life. Just as James comes as the servant of God and the Lord Jesus Christ, so his desire is that his readers might also rejoice with him in their servanthood to their Father-God and his Son and their Saviour, the Lord Jesus Christ. This is both starting-point and ultimate purpose of the epistle: from the knowledge that you, having believed in Jesus Christ, belong to him and the knowledge that he has taken away your sins, you go on to delight to do his will and you strive, in his strength, to conform your life to the blessed pattern of his revealed will and perfect example. All that follows in James' epistle is directed to the great end that we would enjoy Christ by being truly his disciples – the practical Christians we are called to be through gospel obedience and love, through the grace of the Lord Jesus Christ.

The epistle can be divided into three parts, which successively lead us to this happy condition of being practical Christians. Part I – the bulk of the first chapter (1:2-27) – addresses the general problem we all have of coping with the ups and downs of everyday life as Christian men and women. Part II – the body of the letter (2:1 – 5:11) – can be read as a series of case studies which examine specific practical questions drawn from a wide range of life experiences. Part III draws all these threads together and shows us in a nutshell what vital Christianity must mean – it tells us how to live until the return of the Lord Jesus Christ (5:12-20). In this way, James gives us a practical handbook of the principles we are to live by throughout the rest of our lives on this earth, all the while keeping our eyes upon the Lord who is coming again to bring human history to its final consummation and to gather all his saved people into the glory of eternal joy in the presence of God.

An outline of the epistle of James

I.   Introduction (1:1)

II. Coping with the real world (1:2-27)

A. Maturity in the Christian faith (1:2-4)
1. First principle: joy in trials (1:2)
2. Reasons for joy: perseverance and completeness (1:3-4)

B. Wisdom in the face of trials (1:5-8)
1. The need of wisdom (1:5a)
2. Wisdom through prayer (1:5b-8)

C. Wealth and the lack of it (1:9-12)
1. The brother in humble circumstances (1:9)
2. The one who is rich (1:10-11)
3. True riches – the crown of life (1:12)

D. Temptation and sin (1:13-15)
1. Responding to temptation (1:13)
2. Temptation's true source (1:14)
3. Temptation's ultimate destination (1:15)

E. Gifts and their Giver (1:16-18)
1. Good gifts (1:16)
2. The good Giver (1:17)
3. The gift of new birth (1:18)

IV. How to live until the Lord's coming (5:7-20)

    A. Waiting patiently for the Lord (5:7-11)
       1.   The goal of patience (5:7a)
       2.   Examples of patience (5:7b-11c)
       3.   The Lord and your patience (5:11d)

    B. Praising the Lord (5:12-13)
       1.   Reverence for God (5:12)
       2.   Prayer – for times of trouble (5:13ab)
       3.   Praise – for times of joy (5:13cd)

    C. Sharing your burdens (5:14-18)
       1.   Praying for the sick (5:14-15)
       2.   Confession and prayer in the fellowship (5:16ab)
       3.   Effectual prayer (5:16c)

    D. Winning others for Christ (5:19-20)
       1.   Christians caring about others (5:19)
       2.   The blessings of faithfulness (5:20)

Part I
Coping with the
real world

1.
Christian maturity

Please read James 1:2-4

'Consider it pure joy, my brothers, whenever you face trials of many kinds, because you know that the testing of your faith develops perseverance. Perseverance must finish its work so that you may be mature and complete, not lacking anything' (James 1:2-4).

Life is full of 'ups' and 'downs'. In the real world, life can be a roller-coaster ride and most folk would have little difficulty adding their own 'Amen' to the words of the old Negro spiritual,

Sometimes I'm up, sometimes I'm down;
    Oh, yes Lord!
Sometimes I'm almost to the ground;
    Oh, yes Lord!

Everybody knows what this is like. It is a fact of life and it's here to stay, on this side of eternity. Knowing what is happening and coping with the happenings themselves are, of course, two entirely different things.

The first chapter of James' letter is a fairly general overview of how to cope with life's 'ups and downs'. James' perspective is, of course, the Christian perspective. In the face of life's difficulties, a living personal faith in Jesus Christ makes all the difference in the world. It is a faith that acts! It is a faith that surmounts the obstacles and gains victories through following Jesus Christ! Any bird can sing when the sun is shining, to be sure. Christians, more than anybody, should know how to praise God and enjoy life, when everything goes smoothly and the goodness of God is as obvious as it is abundant. But a faith that shines with lustre in the sunshine of

God's favour radiates even greater brightness against the
darkness of the clouds of trial and tribulation. Here is the testing of the Christian's mettle – the trying of the reality of his
faith. This is always the bottom line for faith, because faith is
by definition 'being sure of what we hope for and certain of
what we do not see' (Hebrews 11:1). However great our
experience of God's blessing in the past or in the present, the
essence of our faith is that it rests on the acceptance of the
truth of God's Word as it analyses, interprets and, not least,
directs our experience of life. Faith looks to God's promises
concerning our future and centres everything in God's plan of
redemption in Jesus Christ. The certainty of this faith is not so
much in what we have seen with our eyes to have been
accomplished, but in 'what we hope for' and yet 'do not see'.
Our faith will inevitably be put to the test in the hard experiences of life, because these things always *appear* to be the
contradiction of the positive promises of God's blessing. Living faith is faith in Christ. Faith in Christ is faith that acts in
obedience to him. Such a faith perseveres even when the
earthly props of temporal prosperity and well-being have
been kicked away and the blessings of God seem very far off.

James approaches this most profound of problems by stating a fundamental practical principle. This is in the form of a
command to **'count it pure joy'** whenever we face **'trials of
many kinds'** (1:2). He then goes on to support this with two
reasons that compel a willing and happy obedience (1:3-4).

The joy of trials (1:2)

**'Consider it pure joy, my brothers, whenever you face trials of
many kinds.'** Few statements can be more calculated to raise
the eyebrows than this invitation to what looks like a species
of masochism. It is one thing to believe that some disaster
may be a so-called 'blessing in disguise'; it is quite another to
regard it with *joy*! The standard heroic response to trials is to
keep a 'stiff upper lip' or, in the USA, to invoke the spirit of
the pioneers: 'When the going gets tough, the tough get
going.' But 'pure joy'? This makes the mind boggle. It grabs
our attention. It is certainly not what we hear from the counsellors and psychiatrists of our time.

Facing trials

We must remember that James was addressing the Jews of the Dispersion who had become Christians. As the 'old covenant' people of God they knew the cutting edge of racial prejudice; as the 'new covenant' people of God in Jesus Christ, their new faith exposed them to fresh experiences of the wrath of men – both of the Gentiles and the as yet unconverted Jews. They were a despised minority and they knew it. It cost them a great deal to stand up for Jesus.

The **'trials'** they faced are, to use Dean Alford's definition, 'any kind of distresses that happen to us, from without or within, which in God's purpose serve as trials of us'.[1] The Greek word for 'trials' *(peirasmoi)* is used in the Lord's Prayer (Matthew 6:13). We are to pray, 'Lead us not into *peirasmoi.*' That is to say, we pray the Lord to spare us the tests of difficult experiences. The classic rendering, 'Lead us not into temptation', improperly narrows the focus from testing in general to the specific notion of seductive inducements to outright sin. Testing and trials may indeed issue in sinful failure, but they may simply be the occasion of sorrow and grief. Peter, for example says, 'In this you greatly rejoice [i.e., in living faith in Christ] though now for a little while you may have had to suffer grief in all kinds of trials' *(peirasmoi).* These trials encompass everything considered as tests of character: anything that seems to be a set-back, anything that casts us down, anything that otherwise makes us angry and resentful, things that people say and do that are injurious or annoying to us, even things we imagine to be problems – all are included in James' category of trials. It is these that he says we are to count 'pure joy'!

Pure joy

What is this **'pure joy'**? And how is it to be derived from the cauldron of affliction? Suppose we think of our life experience as a ledger in which we keep accounts. Some items are entered in the credit column, others on the debit side. Obviously, we naturally see our tribulations as negative entries. But it need not be that way! John Calvin suggests that we can decide 'that temptations ought to be so deemed as gain, as to be regarded as occasions of joy'. If we do this then 'There is nothing in afflictions which ought to disturb our joy.'[2] Trials

will always come in on the debit side. We will always tend to
say, 'Why is this happening to me? What did I do wrong?
When will it ever end?' and the like. We will naturally be
tempted to anger, frustration and despair. Sometimes people
take their own lives because they feel their situation to be
irretrievable.

What James is saying is that *as an act of faith* we must put
these trials in the credit column. That does not mean uttering
a glib 'Praise the Lord anyway' and attempting to put it all in
the past. And it doesn't mean smiling the pain away. That just
won't happen. Jesus turned his suffering into our salvation
and his triumphant ascension to glory, but he had to agonize
every inch of the way. So will we, as we grapple with life's
harder realities. The point is that real pain and distress can be
turned into occasions of joy by faith that looks to Jesus Christ
and we can come to see that the Lord is using that distress to
draw us into a closer relationship with him. With the help of
the Holy Spirit, this is how we are to redeem the downside of
life. James is teaching us 'to bear adversities calmly, and with
an even mind' and 'shows that there is a reason why the faithful should rejoice when pressed down by them'.[3]

This is, no doubt, a great paradox. Perhaps you just cannot
fathom how anyone can really turn affliction round into a
blessing. To the Christian, however, this is not only something he can understand – it is something that he can *obey*.
Christians agree with the writer to the Hebrews when he said,
'No discipline seems pleasant at the time, but painful. Later
on, however, it produces a harvest of righteousness and peace
for those who have been trained by it' (Hebrews 12:11). Yet
no one has difficulty understanding the value of training,
however painful it might be. Athletes only become athletes
because they are willing to sweat and suffer. They can even
learn from their injuries and their defeats in competition!
Spiritual growth – including counting trials as pure joy – is the
same principle worked out in the even more intense arena of
a person's innermost being. And just as it takes an act of will
for an athlete to turn his pain into happy achievement, so it
takes an act of will, through faith in Christ, to bring joy out of
pain in the Christian life!

The alternative is to let affliction do the devil's work: lie
down under it; brood on what might have been; feed your

frustration with a festering resentment against others, perhaps even against God himself, and slide into the gall of bitterness, your life crushed by defeat and hopelessness. The Lord Jesus Christ calls us to the very opposite – 'a harvest of righteousness and peace'. However 'victimized' we may be by adverse circumstances, we do not need to add the self-victimization of a decision to feel sorry for ourselves and resentful of all others. God calls us to *choose* the way of life – by his free grace, through personal faith in Jesus Christ.

Whenever you fall

The original Greek text says, 'Consider it pure joy, my brothers, whenever you *fall into* trials...' (NIV has 'whenever you *face* trials'). The Greek word, *peripiptein,* carries the idea of suddenly finding yourself surrounded by unanticipated difficulties. You don't go looking for troubles – they will come to you, and often when you least expect them! The significance of this is twofold.

In the first place it gives no encouragement to those Christians who sometimes seem to go out of their way to bring afflictions on themselves. The Bible speaks often about martyrdom, but it never encourages the so-called martyr-complex. No Christian need feel he is failing his Saviour because he has not so far had a hard life or experienced serious persecution. In fact, Scripture positively forbids Christians from indulging in all forms of religious masochism and goes as far as to call such measures 'self-imposed worship' and 'false humility'! (Colossians 2:23). The true spirit of the gospel of Christ waits upon God's providence and prays for a quiet life (1 Thessalonians 4:11).

Secondly, no one should imagine that the only way to 'pure joy' is through facing trials. This is another pernicious fallacy of asceticism – namely, the notion that 'The more it hurts, the more good it must be doing you!' We are not called to castor-oil Christianity! Our lives ought to be filled with 'pure joy' without the ministry of trials and tribulations. James' point is that the negatives can be turned to positive effect. Meanwhile, the outright blessings of God can speak for themselves. We don't need to be told that *they* are 'pure joy'!

Two reasons for counting trials as pure joy (1:3-4)

There are two substantial reasons for making trials the
occasion of joy in the Lord. The first is that **'The testing of
your faith develops perseverance.'** The other, which we shall
look at shortly, is that this is God's road to our completeness
as whole people (1:4).

1. Perseverance (1:3)
'Affliction,' writes Robert Johnstone, 'lets down a blazing
torch for [the Christian] into the depths of his own nature –
and he sees many things which he little expected to see.'[4] Not
too many years ago, in my native city of Edinburgh, workmen
were starting to repair a crumbling plaster ceiling in a seven-
teenth-century tenement in the heart of the Old Town. As
they scraped off some rotten plaster, they discovered beautiful painted woodwork underneath – the original work of 300
years ago![5] Needless to say, the later plaster was all removed
to restore the original to its former splendour. Sometimes the
opposite can happen. What was thought to be the real thing
turns out to be less than expected. I still remember my
mother's disappointment when she discovered that
Grandma's (supposedly sterling) 'silver teapot' was cheap
electro-plate after all!
   Trials work in these ways. Sometimes they show us that we
are neither as strong nor as wise as we imagined ourselves to
be. At other times they have revealed strengths and graces in
us that we never dreamed could be ours. Tertullian once said,
in his inimitable fashion, that 'Innocence is best tried by
iniquity.' You have to melt the rocks if you want the metal!
Consequently, where there is true faith in the heart, testing
works 'perseverance'. Paul says that 'Suffering produces perseverance' (Romans 5:3). This means, as Calvin comments,
that our experience in grappling with evil and overcoming it
leads us to 'experience how much God's help avails in a
crisis'.[6] Again we have a paradox: in weakness, the Christian
finds true strength in Christ; in darkness, living faith shines
ever brighter; and in need comes the discovery of the abundant grace of God which supplies all our needs. So far from
dampening our devotion to the Lord or stifling our
enthusiasm for living the Christian life, the hard experiences

actually stimulate a deeper commitment and a growing personal holiness. Perseverance is that willingness to keep running the race that is generated in the course of the race at precisely the moment when the muscles are hurting and the lungs are bursting. It is the triumph of the spirit over the felt weakness of the flesh. This is simply a fact of life. And it is a fact of the Christian life. Testing actually produces perseverance! The obverse is that until we are afflicted, we tend to go astray (Psalm 119:67).

2. Completeness (1:4)

If perseverance is the journey, completeness is the destination. **'Perseverance must finish its work so that you may be mature and complete, not lacking anything.'** The whole process is one of growth and improvement towards spiritual maturity. The key words are 'finish' *(teleos)* and 'complete' *(holokleros)*. They speak of the goal and the completeness of the work of *sanctification* – the progressively growing personal godliness of the believer which issues in being made perfectly holy in heaven.

There is an imperative quality to the work. Perseverance **'must…'** To stop being patiently persevering has the practical effect of denying the faith. How easy it is to begin a project with great zeal, only to drop it later as the initial enthusiasm wanes! But the work of the Holy Spirit has a goal, and it will be, it must be achieved. It is a fact of divine revelation that the good work begun by God in every Christian will carry on to completion until 'the day of Jesus Christ' (Philippians 1:6). This is the promise upon which we may act confidently. Our exercise of faith must not be interrupted – it must go forward until it is completed according to God's purpose for our lives.

The goal, then, is maturity and completeness. The central focus is on the fulness, the richness and the well-roundedness of our spiritual character in the eyes of God. 'In regard to evil, be infants,' says Paul, 'but in your thinking be adults' (1 Corinthians 14:20). 'All of us, my brethren,' writes Robert Johnstone, 'in religion as in intellectual culture, are in danger of being one-sided. Yielding to natural temperament, we are apt, whilst cultivating certain departments of Christian thought and activity, to neglect others. The believer of a contemplative disposition, for instance, may shrink from taking his proper share in the church's work; whilst another Christian, strenuous in labour, may forget to some extent that the tree of piety can bring forth fruit to perfection only when watered with the dew of the Spirit through prayer and quiet communion. Thus the new man has deformities, his growth being inharmonious, without fitting proportion of parts. God's varied discipline is designed to produce a perfectly balanced completeness of character. Now there are some elements of holy character which can be acquired only in trouble. The beautiful graces of resignation and sympathy cannot grow but in a soil through which has passed the ploughshare of affliction, and which has been watered by the rain of tears. Therefore it is that God "scourgeth every son whom he receiveth," and "every branch of the true vine that beareth fruit, he purgeth it, that it may bring forth more fruit".[7]

It is no accident that the sequence is trial – pure joy – perseverance – maturity – completeness. We would think it more appropriate to put the joy at the end – after the pain of persevering was past and done! God's point is that joy, in Christ, is the power-house of perseverance. To be sure, that joy looks ahead to the reward which will be garnered at the final goal. But joy is the leading motif of the Christian faith *as it is lived out in daily life*. Our calling is a happy one. Our perseverance in the face of trials partakes of that joy precisely because it is God's gracious purpose to work in us 'an eternal glory that far outweighs them all' (2 Corinthians 4:17).

2.
Wisdom

Please read James 1:5-8

'If any of you lacks wisdom, he should ask God, who gives generously to all without finding fault, and it will be given to him' (James 1:5).

The only problem with everything that is good and spiritual is that it is easier to talk about than it is to do! When James talked about the way to spiritual maturity (1:2-4), he taught us that the trials and tribulations in life are designed to refine our faith and bring us to maturity and completeness as Christians, through the exercise of persevering faith in Christ and an ongoing holy patience with the circumstances of God's providence. We are to count such experiences joy because they are the very means by which we enter more deeply and surely into the meaning and scope of our salvation.

This, so to speak, is the theory. But what about the practice? There is a self-evident beauty, symmetry and genius to this doctrine as set forth by James. It hangs together; it rings true; now that we have read it, it seems the obvious way to handle the problem; indeed, it is exactly what salvation in Christ has to mean for the way we cope with the problems of life. Our difficulty is practical: how to translate this sublime truth into action in the hurly-burly world of our ups and downs? We readily identify with the apostle Paul when he said, 'I have the desire to do what is good, but I cannot carry it out' (Romans 7:18). We would agree with John Calvin when he remarked that 'Our reason, and all our feelings are averse to the thought that we can be happy in the midst of evils.'[1] This is precisely why James immediately introduces us to the need of seeking wisdom from God. Just because our

minds rebel against the idea that we can be happy in the
middle of our troubles, we need the Lord to bring us to a grasp
of this truth. We need this in order to respond with happy
obedience. Otherwise we shall slide into the fruitless ways of
the 'but-Christian' who says to himself, 'I know what the
Lord's will is ... *but* I feel hopeless about ever really doing it.
I know I shouldn't despair in this way ...*but* ... *but* ... *but* ...'

This is where wisdom comes in. Wisdom is more than
knowledge. It is knowledge allied to an active faith in the
Lord. In this context, wisdom issues in a readiness to 'submit
to God in the endurance of evils, under a due conviction that
he so orders all things as to promote our salvation'.[2] James
tells us how we may acquire this wisdom for ourselves.

Realize your need of wisdom (1:5)

'If any of you lacks wisdom,' begins James (1:5). 'If' does not
imply any possibility that some of the readers may have sufficient wisdom already so as to obviate any necessity to seek it
from God. Neither does it suggest a sarcastic tone on James'
part, as if he were rubbing in the impossibility of anyone's
really possessing any genuine wisdom. The purpose of the
Lord's brother is not so much to emphasize the *need* of wisdom – after all, it is the mark of wise people that they freely
confess their desire for even more – but rather to point us to
the *resources* that are available, whenever we do conceive a
felt need of the Lord's guidance. If we lack wisdom, God will
supply our need. He does not ask anything of us that is totally
beyond our capacity, provided that we seek his enabling
strength through the means he has provided for us in his
Word.

The **'wisdom'** referred to is wisdom in the narrow sense
envisaged by the context, namely, that wisdom peculiarly
required in a time of trial to enable us to receive joyfully the
dispensations of God's providence. Such circumstances are,
in their very nature, to be viewed as disciplinary and reforma-
tive, irrespective of their provenance. For example, it may be
that some injustice has been heaped upon us, and with respect
to the perpetrator, we are wholly innocent. Even in such a
case, however, we have occasion to look for the hand of God,

so that we may discern what he is teaching us through this essentially outrageous imposition. God permits the turbulence of a wicked world to rock us and both makes and takes these opportunities to draw us more deeply into fellowship with him. It takes wisdom to accept this and to grow spiritually as a result of it. This is, as one commentator puts it, the 'highest of all [wisdoms] and the most difficult of attainment'.[3] Why? Because it is relatively easier actively to do the will of God – i.e., to keep this or that positive precept – than it is to endure patiently the hard knocks of life. Without this wisdom, people either become fatalistically resigned or they are crushed into a frustrated hopelessness. In both cases the 'fear of the Lord', which is 'the beginning of wisdom' (Proverbs 1:7), is evidently lacking. 'Wisdom,' as Solomon says in another place, 'is supreme; therefore get wisdom' (Proverbs 4:7).

This is how, Christian friend, you can know whether you lack wisdom – assuming there is any real question about the matter. Do you find yourself sliding into confusion of mind and bitterness of soul as you evaluate God's dealings with your life? Any Christian who wallows in complaining self-pity and never breaks from a perpetual litany of 'Lord, why has this happened to me?' has not begun to tap the resources of wisdom which God has made available to the prayer of faith. He provides for the healing of hurt minds, as well as bodies. If, however, we insist on a diet of gnawing dissatisfaction with God's will, when we should be feeding on Christ the 'bread of life', then it can be small wonder that the remedy escapes us. If any of you lacks wisdom, he should ask God.

Seek wisdom through prayer (1:5)

The answer to the deepest cries of the heart is to be found with the Lord. If anyone lacks wisdom, **'he should ask God, who gives generously to all without finding fault, and it will be given to him'** (1:5).

God alone is the source of true wisdom. He is 'the Father of the heavenly lights', from whom comes 'every good and perfect gift' (1:17). The entire twenty-eighth chapter of Job is devoted to this theme. Job asks, 'But where can wisdom be

found? Where does understanding dwell?' After reviewing
the failure of all sorts of sources, he comes in the end to affirm
the exclusive claims of God: 'God understands the way to it
and he alone knows where it dwells.' Furthermore, God has
revealed to us the essence of the matter: 'The fear of the Lord
– that is wisdom, and to shun evil is understanding' (Job
28:12,23,28). God is the source and, says James, believing
prayer is the means of its attainment. To that end, we are
offered two encouragements to prayer.

God gives generously to all

Not only does God *give* – i.e., he pours his blessing upon us,
as grace unmerited and undeserved on our part – he gives
'generously'. God is a giving God. He gives 'immeasurably
more than all we ask or imagine' (Ephesians 3:20). And if
anyone asks, believing, he will answer with his love. He will
respond to 'the prayer of the destitute' (Psalm 102:17). And
he will give more than we ask. Solomon asked for 'a discerning heart' and God replied by granting this request and also
giving him what he did not ask for – riches, honour and a long
life (1 Kings 3:9-14).

Without finding fault

The Lord says he will give to *all* without finding fault. This is
not to say that the Lord indiscriminately gives his blessings to
everybody in abundance without any regard to the spiritual
condition of each individual. The 'all' in the text refers to all
who sincerely and believingly apply to him for help. There is
no comfort for the careless and unbelieving. While we regard
sin in our hearts, the Lord will not hear us (Psalm 66:18).

What, then, does it mean to say that the Lord will answer
prayer **'without finding fault'**? Well, what does a fault-finder
do? He keeps on bringing up past mistakes! He harps on
earlier failures. He never forgets the slightest stain on the
escutcheon. And because he never forgets, he never actually
forgives, for the essence of forgiveness is the complete
erasure of the bad record from the past. God answers prayers
without bringing up our past failures and holding them up as
a reason for reproach or for not giving help on this occasion.
Whereas we, in our imagined magnanimity, would give a
fellow two or three chances to get something right, the Lord

promises to answer prayer again and again without recrimination. He doesn't say, 'Go away! You've asked for that ten times now: ten times I've given it and ten times you thanked me by getting yourself into the same mess! I'm through with this! You're on your own! No more favours!' No! Our Father-God commands us to come in faith to his throne of grace. He will not turn his afflicted people away, however frequently they come to him. God is always ready 'to add new blessings to former ones, without any end or limitation'.[4] As a matter of fact, far from being a reason for cutting off his aid, the past blessings of God are constantly held up to both the faithful and the backslidden as reasons for coming afresh to the Lord! God's ways are not our ways! We have the encouragement never to hold back from coming to God. From his side, he reminds his people, 'I am the Lord your God, who brought you out of Egypt' (Exodus 20:2), and thereby promises to keep them in his loving arms. From the believer comes the response: 'Thus far has the Lord helped us' (1 Samuel 7:12), which breathes the happy expectation that he will continue to be his servant's help on into the future.

These are surely the most powerful encouragements to seeking the Lord's wisdom.

How to pray for wisdom (1:6-8)

The willingness to come to the Lord must be matched by a practical recognition of who he is and, therefore, of how he is to be approached. Anyone who seeks a favour from a potential benefactor is usually keenly aware of the need for a humble and respectful approach. Nothing turns off the taps of human kindness more quickly than arrogant and peremptory demands – as witness the catastrophic state of industrial relations in this country, where all, management and unions alike, 'demand' their 'rights', and the thought of an old-fashioned 'humble remonstrance', or even a polite request, is laughed out of court as evidence of the loss of manhood, if not indeed of the ability to think.

God is to be approached on his terms, not ours. He is to be approached in the way he has prescribed, not 'any old how'! Moses, you will recall, was told to remove the shoes from his

feet before the burning bush because, as the Lord told him,
the ground on which he stood was holy ground. God is holy.

Believe and not doubt (1:6)

'Without faith,' says the writer to the Hebrews, 'it is impossible to please God, because anyone who comes to him must
believe that he exists and that he rewards those who earnestly
seek him' (Hebrews 11:6). Faith is 'the essential condition of
prayer'.[5] In other words, prayer is not a medicine that we
take; it is an expression of what we already are. Prayer does
not work like a magic incantation, the effectiveness of which
is presumed to be in the naked mechanical utterance of a form
of words. There is no virtue or automatic grace in the mere
form. Prayer in the abstract is not true prayer. Why? Because
it has neither a genuine destination nor any assurance of a
genuine response.

   This is where James' stricture about not doubting comes in.
The doubt he has in view is a fundamental lack of faith in the
Lord's promise to answer prayer. Real prayer has to be preceded by some conviction of this truth. John Calvin is surely
correct when he tells us that we will just not be able to pray
unless the Word of God leads our way – unless, in other
words, we believe God is as good as his word. It is either
promise or pretence. Faith looks to the promise of God
with confidence that he will answer prayer to our blessed
satisfaction.

   It should be noted that the word rendered **'he who doubts'**
(*diakrinomenos*) does not mean 'he who is not a true believer
in Christ', as opposed to one who is a Christian. Rather it
means – with reference to those whom James repeatedly
addresses as his 'brothers', i.e., professing, praying Christians – 'he who wavers' and answers 'yes' and 'no' together,
with the practical emphasis inevitably on the negative. His
doubts are a constant contradiction of his faith. They cast a
shadow over his relationship with his Saviour and set his mind
in a turmoil whenever he is faced by a crisis – which, in such
a spiritual state, is quite often. He is 'all at sea' in faith and
life. Yet he is a believer – a believer who is in trouble. He is
'like a wave of the sea, blown and tossed by the wind'. His
prayers – if indeed he can ever decide on anything to pray for
– go nowhere, only back and forth in the indecision of his

doubts. He halts between two opinions. Like a child pulling daisy petals, he goes on wondering, 'He loves me...He loves me not...', without any resolution.

The expectations of double-mindedness (1:7-8)
Vacillation is fatal to effective prayer. Just as no man can serve two masters, prayer cannot flow from a divided heart. The **'double-minded man'** is **'unstable in all he does'**. And it ought therefore to be no surprise to him that he should not expect to receive anything from the Lord. This is not because the Lord is cruelly withholding his blessings; it is simply that there is nothing to answer with blessing. God does not bless at random, nor does he reward the contradiction of his unchanging truth. That man's greatest need is to listen to the Lord as he says, 'Be still, and know that I am God' (Psalm 46:10). He needs to repent of double-mindedness and become single-minded in the Lord.

Walking evenly with God

'None walk so evenly with God,' said Thomas Manton, 'as they that are assured of the love of God.'[6] Elsewhere that wise Englishman shows us that our walk with the Lord is as stable as our grasp of his revealed truth: 'If you love a truth ignorantly, you cannot love it constantly.'[7] The apostle Paul warned the early Christians to avoid being blown about with every wind of doctrine (Ephesians 4:14). That is what happens when people, in Manton's phrase, 'love a truth ignorantly'. If they really grasped the truth, they would be grasped by that truth. It would not let them go. We must, by all means, 'test everything', but having done so, we are to 'hold on to the good' (1 Thessalonians 5:21). To walk 'evenly' with God, you need to be on his level path. Peter concludes his second epistle with a plea which turns our eyes to the One who is able to keep us from falling: 'Therefore, dear friends, since you already know this, be on your guard so that you may not be carried away by the error of lawless men and fall from your secure position. But grow in the grace and knowledge of our Lord and Saviour Jesus Christ. To him be glory both now and for ever! Amen' (2 Peter 3:17-18).

Oh, for a closer walk with God,
A calm and heavenly frame,
A light to shine upon the road
That leads me to the Lamb!'

(William Cowper).

3.
Poverty and prosperity

Please read James 1:9-12

'Blessed is the man who perseveres under trial, because when he has stood the test, he will receive the crown of life that God has promised to those who love him' (James 1:12).

Nothing is more obviously written across the face of our world than the inequalities between the rich and the poor. We don't need to see pictures of the slums of Calcutta, the starving in Ethiopia, the mansions of Beverly Hills or the palaces of Saudi oil magnates to be touched by this reality. Indeed, these extremes – at least for most of us in Western societies – are little more than media images. We have no personal experience of such conditions. What we are keenly aware of in daily life are the more modest circumstances of the various shades of what is called 'middle income', immunized from crushing poverty and the threat of starvation and, less to our liking, relieved from the peculiar burdens of great wealth. What we do experience most keenly are the perennial inequalities within the circles of our job, community and even our church. 'Keeping up with the Joneses' is a far more nagging problem for most people than the annual pre-Christmas media guilt-trip about the homeless and the starving.[1] What really eats up many of us are the relatively petty jealousies and gnawing frustrations associated with a perceived (and actual) lack of 'disposable' income. They go on vacation to the Bahamas; we go to Margate. They have a new Jaguar; we have a ten-year-old Ford. The 'standard of living' and the inequalities we feel between ourselves and our neighbours are the twin fountains of much of the day-to-day frustration that people in this country feel, with respect to things economic. This is not to minimize the genuine pressure to 'make ends meet', especially in a time when economic recession, the third horseman of the Apocalypse (Revelation 6:5-6), spreads its depredations abroad in the land. My point is that, for whatever reason, money is a trial to virtually all of us and the inequalities between us are just the salt that causes the wound to sting all the more.

No one ought to be surprised, therefore, that James' first specific example of the trials of life should be that of poverty and prosperity. He is bringing us a word from God designed to help us cope with life in the real world. The groundwork has been laid: trials in general must become the occasion for joy (1:2-4), while the wisdom necessary to this not undaunting task is to be sought from the Lord in single-minded prayer (1:5-8). So here we are confronted with the one practical problem that hits us every time we need to spend money – the reality of personal economics. Now, James has no programme for increasing our income or eliminating poverty in the world. Neither is he ready at this point to discuss the varieties of wickedness associated with the desire for riches – he will do that later in 2:1-7 and 5:1-6. His immediate concern is to take a look at both poverty and prosperity and, most strikingly, to view them both, equally, as tests of the reality of our personal faith in Christ.

Needless to say, not many people think of wealth as a great test of faith. Poverty as a test we can understand. But wealth? We thought that prosperity was the thing that eliminated real trials and set a person on the primrose path to a worry-free life! Well, says James, let us think again!

James addresses himself to Christians – 'brothers' (1:9-10) – and, in so doing, he first points out the deceitfulness of riches as this affects both rich and poor, and then goes on to emphasize the true riches that belong to those who love the Lord.

The brother in humble circumstances (1:9)

There were probably many Christians in **'humble circumstances'** in the first century A.D. Hebrew Christians in particular – the initial readership of the epistle (1:1) – were

often seriously discriminated against by their former con-
frères in Judaism. As with converts from very tight religious
fraternities in every succeeding generation, these new Christians faced social ostracism which included loss of jobs and
previous financial contacts. For some centuries, the church of
Jesus Christ was, as a general rule, made up of those whose
circumstances were decidedly humble. The sociological
shape of the apostolic church was well assessed by Paul when
he reminded the Corinthian believers of what they were when
God called them (and presumably what they remained there-
after in the eyes of the world): 'Not many of you were wise by
human standards; not many were influential; not many were
of noble birth.' Were they not the 'foolish things of the
world', chosen by God to shame the wise and the strong? (1
Corinthians 1:26-27). This gives us a clue to the deeper
dimension of these 'humble circumstances'. These believers
were, in God's eyes, not simply poor, but, as Thomas Manton
so beautifully puts it, 'poor for Christ'. That is to say, their circumstances were not unrelated to the fact that they were
Christians.[2]

**'The brother in humble circumstances ought to take pride in
his high position'** (1:9). Here is another of these paradoxical
statements with which Scripture abounds. The poor Christian
actually has a 'high position' in which he ought to 'take pride'!

'Take pride' may not, in this context, be the happiest
rendering, in view of the generally negative connotations of
the word 'pride' in our day. James has a positive and holy joy
in view. The idea in the Greek verb *(kauchaomai)* is, however, that of 'any "proud and exulting joy"'.[3] Sometimes this
is sinful, as when Paul scathingly rebukes the Roman Christians as those 'who *brag* about the law' while they 'dishonour
God by breaking the law' (Romans 2:23), and tells the Corinthian believers that there must be 'no more *boasting* about
men' (1 Corinthians 3:21). But more often it refers to a holy,
positive and exultant joy – the Christian rejoicing in his
Father-God (Romans 2:17; 5:11), in Christ (Philippians 3:3),
in believers (2 Corinthians 7:14), in the good works of others
(2 Corinthians 10:15) and in afflictions and weaknesses (Romans 5:3; 2 Corinthians 12:9). Paul sets the standard for
Christian exultation when he declares, 'May I never *boast*
except in the cross of our Lord Jesus Christ' (Galatians 6:14).

But what is this **'high position'**, in which the poorer Christian is to exult? The answer can only be found in the contrast between his outward circumstances, which are humble, and his inward dignity as a child of God, in which he can only rejoice! The humble circumstances are temporary; his exalted personal relationship to the Lord is permanent. Even if he was a slave, he is 'the Lord's freedman' (1 Corinthians 7:22). James' point is this: however desperate or straightened our circumstances may be from time to time, we must not allow ourselves to fall into the trap of being depressed by them. If these things get to us and make us feel helpless, worthless and despairing, it is only because we have been ready to tie our feelings of worth to an essentially material standard. Riches can be as deceitful when we don't have them, but wish we did, as when we have them in abundance! Rather, look to your true status as a child of God and an heir of the covenant promises of the Lord. You belong to Christ! So do your circumstances, for they are within the orbit of his plan for your ultimate good, your full salvation.

The one who is rich (1:10-11)

There would be far fewer rich people than poor in the apostolic church. There were some, however – Lydia is a notable example (Acts 16:14) – and they needed 'a word in season' about their position. In contrast to their poorer brothers and sisters, the rich believers needed to see that they were to glory, not in a high position, but in a low one! James' caution, says John Calvin, 'pertains to all those who excel in honour, or in dignity, or in any other external thing. He bids them to glory in their lowness or littleness, in order to repress the haughtiness of those who are usually inflated with prosperity.'[4]

Pride in his low position (1:10)
Richer Christians must realize that they are called, in Christ, to an essential equality with their poorer fellow-believers. Worldly distinctions of class, involving as they would in the ancient world (and as they still often do today) a conventional obligation to be segregated socially from the poor, must be

completely rejected. This would be a breach of fellowship and a practical denial of the very nature of the Christian salvation. For real fellowship to be maintained, there will need to be a real humility on the part of those who have attained success in the world's terms. The church in Corinth, you will recall, had to learn this lesson the hard way. They had held what they called 'love feasts' prior to the celebration of the Lord's Supper. Evidently the rich flaunted their wealth by the quality and quantity of the food and drink they consumed on these occasions, while the poor had to look on in humiliation. The former got drunk; the latter remained hungry. This was, said Paul, in one of the most solemn comments on the temporal judgements of God upon the church, the reason why many of them had become sick and some had even died! (1 Corinthians 11:17-34). Here, then, is the burden and challenge that riches pose for the Christian. The rich Christian has to face and conquer 'the deceitfulness of riches'. He is not to tie his sense of self-worth to his possessions and successes. He is not to look for his happiness in the riches he enjoys.

He is therefore to take pride in his **'low position'**, that is to say, in the realization that riches are nothing in themselves, that they will pass away and that those who are privileged to posses wealth are truly no better than anyone else. The rich man who humbles himself in these realizations is, therefore, consciously adopting a 'low position' and is rejoicing that Christ has revealed it to him. In absolute terms, both the rich and poor believers share the same high ground of salvation in Christ. Both are equally members of the royal priesthood which the body of Christ is (1 Peter 2:9). But in terms of the dynamics of practical Christian experience in the present realities of a fallen world, they are affected in opposite directions by the poverty-prosperity tension and must consequently respond to the Lord in contrasting ways: the poor need uplifting, the rich humbling.

Like a wild flower (1:10-11)
The fact is that the wealth of the rich is every bit as temporary as the poverty of the poor. The rich Christians face a great spiritual danger, namely, the fallacy that riches guarantee security. The siren seduction of 'things' is always that they will provide us with the settled comfort, satisfaction and status in

life which we so naturally desire. But like Jonah's gourd, it is all here today and gone tomorrow (Jonah 4:6-11). In the same way the rich man **'will pass away like a wild flower'** (10). This, of course, is simply an application of the general truth, as stated by the apostle Peter, that 'All flesh is as grass and all the glory of man as the flower of the grass' (1 Peter 1:24). Over a century ago, Robert Johnstone commented, 'As amid the monotony of green the gay wild flowers, by the richness and variety of their hues, attract the eye, so riches and rank give prominence to their possessors among the crowd of mankind. But the "flower of the grass" fadeth with the grass; so the honoured and the mean pass alike to the grave.'[5]

The image is drawn from the prophecy of Isaiah, which is also the source of 1 Peter 1:24. The prophet is speaking of the only source of comfort for the people of God, namely the gospel message of the coming of the Messiah. He cries out the word of the Lord:

'All men are like grass,
    and all their glory is like the flowers of the field.
The grass withers and the flowers fall,
    because the breath of the Lord blows on them.
    Surely the people are grass.
The grass withers and the flowers fall,
    but the word of our God stands for ever'

(Isaiah 40:6-8).

'In the same way', says James, **'the rich man will fade away even while he goes about his business.'** Take note! This is not only a statement of the fact that riches do not endure, but also the intimation of 'the certain destruction of those who are rich only in this world's goods'.[6] But God's Word will stand for ever and Jesus is both Saviour and Lord! In Jesus Christ, God's poor are the 'rich poor' and his rich are the 'poor rich'! Both are 'rich towards God' (Luke 12:21).

The crown of life (1:12)

The heart of the matter – being 'rich towards God' – is in the universal truth that 'The same Lord is Lord of all and richly blesses all who call on him, for "Everyone who calls on the name of the Lord will be saved"' (Romans 10:12-13, quoting Joel 2:32). It is not *our* resources or our capacity to endure trials that is the root of the matter: it is the richness of God towards us in gospel grace. We love him because he first freely and sovereignly loved us and sent his only Son to atone for the sins of everyone he will save to be his people! (1 John 4:10).

Blessed is the man

For this reason, there is a sense in which persevering under trials is its own reward – although, as we shall see in a moment, it is far from being all of the reward. The man who **'perseveres under trial'** is described as **'blessed'**. The present tense of the verb (*upomenei* – 'perseveres') indicates that there is joy for the one who is faithful in the act of persevering while the trials are upon him. He endures and, as he endures, he conquers! He doesn't just, as the Scots say, 'thole it' – i.e., put up with it, tough it out, suffer through or grit his teeth and bear it. 'The wicked man *suffers*; he does not *"endure"*, in the Scripture sense of the word.'[7] Christian joy is not merely future; it is a present experience even in this vale of tears. We have turned full circle: the exhortation of the second verse, 'Count it pure joy...whenever you face trials', has issued in the reality of God's blessing upon faithfulness: 'Blessed is the man who perseveres under trial.'

The promised crown of life

For the Christian, the blessings of the present are always related to the promises of the future. Our Lord 'endured the cross, scorning its shame', because of 'the joy set before him'. Therefore, we are called to 'throw off everything that hinders and the sin that so easily entangles, and...run with perseverance the race marked out for us,' fixing our eyes on 'Jesus, the author and perfecter of our faith' (Hebrews 12:1-2). There is a **'crown of life'** ahead for the believer. Although the image is taken from the crown a victor would gain in a sports competition, where there would be only one winner, in the Christian race all are winners. Adamson points out that the heart of the illustration from sports focuses on the element of endurance. Thus, in Hebrews 12:1, the Christian is portrayed as stripping down to his athletic gear and, cheered on by a 'cloud of witnesses' (the faithful who have run the race in the past) and looking steadfastly to his Saviour Jesus (who stands, as it were, stop-watch in hand at the tape), he runs the distance marked out on the track.[8]

The 'crown of life' is life. It is both now and not yet, in that every believer has eternal life now in Christ (John 3:16), and yet looks forward longingly to the fulness of the life in heaven, which is obviously 'not yet'. The 'crown' in this context refers to the consummated reward of the Christian in heaven, in which the Lord's people will reign with Christ as his kings and priests (Revelation 1:6; 3:21).

This is the promise of God **'to those who love him'**. Loving the Lord is the point at which, as the saying goes, 'the rubber hits the road'. In the final analysis, the Lord does not say 'to those who suffer', but 'to those who love'.[9] If I 'surrender my body to the flames', says Paul, 'but have not love, I gain nothing' (1 Corinthians 13:3). James is making a plea that his readers simply love the Lord, for it is only through the Saviour's love that we will both cope with life and enter into glory.

4.
Temptation

Please read James 1:13-15

'When tempted, no one should say, "God is tempting me." For God cannot be tempted by evil, nor does he tempt anyone; but each one is tempted when, by his own evil desire, he is dragged away and enticed' (James 1:13-14).

In my student days in Aberdeen, I lived in 'digs' in which the landlady provided our evening meal. On one occasion, one of our number did not like the look of the cook's efforts. In that abusively humourous tone so characteristic of student banter, he wondered what 'this dirt', as he called the main dish, was going to do to his insides. 'Och!' said another, with a droll Glaswegian chuckle, 'You dinnae need to worry about that! It isn't the dirt that goes into a man that defiles him, it's the dirt that comes out!' This young man, who today is a faithful minister of the gospel in his native Scotland, was in fact paraphrasing Jesus' words, as recorded in Mark 7:15. For all the general hilarity of the moment, a nightly occurrence in that boisterous company, there was a serious witness to a profound truth – the truth that the deepest problems of the human race come, not from external factors, but from within, from our innermost being.

Up to now, James has been discussing those trials which originated in outward circumstances, both the 'abnormal' (personal disasters, 1:2-8) and the 'normal' (economic inequalities, 1:9-11). He concluded with the declaration that those who persevere faithfully under such afflictions would 'receive the crown of life that God has promised to those who love him' (1:12). Now James addresses trials that come from *within* – specifically, temptation and sin. Many of those he pastored would sometimes have experienced failures in their responses to the trials of verses 2-12. Perhaps some of the brothers 'in humble circumstances' had gone on feeling bitter over their circumstances; perhaps some richer Christians had continued to be very tied to their wealth and still flaunted it in the church; others had not found joy in their afflictions. Why did these things happen? Why did these problems resist solution? Because there was another problem – an inward one, a problem of the heart, a problem called sin!

When you think about it, trials and temptations are inseparably linked with one another. Whenever we face some trial, we are inevitably confronted with choices that touch our deepest dispositions and principles. The most obvious aspect of this has already been mentioned by James: when afflicted, do you 'consider it pure joy'? Or would you rather flail around in frustration and bitterness? Will you follow God's way – to joy – or yield to the temptation to go in the opposite direction – to anger and/or despair? Trials involve temptation. Conversely, temptation to specific sin has to be a trial of our faith, one in which we also are called to perseverance and victory leading towards receiving God's 'crown of life'.

James' discussion of temptation goes right to the heart of the matter. How do we respond to temptation? Who is responsible for temptation? What is the nature and what are the consequences of temptation? Upon the answers to these questions hangs the very reality of our relationship to the living God.

How do you respond to temptation? (1:13)

'The Christian is God's man,' writes James Adamson, 'not the world's; and so, as his loyal child, he is bound by God's law.'[1] This has the clearest implications for the way we respond whenever we are tempted to some particular sin. James makes two points in 1:13.

Don't blame God
'When tempted, no one should say, "God is tempting me."'
Curiously, perhaps, the most natural response to being confronted with our own sin is not to deny the facts of sin, but to excuse ourselves by shifting the blame onto somebody or

something else. One does not need to sit on a jury or be a pastoral counsellor to discover this fact of life. It is everywhere in human life. It can easily be illustrated from songs and poetry. For example, one of the songs made famous by the legendary tenor Richard Tauber contains the deceptively innocent thought:

> Girls were made to love and kiss,
>   And who am I to interfere with this?
>   Is it well? Who can tell?
> I'm a man and kiss them when I can!

In a similar vein, but with greater honesty, Robert Burns gives his excuses for a short life packed with sexual sin. In his poem, 'A prayer in the prospect of death,' he says to God,

> Thou know'st that thou hast formed me,
>   With passions wild and strong;
> And listening to their witching voice
>   Has often led me wrong.

The same poet says elsewhere, with even greater boldness, that 'The light that led astray was light from heaven.'

Whether we blame our 'passions wild and strong' or the attractiveness of the temptation itself, or, like the American comedian Flip Wilson, we say, 'The devil made me do it,' we are ultimately saying that we are not really responsible, for God made us this way or allowed things to happen as they did. Ultimately – and this is James' point – we are saying, 'God is to blame. He is responsible for the bad things in my psychological make-up, my environment, my friends... everything!'

Why do people respond in this way, always seeking to excuse themselves for their evil actions! We need only look into the first human sin for the answer. Eve was tempted by Satan. She willingly sinned. The devil did not make her do it (but she blamed it on him anyway!). Adam, who was tempted by Eve and duplicated her sin, also attempted to excuse himself. He seems to blame his wife but in fact puts the blame upon God! 'The woman *you put here with me* – she gave me some fruit from the tree, and I ate it' (Genesis 3:12-13).

Again, think of Jesus' parable of the rich man and Lazarus
(Luke 16:19-31). The rich man Dives is in hell (v.23). He asks
Abraham, who is, of course, in heaven, to send Lazarus to his
father's house to warn his five brothers 'so that they will not
also come to this place of torment' (vv.27-28). Note the subtle
tilt at his 'father's house' as the environment in which his
brothers have come to need the warning to flee the wrath to
come. Dives makes no mention either of his own, or his
brothers' responsibility for their own spiritual condition. The
only hint of a source for their predicament is the expression
'my father's house'. But was it their upbringing and their
environment that was to blame? 'Abraham replied, "They
have Moses and the Prophets; let them listen to them"'
(v.29). No! Their problem was that they had rejected God's
clearly revealed Word. They could not evade responsibility
by passing the blame off onto somebody else!

In summary, we may declare, with the absolute authority
of the Word of God, that all attempts to blame our sins on
God, or his sovereignty (the biblical doctrine of predestination), or the way he made us (our temperament), or our circumstances in life ('the breaks,' people call them), or other
people, must be rejected. These are no more than attempts at
self-justification. And when God is blamed, they are blasphemies against his perfect righteousness. James now adds a
word of explanation for the truth of this assertion in verse 13.

God is neither temptable nor a tempter
It is utterly wrong to blame God for your temptations, **'For
God cannot be tempted by evil; nor does he tempt anyone.'**
God is and does the exact opposite from evil. He commands
us to be perfect, as he is perfect (Leviticus 11:45). God is
'beyond the reach of temptation. There is no point of contact
in the divine nature for the enticements of temptation.' John
Calvin sums up the matter succinctly: 'For it is the devil who
allures us to sin, and for this reason, because he wholly burns
with the mad lust of sinning. But God does not desire what is
evil: he is not, therefore, the author of doing evil in us.'[2]

To try to excuse our sins by shifting the blame onto God, in
whatever way we choose to do this, is the crime of *lèse-majesté*
– it is treason against the righteous lordship of God. There is
only one person responsible for the temptations into which

we fall. As the prophet Nathan said to David, over the sin with Bathsheba, so God says to us in rebuke of our sins, '*You are the man!*' (2 Samuel 12:7).

Temptation's true source (1:14)

What is the true source of temptation? James goes on, '**...but each one is tempted when, by his own evil desire, he is dragged away and enticed**' (1:14).

Evil desire
The problem is 'evil desire'. The NIV is to be preferred to the AV and NASB at this point, for the AV renders the Greek word *epithumia* as the English 'lust' – a word that has since become too narrow for the breadth of the Greek, since it has come to be equated with illicit sexual desire. Not all *epithumia*-desire is evil. It was with 'desire' that Jesus wished to celebrate the Passover (Last Supper) with his disciples (Luke 22:15). In James the concern is with evil desires in general – desires for anything that is contrary to God's revealed will for our lives.

Personal responsibility
Individual responsibility is embodied in the expressions '**each one**' and '**his own**'. James does not say anything about the role of Satan and demons. He does not talk about external forces which, to be sure, can contribute very powerfully to temptation. He puts the responsibility where it ultimately resides. This points to a fact that is often overlooked, namely that no power on earth, Satan included, can make you *want* to be wicked. You have to want to do it yourself, however great the seductions and inducements heaped upon you. There are cases when people are coerced into sinful acts against their will, or do things which appear to be wicked, because they are under the influence of chemical imbalances or certain kinds of mental illness. This in no way detracts from the basic thrust of the text. People sin because they want to. The powers of darkness and the circumstantial opportunities just make it a more attractive proposition. It is worth pointing out, however, that a sinful life-style makes hearts harder and sin easier. Paul

warns of the consequences of this in Romans 1:18-32. Sin takes over, the longer you give yourself to it. But even then, your responsibility to repent and turn to the Lord is not lessened one whit.

Temptation drags away and entices
Initially temptation is not sin itself. But it speedily leads to sin because of two distinct effects. It 'drags away' in that it distracts us from the true pleasures to which we are called by the Lord. And it 'entices' in that it draws us to the illusory pleasures of sin by presenting them in a false light. Temptation flatters to deceive. It is attractive and appealing. At first, it is neither tawdry nor repulsive. Indeed, it only becomes repulsive to the heart that is convicted of the sinfulness of sin.

Temptation's ultimate destination (1:15)

'Then, after desire has conceived, it gives birth to sin; and sin, when it is full-grown, gives birth to death' (1:15). The use of the process of birth as an illustration is brilliantly ironic. The very notion of the birth of death conveys a sad and sickening air of disaster and meaninglessness. A still-birth is self-evidently a tragedy. A deliberate abortion is a search-and-destroy mission aimed at life itself. It terms of James' illustration, temptation is the abortion of the human soul. Temptation kills; sin *is* death itself. The progression is temptation, sin, death. The wages of sin is death (Romans 6:23).[3]

The seriousness of sin
The gravity of the mere inward entertainment of sin was forcefully stated by Jesus in the Sermon on the Mount, when he said that 'Anyone who looks at a woman lustfully has already committed adultery with her in his heart' (Matthew 5:28). John extends the application of the principle to the hatred of a brother: 'Anyone who hates his brother is a murderer' (1 John 3:15).

This is further emphasized by the nature of death. 'Death,' as Thomas Manton notes, 'is but a modest word for damnation.'[4] All sin works death in us. No one escapes the first death and that is because of sin – our personal sin. That first death is also the 'last enemy' and it is subject to redemption in Christ for all believers. But for those who go their own way apart from Christ, the first death issues in the second death of a lost eternity.

There is nothing arbitrary about God's definition of what is righteous and what is not. The practical consequences of sin in the world give ample evidence of the hand of death being upon them. Fornication produces teenage pregnancies and abortions; unfaithfulness in marriage multiplies broken homes and children raised without (mostly) a father; hatred engenders violence and death at every level; covetousness issues in stealing, lust in rape; homosexuality has its own diseases and has been the means of introducing AIDS to Western society. Biblical ethics, flowing from love for Christ, would all but eliminate these scourges from our communities, but men love 'darkness instead of light, because their deeds [are] evil' (John 3:19).

A purpose of grace

Even so, the tragedy of the unconverted is that they also hate what they love. They protest too much their happiness with their godless Christ-denying life-style. Manton is surely right when he says that God 'made man of such a nature that all carnal delights leave impressions of sorrow at their departure'.[5] Sin begins as novelty, slips into drudgery and ends in slavery. Sinners are addicted to their way of life. Sin is their 'fix'. They know it is killing them, but they cannot do without it.

Yet, paradoxically, this is a powerful point of contact that the gospel of Jesus Christ has with lost, hurting people, even when they are not at all interested in Christ. Underneath the world's outward joy, there is sadness and pain, hopelessness and despair. You can only be a fun-loving sinner for so long. Soon the bill has to be paid. If you are filled with emptiness long enough, you begin to hear the rattle. When, like the prodigal son in Jesus' parable, you are reduced to putting your snout in the pig-trough, you know you need a new beginning.

James has a purpose of grace in speaking as he does of sin

and death. The purpose is to call us to the Lord, to love him
and gain a crown of life. But we must forsake that disastrous
complex of desire-sin-death and commit our lives to the Lord
Jesus Christ. It was he who said, 'Unless you repent, you too
will all perish' (Luke 13:3).

5.
Gifts

Please read James 1:16-18

'Don't be deceived, my dear brothers. Every good and perfect gift is from above, coming down from the Father of the heavenly lights, who does not change like shifting shadows' (James 1:16-17).

Having made clear that God could never be the originator of sin or temptation, James turns to the positive side of the question. His address to his readers, **'Don't be deceived, my dear brothers...'** (1:16), indicates the connection with what has gone before (cf. 1 Corinthians 6:9; 15:33; Galatians 6:7) and prepares them for the foundational truth that God is the source of all good gifts. There is an intensity about the way James introduces his teaching about God's gifts and we ought not to miss the richness of its content.

The first point to notice is the seriousness of being **'deceived'** as to God's relationship to sin. To deny the perfect righteousness of God is tantamount to rejecting him altogether. The man who can shuffle off the blame for his sins onto God is a man who is effectively declaring that he not only does not need a God who saves sinners, but also that this God is actually a menace to human morality, since he made things the way they are! To be deceived into thinking that God could be the author of temptation and sin is an act of self-justification at the expense of God. It is a tacit denial of faith and, with it, of the truth as so clearly revealed in Scripture. It is the denial of the Father-God of the everlasting covenant, who loved the world so much that he sent his only-begotten Son to be the Saviour of the world.

Secondly, James is speaking to his **'dear brothers'**. This balances the stark urgency of the exhortation not to be deceived. The juxtaposition of a tough command and a warm expression of brotherly love indicates James' attitude to his readers. He speaks as a true pastor to a flock of fellow-believers for whom he has the deepest affection in the Lord. This puts in perspective all the hard sayings about sin and death. James tells them the truth because he loves them. There is no mere denunciation of sin and sinners. He is not flogging the sheep, as if he didn't really believe they were Christians and they had to be bullied into toeing the line! James sets out the truth with that combination of clarity and gentleness that seeks to win men's and women's hearts for the Lord!

A more general connection between 1:13-15 and 1:16-18 is the continuation of the metaphor of childbirth. In verse 15, the conception of evil desire gave birth to sin, and sin gave birth to death. Contrasted with this is the emphasis in verses 17-18 upon the fatherhood of God and the regeneration, or new birth, of believers through the word of truth. On the one hand, we have the birth-experience of rebellious unbelieving humanity, which aborts into eternal death, and on the other the rebirth of the new redeemed humanity to eternal life in Jesus Christ, by the free grace and sovereign power of God in salvation. James has shown us the way of death; he now opens up the way of life.

Good gifts (1:17)

'Every good and perfect gift is from above, coming down from the Father...' (1:17). We are immediately presented with the doctrine of the perfect righteousness of God in his dealings with the human race. All our English versions lose something in translation because the original Greek does not merely repeat itself, to say 'good' gift and 'perfect gift'. A more accurate picture of the thrust of the text can be given if it is paraphrased as follows: 'Every act of giving that is good *(Pasa dosis agathe)* and every perfect gift *(pan dorema teleion)* is from above...' This expresses the completeness of the goodness of God – both *what he does* and the *way that he does it* – both the gifts and the giving. When God gives, he gives lovingly and he gives wonderful gifts. Both gifts and giving express his character. This is further reinforced by the fact that, in context, the emphasis is not so much upon the temporal, material, providential gifts of God, which are good and perfect even in a world marred by sin (food, shelter and the like) but on God's gifts as they relate to spiritual life – the triumph of faith over trials and temptations. The thought is this: God is not the author of any evil whatsoever; rather, his dealings with us are good and complete – he would never incite us to sinful behaviour. He is our heavenly Father and he knows how to give us good gifts. So although all of God's material gifts are good and perfect, it is his spiritual gifts that are primarily in view here. God gives his people the Holy Spirit to lead them into all truth (John 14:26; 16:13) and to bring forth abiding fruit in their lives. He teaches and guides us to the end that we should be transformed after the image and example of our Saviour and that glory might accrue to his name. And because these are the dealings of the Holy Spirit within our innermost being, this means that we respond in a predictable way to his good giving and his perfect gifts. A deep sense of the goodness of God accompanies his work in our hearts. Believers recognize true spiritual blessings for what they are and are strengthened in their faith. Indeed, the Christian declares these gifts to be 'better than life' (Psalm 63:3). He never tires of God's ministrations – his mercies are 'new every morning' and call forth the confession, 'Great is your faithfulness!' (Lamentations 3:23). Christians are conscious in a most personal way that the Lord is the source of their lives and the ever-loving guardian of their times. We confess that God will be our God 'through all eternity'. We know him as the God and Father of our Lord Jesus Christ, who has reconciled us to himself through the blood of his own dear Son. And we remember the words of our Lord when he assured us of the bountiful love of the Father towards his believing people: 'If you, then, though you are evil, know how to give good gifts to your children, how much more will your Father in heaven give good gifts to those who ask him!' (Matthew 7:11).

The good giver (1:17)

The gifts of God, says James, come **'from the Father of the**

heavenly lights, who does not change like shifting shadows'
(1:17).

The Father of the heavenly lights
God is called, literally, 'the Father of the lights'. The **'lights'**
are the stars and the connection is that he, as the Creator of
all the light sources in the universe, is himself the eternal
uncreated light. 'God is light; in him there is no darkness at
all' (1 John 1:5). Light and darkness correspond to good and
evil. Men love 'darkness instead of light' because their deeds
are evil (John 3:19). But the Father has sent his Son into the
world, 'the true light that gives light to every man' (John 1:9).
The redeemed of the Lord sing together, 'The Lord is my light
and my salvation – whom shall I fear?' (Psalm 27:1). Salvation
is being taken 'out of darkness into his wonderful light' (1
Peter 2:9). Every believer acknowledges with thanksgiving
that God's Word is a lamp to his feet and a light for his path
(Psalm 119:105). The glory of the Lord is called 'unapproach-
able light' (1 Timothy 6:16). And the witness of believers is
described by Jesus himself as letting our light shine before the
world, because, as he says, we are the 'light of the world'
(Matthew 5:14-16).

All of this scriptural usage of the imagery of light emanates
from the one Father who is light in himself. And James' argument is simply asking, how can the gifts which are given by
such a Father God be anything less than good and perfect?
When God created the world, he said, 'Let there be light.'
When he sends forth his gifts, his light shines forth. It is
inherent in his very character as the infinite-personal God.

Who does not change
The fact of God's unchangeableness – in theology, the 'in-
communicable attribute' called immutability – underscores
James' argument that his gifts are good and perfect. Unlike
the sun, moon and stars, which come and go and cast
shadows, God never changes and never moves in such a way
as to cast shadows. 'I the Lord do not change' (Malachi 3:6).
Change is characteristic of created things – immutability is a
divine attribute. He is the same, 'yesterday and today and for
ever'. His mercy endures for ever.

The question is often raised as to how this squares with the changes which the Lord brings into our lives. The course of human life is a constant process of change. And what is that life but the providential activity of God? Both trials and gifts are changes which affect us very significantly. Are they not the acts of God and are they not, by the same token, changes in him? The answer is that the changes we experience do not imply any alteration in the eternal purpose of God. God is active, but all his actions are the outworking of his unchanging purpose and immutable will. His will is like 'a silken string' running through a 'chain of pearl' (his actions), says Thomas Manton. 'He may will a change, but not change his will.'[1]

Change is so much a part of human experience that we take it for granted. Indeed, our day-to-day hopes are bound up with an effort to change things for the better. It is difficult for us to get our minds round the immutability of God, far less to accept the rather obvious implication of this truth that mutability (change) is a bad thing. Indeed, it seems to contradict the whole thrust of the gospel, which is to change lives radically – and even transform societies, nations and human history itself! Clearly, we are dealing with different levels of change. In terms of the infinite-eternal character of God, there can be no change. There ought to be a reflection of this in men and women, in terms of their bearing the image of God, namely, 'knowledge, righteousness and true holiness'.[2] In this sense – the spiritual, moral and ethical – changeableness (away from God's perfect precepts) is sinful and self-destructive. Manton is right to say, 'The more mutable [changeable] you are, the less you are like God.' We are called to 'establish and settle [our] spirits' as God brings us to an unchangeable 'state of grace, against which all the gates of hell cannot prevail'.[3] Stability, maturity and sober- and single-mindedness are the evidence of the grace of 'unchangeableness' bearing fruit in a life buffeted by sin from without and within.

At the nuts-and-bolts level of daily living, change is simply the way we act as successive moments present us with different choices. In this respect, time is no different from eternity, earth no different from heaven. Heaven is not some ethereal environment in which time is suspended and nothing moves. Sin-related change – as with decay and death – is absent from heaven. But the finite nature of men and angels means that even in heaven they experience the succession of moments and actions that characterize our life on this earth. In this sense, change is inescapable. We cannot think or be conscious without such change. This, however, is not spiritual or moral changeableness; it is merely the transitional development of thought and action inseparable from the finitude of the creature and the sequential nature of the experience of living in time. We are changeable by nature and experience; God is unchangeable by nature, but he acts to change us by his everlasting love and irresistible power.[4]

The gift of new birth (1:18)

James now appeals to his readers' personal experience of the Lord's grace: **'He chose to give us birth through the word of truth, that we might be a kind of first-fruits of all he created'** (1:18). There is one 'special proof of the goodness of God', says John Calvin, which 'every one of the faithful feels in himself'.[5] This is the new birth – the regeneration by the Holy Spirit of the innermost unrenewed nature, which creates a new disposition to receive, rather than oppose, the message of the gospel and the person of Jesus Christ. To have been 'born again' (John 3:3-8) and subsequently to be converted to Christ through repentance and saving faith (John 3:16; Acts 16:31) cannot but impress upon us, at the deepest level, the goodness of God towards us in Christ. James' argument is plain: if being a true Christian inescapably proves to us that God is good, then there need be no doubting his goodness in respect of everything else that he does for his people. The argument is from the greater to the lesser: once we have experienced spiritual rebirth – i.e., saving grace in the renewal of the heart – then we know that our Saviour can give us nothing but good and perfect gifts and is in no way to be held responsible either for our trials or our temptations. The Christian who seriously attributes bad motives and evil providences and temptations to God is a contradiction in terms. Truly to know the grace of God is to know the God who is truly all of grace. This is not to say that doubts and errors about the Lord are impossible in a Christian. The greatest of saints have their failings and inconsistencies. The point is that wherever God has regenerated a sinner, the bedrock reality is that his goodness will inevitably be recognized and confessed. And however far that believer may stray, he will return to the truth that God is perfectly holy and good in both his gifts and the manner of their bestowal. Four aspects of this gift lend force to James' assertion in 1:17.

Birth

To become a Christian required nothing less than a new birth of our sin-sick human nature. James states the fact. He assumes the theology which Jesus taught to Nicodemus (John 3). The image of childbirth is apt. Just as we did not bring ourselves into the world, neither did we bring ourselves into God's kingdom. We cannot bear ourselves again. When Jesus told Nicodemus, 'You must be born again,' he was stating a fact, not issuing a command. He was, in effect, saying that entrance into his kingdom required a change of heart so profound as to be beyond the capacity of the human will to effect. Nicodemus was being told how helpless he was to save himself. New birth was the secret work of the Holy Spirit (John 3:8) that created the disposition to turn in faith to Christ as Saviour and Lord. The secret refers, of course, to the moment of the Spirit's regenerating intervention in our lives. The moment it happens, it is no secret to our awareness of God's gracious outreach towards us. We then want to hear, want to repent, want to believe and want to follow him as his disciples.[6]

Through the word of truth

From the viewpoint of our personal experience of the new birth and its consequences (i.e., conversion to Christ), the gift of the new birth comes to us by means of the Word of God. The breath of the Holy Spirit may come at the time he sovereignly appoints; his regenerating work may be unlooked for by us; it may come against our virulent opposition to the Lord; but the Holy Spirit invariably works in human hearts in connection with the hearing of God's Word – that word which is 'living and active' and 'sharper than any double-edged sword, … dividing soul and spirit, joints and marrow', and judging 'the thoughts and attitudes of the heart' (Hebrews

4:13). Our knowledge of the Lord does not come out of thin air, but from the declaration of God's Word. This is why the Scriptures themselves are so utterly indispensable to evangelism. The written Word declares the Word made flesh. The witness of the church is Christ in all the Scriptures (Acts 8:35).

He chose

The source of the gift of salvation is the eternal decree of God. He **'chose'** or **'purposed'**. He did not merely see ahead of time what was going to happen on its own. His omnipotent will preceded every act. He chose. Sinners are saved because God elected to save a people for his own glory and their eternal happiness. They deserve eternal death but he decides to give them new life. Furthermore, 'It is from his *spontaneous kindness* that God originates this new life.'[7] How then can the God who has given such a gift – and that given purely out of his free grace – ever be conceived of as giving temptations, sins and spiritual death to anyone? It is impossible! And it is blasphemy!

A kind of first-fruits of all he created

The purpose of the gift of new life is that believers would be **'a kind of first-fruits'** for the Lord. The idea of the first-fruits was rooted deeply in the consciousness of the Lord's people (James, you will remember, is speaking to the Christians of the Jewish Diaspora). The bringing of the 'first-fruits' of the harvest to the Lord (Deuteronomy 26:1-10) was an acknowledgement that the whole of the harvest belonged to him. So Christians in any given generation are the first-fruits to God and to the Lamb (Revelation 14:4). They indicate the crown-rights of the Lord Jesus Christ over all creation and are, in themselves, a witness to his personal claims over every single human being – hence the blessing of coming to Christ by faith and the awful loss of rejecting him. He will be your Saviour or he will be your Judge – in either case, his mediatorial authority is fully exercised.

The focus of the 'first-fruits' is, however, upon redemption itself. Christ himself is described as 'the first-fruits of those who have fallen asleep' (1 Corinthians 15:20). That is to say, Christ first rose from the dead and is therefore the guarantor that those believers who die before he returns will themselves be raised from the dead. The same Greek word (*aparche*) is used in Romans 16:5, where Epenetus is called the 'first-fruit' in Asia, and in 1 Corinthians 16:15, where Stephanas and his household were described as the 'first-fruits' in Corinth. A great harvest was to follow. And so the gift of new life in Christ brings forth 'first-fruits' in those who are converted to Christ. In their turn, they are a gift to the world in which they are called to shine as lights for their Saviour, so that more and more people may come to Christ and receive the gift of eternal life through his fully atoning sacrifice for sin. God is the giver of good and perfect gifts – and *only* good and perfect gifts – and the giving of his Son to be the Saviour of his people is the confirmation of this truth in the experience of everyone who has been saved by his grace.

6.
Listening

Please read James 1:19-21

'*My dear brothers, take note of this: Everyone should be quick to listen, slow to speak and slow to become angry, for man's anger does not bring about the righteous life that God desires. Therefore, get rid of all moral filth and the evil that is so prevalent, and humbly accept the word planted in you, which can save you*' (James 1:19-21).

Every Christian will freely admit that his greatest problem in living the Christian life is being consistently obedient to what he knows to be the clear teaching of God's Word. Sins against 'light' – what we know to be true – are a vastly greater problem than sins of ignorance. We sometimes feel that the more we know of the Bible's teaching, the more we find ourselves falling short in our actual practice. We find it relatively easy to listen to God's Word, sincerely and enthusiastically at the time, only to go on living in the same old way, largely unaffected by what we have heard. And so we drive a wedge between the hearing and the doing of the Word of God. Theory and practice do not mesh. We are hearers and not doers.

This problem in the Christian life and its cure are the subject of James' next section (1:19-25). Taking his starting-point from the new birth (1:18), he first addresses the subject of how we are to *listen* to what God is saying to us (1:19-21), and then turns to the *doing* of that Word in practical discipleship to Christ (1:22-25). Then, in 1:26-27, he will draw all these threads together and present what is in effect the theme of his whole epistle: namely, that 'true religion' consists in practical holiness and devotion to the Lord that evidences itself in a clean life and loving service to others.[1]

Cultivating the right attitude (1:19-20)

Problems will not disappear just because you become a Christian. Some Christians, however, believe that Jesus wants them to be happy all the time. A well-known evangelical chorus gives voice to this unscriptural aspiration:

> At the cross, at the cross,
>> Where I first saw the light
>> And the burden of my sins fell away.
> It was there by faith I received my sight
>> And now I am happy all the day.

The whole chorus is a regrettably trite expression of what it means to be converted to Christ. The last line, however, offers a positively misleading impression about the Christian life – one which has been productive of great evils in many a Christian's thought and practice. It is a short hop from the idea that I ought to be happy all the time to the notion that whatever keeps me happy is all right with God. If God wants me happy and this particular action makes me happy, then it must be all right for me! I have heard, first hand, this doctrine of the primacy of 'happiness' used as an excuse for extra-marital sexual relations! The fact is that when personal happiness is king, the righteousness of God soon takes a back seat. Holiness soon melts away before the fervent heat of baptized lust! This is practical antinomianism (*anti* – against; *nomos* – law) in action and its evil genius is that it clothes immoral behaviour with a cloak of false sanctity. It is a way of redefining your favourite sins as good!

More often, however, Christians just feel bad because they experience troubles. Because they feel they ought to be 'happy all the day' and aren't, they feel all the more guilty and depressed. We have seen, however, that James' *expectation* for the Christian life means facing 'trials of many kinds' (1:2). Trials, however distressing and inconvenient, are a thoroughly normal component of the Christian life and no one need feel guilty on that count. Jesus told us we would have to face troubles in this fallen world and indicated that following him could only draw the fire of his enemies (John

16:33; 13:16). Scripture calls this the 'fellowship' of his sufferings (Philippians 3:10). James' point was that it is possible to find real joy in the face of both outward trials and inward temptations. And that joy would come only in faithful perseverance in righteousness. Holiness first; happiness second. And not the Pollyanna happiness of bubbly superficiality, but the heart-shaking joy that comes from crying to the Lord, even 'out of the depths', and realizing with rising hope that 'He himself will redeem Israel [i.e., his people...even me!] from all their sins' (Psalm 130:1,8).

James' train of thought is clear. He reminds the believers of all that God had done for them. They had been reborn by his sovereign grace 'through the word of truth' to be new people for the Lord – 'first-fruits' devoted to God and precious in his sight (1:18). James was well aware that this new life, for all its blessings in terms of peace, joy and new obedience to the Lord, did not mean instant perfection and an end to all the ills of life. A train can be on the right tracks but still carry a lot of excess baggage. Bad habits, unclean thoughts, unhallowed desires, gross ignorance and unsubdued passions didn't all jump the train when the Lord changed the points and put it on his tracks! There is still work to be done to fit it for its arrival at God's destination. Every Christian life needs work. Spiritual growth means progressive sanctification – both separation to God and 'putting to death' the sins of the person we once were (Romans 8:13).

To this end, James says there are three basic things we must do: we must **'be quick to listen, slow to speak and slow to become angry'** (1:19). This will cultivate the attitude of heart in which the fulness of salvation will be embraced and enjoyed in the course of the Christian life.

Be quick to listen (1:19)
The context is 'the word of truth', as that has brought someone to saving faith in the Lord. The focus is on spiritual things. The new Christian is a novice. He naturally wants to talk about his new faith, his new hopes and his new Saviour. But he must rather be as quick to listen. He must restrain his quickness to speak out. He must open his ears rather than his mouth! This principle applies to every Christian, of course,

the point being that the Word of God must first be *heard* before anyone can respond in faith to its claims. And the principle extends to our use of all the means by which we may increase our knowledge of the things of God, whether by listening to preaching, good conversation and wise counsel, or reading the Scriptures and good literature. At the heart of it is the humble realization of the need to learn and the concomitant awareness that if I'm endlessly spouting my ignorance, I can't be absorbing your wisdom...or the Lord's.

Like everything that involves suppressing egotistical impulses, good listening is a discipline that can involve a great deal of hard work. Some people can't sit still long enough to hear what is being said. In one of my classes in Westminster Seminary, we had a fellow who liked to ask his questions before the professor had lectured! On one occasion – our teacher was the eminent New Testament scholar, Philip Edgecumbe Hughes – the echo of the opening prayer had not died before this chap's hand was up and waving, asking opportunity to speak. Dr Hughes, whose puckish English wit was altogether equal to the occasion, looked bemusedly over his half-spectacles and brought the house down by saying, 'I say, old boy, do you think I could say something before you ask me what I meant?' The serious point was, of course, that if you are the student, you are supposed to listen to your teacher before you ask your questions or dispense your insights!

If you can't listen because you're doing the talking, neither can you listen if you aren't paying attention. I once made the mistake of dozing off in one of Cornelius Van Til's apologetics classes.[2] The genial Dutchman was a crack-shot with a piece of chalk! As it bounced lightly off my cranium, I awoke to a loud, chuckling, 'Wake up, Scotchman!' and a face creased with the elfin delight of a successful practical joker. I listened after that!

You can't be listening to the right things, if you waste your attention on unprofitable things. An example of this problem is the modern enthusiasm of many Christians for reading works of fiction and fantasy, without the countervailing benefit of reading in the literature of biblical exposition, theology and devotion. Robert Johnstone, writing a century ago in words far more urgently required today, deplored the habit of spending the larger proportion of our time in 'talk and literature which is simply light, not wicked' – often merely to 'kill time' in an entertaining way. 'Those whom God has taught the value of time,' he said, 'feel that it has little need to be "killed" – it goes away from us all too quickly without that. The wise apostle Paul would have us *"redeem the time"* – buy it back from worldliness and indolence at the cost of self-sacrifice.'[3] Johnstone's point was not to condemn recreational reading, but to call Christians to a sense of proportion and balance with respect to their informational intake.

This gauntlet also ought to be thrown down at our TV and video-watching habits. Quite apart from the content of what is being watched hour after hour, night after night, there is the modern phenomenon of the 'attention span'. For the TV-generation, this is now approximately the time between the commercials, maybe ten to fifteen minutes! Decline in reading and, incidentally, the pressure for fifteen-minute sermons in the churches are laid at this door. We are told this as if there were some deterministic force in modern man which makes this inevitable and implies that we must all accept the reality and adapt. The answer to that is that listening – call it 'the attention-span' if you like – is a discipline which involves will and motivation. People who merely want to be entertained have chosen to reject that discipline and deny themselves the personal growth that it promises. For the Christian, this discipline is an indelible part of his spiritual growth in love for God. Being 'quick to listen' does not take away the hard work that is entailed, but it clothes it in the garments of praise and produces a harvest of blessing in closer fellowship with the Lord!

Slow to speak (1:19)

As with all things there must be balance and proportion. It is not wrong to speak! Some folk are so quiet they never say a word; others are never silent. What James has in mind is a sensitivity to the dangers of speaking too hastily or too passionately. 'Our civilization,' writes Earl Kelly, 'is a civilization without a silencer.'[4] The rise of radio talk-shows has revealed a nation of 'instant experts'. Even in the church, a man is no sooner converted than he is urged to teach others in Sunday School. The Scriptures consistently warn against any rush into speaking or teaching:

> 'A man of knowledge uses words with restraint,
>   and a man of understanding is even-tempered.
> Even a fool is thought wise if he keeps silent,
>   and discerning if he holds his tongue'
> (Proverbs 17:27-28).

Not many of us 'should presume to be teachers', James will say later on (3:1). As the inspired preacher says,

> 'Do not be quick with your mouth,
>   do not be hasty in your heart
>   to utter anything before God.
> God is in heaven
>   and you are on the earth,
>   so let your words be few.
> As a dream comes when there are many cares,
>   so the speech of a fool when there are many words'
> (Ecclesiastes 5:2-3).

Slow to become angry (1:19)

Anger very often wells up in connection with both poor listening and hasty speaking, but it is a problem in its own right. Anger is dangerous. Even righteous anger is to be restrained, just because it so easily tends to be sinfully diverted into vindictiveness and an escalating fury that goes way beyond the original cause of offence. Therefore, said Paul, 'In your anger do not sin. Do not let the sun go down while you are still angry' (Ephesians 4:26). How much more, then, do we need to sit on the sinful resentments and flashes of rage that so easily flare up if someone says something we don't agree with, if our consciences are pricked or even if we brood on what we think somebody is thinking about us? 'He who is slow to anger is better than the mighty, and he who rules his spirit, than he who captures a city' (Proverbs 16:32 NASB).

The practical reason for this is that **'Man's anger does not**

bring about the righteous life that God desires' (1:20).
'Anger,' observes Manton, 'is not to be trusted; it is not as just
and righteous as it seems to be.'[5] We all know this to be true
in our own experience. Only a quiet and calm spirit produces
personal holiness. Steady perseverance and patience, not agi-
tation and anger, are the hallmark of the work of God in
human hearts (Romans 5:3-5).

These, then, are the basic elements in any cultivation of a
Christ-like attitude to spiritual things – quickness to listen,
slowness to speak and slowness to anger. These will, in Jesus
Christ, bring forth the righteous life that God desires.

Eliminating hindrances to growth (1:21)

**'Therefore, get rid of all moral filth and the evil that is so
prevalent'** (1:21). Avoid all spiritual pollutants! Get rid of
everything displeasing to God! The point is that sin always
comes between us and the Lord. It is the bad *habitus* of the
'old man' – the spiritual deadness and darkness that estranged
us from God in the first place.

The word translated 'moral filth' *(rhuparian)* emphasizes
the polluting effect of sin – evils like envy, lust and malice that
eat away at the soul like cancers. The second expression, 'the
evil that is so prevalent' *(perisseia kakias)* reminds us that
there is, as Manton puts it, an 'abundance of wickedness to be
purged out of the heart of man'.[6] There is an echo of Genesis
6:5: 'The Lord saw how great man's wickedness on the earth
had become, and that every inclination of the thoughts of his
heart was only evil all the time.'

Getting rid of sin in all its manifestations is an urgent
necessity. The 'old yeast' of 'malice and wickedness' needs to
be purged out; the 'old self' must be 'put off' and we must
count ourselves 'dead to sin but alive to God in Christ Jesus'
(1 Corinthians 5:8; Ephesians 4:22; Romans 6:11). 'A little
yeast works through the whole batch of dough,' says Paul (1
Corinthians 5:6). Therefore, all must go. 'Let us purify ourselves from everything that contaminates body and spirit,
perfecting holiness out of reverence for God' (2 Corinthians
7:1).

Receiving the means of growth (1:21)

The elimination of the negative only has meaning when the positive is emphasized. With the rejection of sin must come the receiving of the Word of God. Therefore, says James, **'humbly accept the word planted in you, which can save you'** (1:21). This tells us *what* we are to receive, *how* we are to receive it and *why* we are to do so.

The word planted in you
What are we to accept? The **'word planted in you'**. This recalls the parable of the sower and the seed (Matthew 13:1-23). The gospel of Christ is the seed. You are the soil. The seed is to be received into the soil. The Lord is speaking to your heart about your deepest commitments. He is not providing you with an entertaining diversion (a story). Neither is he feeding you with some useful information (study). It is a word of life to be assimilated. It is a life-giving Word to divide 'soul and spirit, joints and marrow'; it judges 'the thoughts and attitudes of the heart' (Hebrews 4:12). Do you welcome the Word, 'not as the word of men, but as it actually is, the word of God'? (1 Thessalonians 2:13). Do you receive it with 'great eagerness' like the Berean Christians, who 'examined the Scriptures every day...'? (Acts 17:11). Notice, too, that the Word is described as 'planted in you'. The idea is that the Word takes root, indeed becomes our root. We become rooted and built up in Christ and his love, as the Word takes root in us (Colossians 2:7; Ephesians 3:17).

Humbly accept
How are we to accept the Word? With humility of mind. God may reason with us (Isaiah 1:18), but he does not negotiate. There is no middle way, no compromise, no give and take on both sides; only unconditional surrender to the gospel of saving grace. He gives; we must accept. It is all of God's free grace in Christ. Therefore, a spirit of childlike acceptance and an attitude of happy meekness animate the way in which the believer responds to the Word. Many Christians talk about 'wrestling' with the Word or with a particular doctrine of Scripture, when what they are really doing is resisting it, as

they try to find a way round accepting teaching that has rub-
bed them up the wrong way. It must be admitted that there
are difficult points of interpretation at various places in Scripture. In such cases, we ought to heed the apostolic warning
about 'doubtful disputations' (Romans 14:1 AV). By and
large, however, contentiousness is most evident on the main
points of revealed truth as these cut across what people actually want to do in their lives. For example, no doctrines in
Scripture are clearer than those of the absolute sovereignty of
God (predestination), the deity of Christ, the total inability of
man to save himself, the divine election of sinners to salvation, the perseverance of the saints and, with respect to the
church, its government by elders/presbyters who must be
men! Yet these are hotly disputed and all the 'wrestling' that
goes on is touted as an evidence of grace! Brothers and sisters,
these things ought not to be! 'Humbly accept the word
planted in you.' Surrender in simple faith.

Which can save you
The effect of the Word, humbly accepted, is salvation. It is,
literally, 'able to save your souls'. James is taking the long
view, towards the great day when salvation in its fulness will
be enjoyed in heaven itself. The gospel is the power of God
unto salvation for all who believe. And that deliverance is
being worked out now, in this present life. Growth in grace
and in the knowledge of the truth is the evidence of the
advance of Christ's redemption in our hearts. 'Like newborn
babies,' says Peter, 'crave pure spiritual milk, so that by it you
may grow up in your salvation, now that you have tasted that
the Lord is good' (1 Peter 2:2-3). This is what becoming 'mature and complete, not lacking anything,' is all about (1:4).
'By thoughtful, prayerful, earnest effort to vanquish sin, the
dimming, begriming, incrustations which have gathered on
the windows of the soul are removed and the beams of
heavenly light shine in.'[7] Let us wash the windows of our
souls. Let us hear what God has said to us!

7.
Doing God's Word

Please read James 1:22-25

'Do not merely listen to the word, and so deceive yourselves. Do what it says' (James 1:22).

One of the most wonderful facets of the way in which the Lord reaches out towards us is the patience with which he takes the time to reason with us, to persuade us in our own minds about what he wants of us. '"Come now, let us reason together," says the Lord. "Though your sins are like scarlet, they shall be white as snow; though they are red as crimson, they shall be like wool"' (Isaiah 1:18). He is the great Shepherd of his sheep and leads the lambs gently, notwithstanding the authority and the searching nature of his message. Line upon line, precept upon precept, he leads our thoughts into his perfect will. This is what we are seeing in the first part of James' epistle. James is leading us from conversion to Christ, through steps that will issue in the fruit of practical godliness and finally to the conclusion that living Christianity is a faith that is expressed in purity of life before God and the world and in practical and loving service to others (1:27). We are called to show forth the redemption which Christ has purchased by his atoning death and victorious resurrection. We are called to grow in the Christian life through godly self-control and dying to sin, together with the humble acceptance of the Word of God, which is the very instrument of our salvation.

Here is the crux of the matter: the Word heard must become the word done! This is the message of 1:22-25. James first states the principle by which we are to live (1:22), and then illustrates it by sketching out the contrast between the person who is only a hearer of God's Word and the one who is both a hearer and a doer (1:23-25).

The true hearer is always a doer (1:22)

The pedestrian paraphrase of 1:22 in the NIV must be set aside for the splendid accuracy of the AV (or any of RAV, NASB and RSV): **'But be ye doers of the word, and not hearers only, deceiving your own selves.'**

We are better at spectating than participating. We love to watch others, but prefer to do nothing ourselves. I believe the greatest sorrow of true ministers of God, after their own sense of personal unfruitfulness, is the experience of preaching year after year to people who evidence little positive response to their messages. They yearn for visible spiritual growth among their people. Every preacher's 'great joy' is to see people 'walking in the truth' (2 John 4).

But be ye doers of the word
These words come first in the Greek text (the NIV inexplicably reverses the order) thus emphasizing the truth that faith is nothing at all if it does not go into action immediately! 'Doers are the best hearers,' says Manton.[1] The language suggests a continuing effort to be in our practice what we already are in Jesus Christ through faith. It tells us that 'doing' the Word of God is the great aim of our lives. The goal is that this should so pervade every aspect of our being that we will be characterized by this habit of active obedience to Christ.

The 'but' (*de*) at the beginning of the verse tells us that a contrast is intended with what has gone before in 1:19-21 about 'hearing' the word. This is confirmed by the words **'and not hearers only'**. Hearing is good, but it means nothing if it is not matched by doing. That is why the person who only hears is said to be self-deceived. In one of the most searching passages in his preaching from James, the Scottish pastor Robert Johnstone challenged his people on this point: 'Yet, alas, brethren, there is reason to fear that, with great numbers of professing Christians...persons who attend the house of God, listen with a fair measure of diligence to the proclamation of truth and...rather love to talk of sermons and ministers and orthodoxy – this is *all*.' Nevertheless, they go on all the while 'with the conviction that they are certainly Christians' and forget 'that any degree of religious profession, where the heart is destitute of the love of God, and the life not consecrated to his service, is in his sight utter mockery'.[2] He then reminds us of Jesus' story about the wise and foolish builders, as he pressed home the teaching of the Sermon on the Mount. Those who hear the Lord's words and put them into practice are like the wise man who built on the rock but, says Jesus, 'Everyone who hears these words of mine and does not put them into practice is like a foolish man who built his house on sand. The rain came down, the streams arose, and the winds blew and beat against that house, and it fell with a great crash' (Matthew 7:26-27). Hearing and not doing is spiritually suicidal. It is to reject the truth of God at the very point where it must take effect. Not to embrace and act upon God's Word is merely to use it as an empty form. To believe that this is what it means to be right with God is nothing more than an illusion. Yet many rest very comfortably in their fantasies and, though they are 'all talk and no walk', they think themselves 'good Christians'. The Greek word translated 'deceiving' (*paralogizomenoi*) means literally, 'reasoning beside' – i.e., it is reasoning that is off to one side, off on the wrong track. It took a wrong turn somewhere along the line. And at least one component of that error was not grasping that hearing is only a means (albeit a very essential means) and not an end.[3]

Looking in the spiritual mirror (1:23-25)

Mirrors are everywhere in our daily lives. We use one every morning after we get up to make sure we are neat and tidy for the day's obligations. We need them in our cars to negotiate safely that rush-hour traffic on the way to work. Mostly, we use them to check that we are as presentable as we can be day by day. Mirrors are so much part of modern life that we forget that without them – including natural mirrors like pond surfaces on still sunny days – we could hardly know what we look like! With them we have an image of who we are. We have a greater sense, perhaps, of our total identity.

Looking...but forgetting (1:23-4)

It would, of course, be silly to look in a mirror, only to go away and forget what we look like. The absurdity of this is in the fact that this would be the contradiction of the very purpose we had in looking in the mirror in the first place. It would defeat the object of the exercise! Well, says James, the person who hears the Word of God and does not put what he hears into practice is just like that! **'Anyone who listens to the word but does not do what it says is like a man who looks at his face in a mirror and, after looking at himself, goes away and immediately forgets what he looks like'** (1:23-24). He 'immediately forgets'. It goes in one ear and out the other. He never had any intention of doing anything about it. The Word did perhaps impinge on his conscience. It did touch something in his life, but he sloughed it off as quickly as it had come. Like the man in the sixth chapter of the letter to the Hebrews, this non-doing hearer has been enlightened to some degree, has tasted of the heavenly gift, has shared in the things of the Holy Spirit, has tasted of the goodness of God and the powers of the age to come, and yet is in terrible danger of that falling away for which there is no repentance.

The mirror illustration is apt, for the Bible is a spiritual mirror in which we are shown both ourselves as we really are and the Lord as he really is. God's Word is his edition of *This is your Life!* In his light, we see light. And both our sins and the Lord's grace in the gospel are reflected into our hearts from the Word. 'Whatever is hidden,' says Jesus, 'is meant to be disclosed, and whatever is concealed is meant to be brought out into the open' (Mark 4:22). 'But we all, with unveiled face beholding as in a mirror the glory of the Lord, are being transformed into the same image from glory to glory, just as from the Lord, the Spirit' (2 Corinthians 3:18 NASB). The 'mirror' remarks Manton, implies 'the clearest representation that we are capable of here upon earth'.[4] That is why it is also used to denote the relatively limited view we have of the risen and exalted Jesus now, as compared to what will be the case in heaven: 'For now we see in a mirror dimly, but then face to face; now I know in part, but then I shall know fully just as I also have been fully known' (1 Corinthians 13:12 NASB). This is neither to minimize the clarity of the Word of God nor to diminish the quality of the fellowship which believers enjoy with their Saviour. The spiritual mirror of Scripture is the fully sufficient revelation of God until the Lord Jesus Christ returns at the end of the age. But the glory yet to be revealed in heaven will bring all God's people into his very presence and we 'shall see him as he is' (1 John 3:2).

Not forgetting, but doing (1:25)

It follows that the person who looks **'intently'** into this spiritual mirror, **'and continues to do this, not forgetting what he has heard, but doing it – he will be blessed in what he does'** (1:25). The mirror is now described as **'the perfect law that gives freedom'**. 'The perfect law of liberty' (AV, NASB) is to be preferred to NIV's paraphrase.[5] It is an accurate rendering which allows the text to carry its full meaning, which is that 'The divine law, as seen by the Christian, exhibits liberty, gives liberty, is liberty.'[6] God's Word shows that sin is slavery, that his will is the way of freedom from sin and to salvation and that, in Christ the incarnate Word, it is the instrument of liberation in the believer's experience. Paul's whole theology of law and grace is contained within this concept of law as liberty. The **'law of liberty'** is the gospel. It is the whole of God's Word understood in terms of its fulness as Christ-centred good news. To receive Christ is to receive freedom from the law in the narrow sense – freedom from the necessity of keeping all God's precepts perfectly as the way of earning our own salvation (i.e., works-righteousness, which is impossible anyway because of our sin). In this sense we are free from the law, because we are under grace (Romans 6:14). And yet, in another sense, we embrace the actual keeping of the law as a freedom we can now enjoy, not because it can earn salvation for us, but because in Christ it can be the practical rule for a free life of holy and willing discipleship to him! Thus Paul says, 'I am not free from God's law but am under Christ's law' (1 Corinthians 9:21). What was the proof of our bondage prior to our conversion to Christ then becomes the instrument of our liberation throughout life. Why? Because Christ kept the whole law in our place and so secured the salvation which, when applied to our hearts and lives, radically altered our natural dispositions *vis-à-vis* God and his Word (the new birth), drew us irresistibly to repentance and faith in Christ as our Saviour (conversion) and renewed our lives by the progressive implantation, cultivation and fruition of new life (sanctification). This is true freedom and it is all in the gospel. As 'the perfect law of liberty,' the Word of God (both Old and New Testaments) is not a mere code of ethical restrictions, but a blueprint for a happy life of faith in Christ! That is why the Christian 'looks intently' into the Scriptures. That is why he puts what he learns into practice, 'not forgetting what he has heard, but doing it'.

The promise is that **'He will be blessed in what he does.'** God gives the rewards of his free grace *in,* and not only *as a result of,* the free faithfulness of the doers of his Word. 'The act of obedience,' observes Curtis Vaughan, 'carries in itself a blessing.'[7] Let us all take the Lord at his Word. The psalmist reminds us:

'The law of the Lord is perfect,
     reviving the soul.
The statutes of the Lord are trustworthy,
     making wise the simple.
The precepts of the Lord are right,
     giving joy to the heart.
The commands of the Lord are radiant,
     giving light to the eyes.
The fear of the Lord is pure,
     enduring for ever.
The ordinances of the Lord are sure
     and altogether righteous.
They are more precious than gold,
     than much pure gold;
they are sweeter than honey,
     than honey from the comb.
By them is your servant warned;
     in keeping them there is great reward'

                                        (Psalm 19:7-11).

8.
True religion

Please read James 1:26-27

'Religion that God our Father accepts as pure and faultless is this: to look after orphans and widows in their distress and to keep oneself from being polluted by the world' (James 1:27).

Religion is a funny thing. Everybody has an opinion about it but not too many admit to having it. 'Religion' is what other people have. 'Religious' is what other people are. In other words, 'religion' is not a word or a concept with which most people feel especially comfortable. To those without a particular 'faith', it is something to be despised as primitive or superstitious. But even to earnest Christians, 'religion' can seem to be a kind of substitute for the real thing – an empty parody of the biblical faith 'that was once for all entrusted to the saints' (Jude 3). 'Religion,' then, has become a bad word in the popular mind – to non-Christians and Christians alike it represents what is wrong with human spiritual life.

When the *theme* of a New Testament epistle is this thing called 'religion' – James calls it 'pure' religion – we inevitably have some explaining to do! We have to define our terms afresh in order to distinguish between **'the religion that God our Father accepts'** and the multifarious prejudices of men and women. Yes, there is such a thing as **'pure'** religion! And it is nothing less than the way God wants us to live!

What is religion? (1:26)

The original Greek words translated 'religion' and 'religious' (*threskos, threskeia*) occur only five times in the New Testament: three times in James 1:26-27 and once each in Acts 26:5 and Colossians 2:8. In each case, the meaning is very specific. It always refers to the proper outward form of religion. We would naturally think of what we call religious observances, perhaps particularly the external manifestations of worship and the paying of scrupulous attention to the exercises of Christian piety.

Our difficulty in understanding what James has to say is rooted in the unfortunate fact that our English word 'religion' does not adequately convey the meaning and scope of the Greek *threskos*. 'Religion' is, for us, our whole faith, inside and out. The Greek word, *threskos,* is more precise and focuses upon only the latter – the outward actions of faith. (Greek, of course, also has a word for the inward aspect of faith – *pistos*.) And this is the key to our understanding of James 1:26-27. James says, **'If anyone considers himself religious and yet does not keep a tight rein on his tongue, he deceives himself and his religion is worthless. Religion that God our Father accepts as pure and faultless is this: to look after orphans and widows in their distress and to keep oneself from being polluted by the world.'**

First of all, *this is not a definition of the whole of Christian faith.* James is not saying that the sum total of faith is doing good for widows and orphans and keeping clear of gross sins. It would be quite wrong to use this text as a basis for reducing Christianity to a combination of social action and abstinence from big sins. In practice, many people do think of the Christian faith in these highly compressed terms. As a result, they do not think of themselves as 'sinners' and they do not believe that God would do anything but accept them just the way they are. This minimalist faith offers a conveniently cheap salvation. That is its attraction. Do some good deeds and don't be a mass-murderer and you can have a clear conscience and persuade yourself that you are right with God! It also sweeps away at one stroke the evangelical claims of the New Testament: namely, that to be a Christian necessarily involves a personal spiritual experience of faith in Jesus Christ as Saviour and Lord and repentance towards God. James 1:27 cannot be regarded as an exhaustive description of what it means to be a Christian, although, as we shall see, it does focus upon a vital element, and evidence, of true faith in the Lord Jesus Christ.

James, then, is talking about *the proper form of religious observance* – the outward actions of true godliness. He is speaking to the Hebrew Christians of the Dispersion, who were well acquainted with the traditional Jewish concern about the details of the form of worshipping God. James is not finding fault with this basic concern. After all, the form of worship, the pattern of prayer and so on are set out in the Word of God. Rather, his point is that the forms of religion which are to be carefully observed according to God's Word must never be thought of as the 'be all and end all' of biblical faith. We are never to think that the cultic aspects of religion – public worship, prayer, Bible reading, pious vocabulary and giving to the Lord's work – are the sum and substance of the outward, visible activity of religious devotion. The actions of true religion go beyond a punctilious – and sincere – observance of the properties of public and personal worship of the Lord. 'Religion' does not equal 'ritual'! Biblical religion encompasses all the actions of the believer. *All* must be subject to Christ. Together, these constitute the religion acceptable to God our Father.

At this point, James is not discussing the inward spiritual aspects of the Christian experience and faith. This will come up later when he talks about the relationship between faith and deeds (2:14-20). Here, his concern is with *what we are actually doing* – or, more likely, what we are *not* doing but should! In so far as we observably conform to God's pattern for practical obedience, we give evidence of a living faith within our innermost being. Visible obedience argues invisible commitment. Outward wickedness suggests an inward rebelliousness against God. Perhaps the classic biblical example is that of the Pharisees in our Lord's day. Jesus denounced them in no uncertain terms (Matthew 23:1-39). The common misconception is that this was because they were outwardly correct, but inwardly rotten. The reality was that their *whole* system of behaviour proved their inward rottenness. They were both outwardly and inwardly rotten! In other words, they could be seen for what they really were! They were, to be sure, correct in many of their actions, as are the very worst of men. They tithed of their spices – outwardly and correctly – but they 'neglected the more important matters of the law – justice, mercy and faithfulness' – outwardly and incorrectly! (Matthew 23:23). It was their actual practice that made people realize that they were hypocrites. And it was the evident inconsistency between their outward actions and the full balance of God's law that condemned them, because it was indeed an accurate transcript of the unrenewed depravity of their hearts. This is why James later says to the person who excuses his lack of practical godliness by saying he has faith in his heart: 'Show me your faith without deeds, and I will show you my faith by what I do!' (2:18). Obviously, you cannot show your faith without deeds. You can talk, but talk is cheap. Deeds are the only true evidence of faith. The question always is 'What are you going to *do?*' The religion that James wants to promote is that which *does*. True religion is the practical outworking of the rule of Christ in the whole of life's activities. It is as simple – and as challenging – as that!

The proof of pure religion (1:26-27)

James' goal is that we might be led to a full consistency between our heart-commitment to the Lord and the way we actually conduct ourselves in daily life. In the development of his first chapter (as we shall see in detail in successive studies), he takes us from *trials* and temptations (1:2-18), to *perseverance* in practical obedience to the wisdom of God (1:19-21), and then to the challenge of *consistency* (1:22-25). Are we doers of the Word, as well as hearers? Having thus probed our consciences, he faces us with three basic evidences of true religion (1:26-27). The list is not exhaustive, as has been noted already. But it is a very telling one, for these are three salient points in the spectrum of our ethical response to God's Word. They represent, in microcosm, the thrust of the entire epistle. One way and then another, these surface in greater detail as James expounds his theme and applies it to our hearts and lives.

The control of the tongue (1:26)
'If anyone considers himself religious and yet does not keep a

tight rein on his tongue, he deceives himself and his religion is worthless.' The tongue is often the last bastion of open wickedness in the lives of Christians. John Calvin, with his characteristic perspicuity, remarks, 'He who is neither an adulterer, nor a thief, nor a drunkard, but, on the contrary, seems brilliant with some outward show of sanctity, will set himself off by defaming others, and this under the pretence of zeal, but really through the lust of slandering.'[1] In mentioning 'defaming others' and the 'lust of slandering', Calvin is not thinking merely of 'bad language'. Neither does he have false teaching in mind. The specific problem is rather a boastful self-serving spirit that uses the tongue to put other people down, and, at one and the same time, to puff up the speaker himself. There is no easier way to cover yourself with stolen glory for your alleged gifts and graces than by assassinating the character and gifts of your Christian brothers and sisters. Sometimes this is done with honeyed words which seem at first to express appreciation and praise for those who are about to be criticized. Such critics, writes Thomas Manton, 'make their praise but a preface to their reproach'. This, says Manton, is like an archer who draws back his hand, 'that the arrow may fly with the more force'.[2] It is the art of 'damning with faint praise' – the praise is only the prelude to the most piercing of censures. It merely masks a malicious purpose.

It goes without saying that all forms of unrestrained speech – swearing, lying, foul-mouthed joking, invective, boasting and the like – fall under God's ban, as the evidences of a proud spirit and an unholy attitude of heart. They all suggest, with not inconsiderable force, that the person who talks this way and imagines it is all right with God, 'deceives himself and his religion is worthless'. An unhallowed tongue bespeaks an unhallowed heart.

In contrast, the person who truly loves the Lord Jesus Christ is not *habitually* the person of James 1:26. He may fall into sin from time to time, as all of us do (too, too frequently). But as a believer, he is consciously striving to bring his tongue into subjection to God's Word. In fact, the actual experience of believers is to see the growth of practical discipleship to Christ in the normal course of life. The evidence of sanctification (progressive dying to sin and living for Christ) is, with respect to what we say, to see the tongue controlled and the

mouth more and more speaking out of the abundance of a
heart in which the Holy Spirit lives and works with renewing
power (Matthew 12:34).

A practical love for those in need (1:27)

**'Religion that God our Father accepts as pure and faultless is
this: to look after orphans and widows in their distress...'** The
Authorized Version renders this 'to *visit* the widows and the
fatherless...' thereby giving the impression that visiting is the
central thought in the text. This is, however, a case of an
English word that has a much narrower meaning today than it
had in 1611 and is now unable to carry the full meaning of the
original Greek (*episkeptesthai*). *Episkeptesthai* means 'to
look after' or 'to give relief'. Much more is involved than
merely going to see people. The whole scope of the ministry
of mercy is in view – although not so much the official
diaconal work of the church as the personal love and care of
individual Christians for others, as they have and make
opportunity. This would clearly be relative to the gifts and circumstances of these individuals. One Christian or a group of
Christians might commit themselves to looking after an
elderly person in the fellowship. A Christian couple might
foster or adopt a child who had been deprived of parents and
a home. James challenges the Christian community to pour
out the love of Christ in the most practical ways, to the end
that the deepest of needs might be touched for blessing, both
temporal and spiritual.[3] Have we not received salvation in
Christ? It is love received that is, in turn, the cornucopia of
love that is shared. Such commitment is rare, yet it ought not
to be. There must be an 'active love to the needy'.[4] And this
means using the gifts and opportunities that the Lord has
given in ways which most effectively minister to real need.

Separation from the world (1:27)

**'Religion that God our Father accepts as pure and faultless is
this:... to keep oneself from being polluted by the world.'**
James tells his readers, 'Don't be deceived...' (1:16). Sin
when it is full grown, gives birth to death (1:15). The apostle
Paul uses the same expression when warning the Corinthians
about the consequences of going along with the way of the
world. 'Do you not know that the wicked will not inherit the

kingdom of God? Do not be deceived: Neither the sexually immoral nor idolaters nor adulterers nor male prostitutes nor homosexual offenders nor thieves nor the greedy nor drunkards nor slanderers nor swindlers will inherit the kingdom of God.' Then, to emphasize the positive side of their obligation to live holy lives, Paul goes on to say, 'And this is what some of you were. But you were washed, you were sanctified, you were justified in the name of the Lord Jesus Christ and by the Spirit of our God' (1 Corinthians 6:9-11). The ethics of Christ must be the heart and soul of our daily lives. We need always to be sensitive to the fact that 'The very things of the world leave a taint upon our spirits.'[5] Our consciousness of sin and its effects ought to move us powerfully to draw back from the pollution of the world. But far more powerful is the Christian's awareness of the love of his Saviour which persuades him of the joy and privilege of separation from the world and union with Christ.

This, in a nutshell, is the Christian's calling in Christ. It is the practice of 'pure and faultless' religion. It is not we who are pure and faultless, even in our discipleship to Christ. It is the Lord's righteousness which is the purity and faultlessness implanted in the faith-experience of all he has saved. So, our response in faith and in Christ is acceptable to our heavenly Father because Christ, having died in the place of sinners for their sins, is acceptable to his Father as their sin-bearer. Christ's righteousness is ours. And it breaks out into vibrant spiritual devotion when self-control bears fruit in a sanctified tongue; when active love reaches out to the real needs of others; and when a decisive ethical separation from the norms of the world of unbelief issue in a transformed life, consumed with love for the Lord Jesus Christ. This is the 'religion' that God wants to see us living. This is what it means to be a practical Christian.

Part II
Case studies of faith in action

9.
Favouritism

Please read James 2:1-7

'Listen, my dear brothers: Has not God chosen those who are poor in the eyes of the world to be rich in faith and to inherit the kingdom he promised those who love him?' (James 2:5).

The first chapter of James establishes the central theme of the Christian life, by means of a chain of very practical arguments. The real, living faith to which believers have been born through the word of truth (1:18) is a faith that both hears what God says and does it with a willing heart. It consists in a practical service to others and a personal holiness before the Lord (1:26-27). Its reality is underscored by the fact that it meets trials and temptations head on, sees them as the tests of perseverance designed to produce spiritual growth and maturity, and goes on to gain the victory in dynamic dependence upon the Lord Jesus Christ.

In his second chapter, James begins to outline specific case-studies of faith in action. This makes up the body of the epistle (2:1-5:11). The central assumption is that the reality of Christian faith will evidence itself plainly in practical behaviour in the normal course of life. It will be possible to work through the doctrine we believe in terms of observable conformity to Jesus Christ. In the final analysis, this is the only way anyone will ever grow in the knowledge of Christ. Accordingly, we ought always to welcome the exposure of our consciences and our practices to the searchlights of God's Word. Interaction with the Word and the Holy Spirit is the leading edge of spiritual growth and maturation.

The first case is favouritism within Christian churches. Favouritism – 'respect of persons' in the older Bible versions

– does not immediately strike us as the natural first choice for
any discussion of the problems of the Christian life. We may
well wonder what the connection is with all that has gone
before. How did we get from trials and temptations and the
lofty themes of personal holiness and caring for widows and
orphans to 'favouritism' in the local church? Favouritism
seems more like a sub-set of general spiritual etiquette than a
major starting-point for a discussion of 'faith in action'.

No doubt many explanations could be proposed for James'
choice of opening subject. Was he just changing the pace? Or
grabbing the attention with a startling change of subject? Did
he feel the time had come for an injection of some down-to-
earth practicality? Without discounting these, I would like to
suggest that the key is at the heart of the story he tells in 2:1-7.
Having sketched out the main issues concerning the Christian
life in the general terms of 1:1-27, James begins his application to the practical specifics by asking us what happens at
the church door! Christians make up the church. They are the
body of Christ – the Lord's people in this world. Well, suppose someone comes to one of our gatherings. How is he
greeted? How does our Christian faith, in practical terms,
translate into how he is received? The church is, as it were,
the most public point of contact between the assembled
people of God and the surrounding world. As such it is the
arena of a simple practical test of the reality of faith: how do
we treat newcomers? Once we have dealt with this question,
we can go on to look at the wider theological truths about the
relationship of faith and works (2:14-26) and follow that up
with further specific areas of application, such as the way we
speak to and about people (3:1-12), quarrels among Christians (4:1-12) and the like. So the choice of 'favouritism' as
the opener is not so odd or illogical after all. It faces us from
the start with the implications of the gospel for the way we live
as Christians in the world, day by day.

Don't show favouritism (2:1)

**'My brothers, as believers in our glorious Lord Jesus Christ,
don't show favouritism'** (2:1). Our English translations cannot adequately convey the intensity of the original Greek of

the first verse. Because of normal English sentence structure, the phrase rendered 'don't show favouritism' is put last in our Bible versions, whereas in the Greek text it comes at the beginning – in the place of greatest emphasis. The text reads, literally, 'My brothers, *not with favouritism* hold the faith of our Lord Jesus Christ the glory.' This is a vigorous expression of the utter contradiction of being a believer in Jesus Christ while at the same time being given to the practice of favouritism and a spirit of partiality. The 'faith of our Lord Jesus Christ the glory' – that is, faith in the Lord Jesus Christ who is the glorious one, or the Lord of glory – is the root of all spiritual life and of all the good works that are pleasing in the sight of God. Favouritism is wholly inconsistent with discipleship to the Lord.

My brothers...

James speaks to those who think themselves Christians. He appeals to our confessed faith in Christ. He thereby touches the question of the reality of our personal love for the Lord. In this quiet, but unmistakable way, the Lord's brother establishes an irreducible standard of the Christian life – that a believer is committed to a very definite pattern of behaviour, which is taught by the Word of God and the Holy Spirit and which flows in his own innermost being from the experience of being converted to Christ in a living faith. To address his readers as **'brothers'** immediately makes contact with their consciences. Anyone who is called 'brother' cannot evade an internal response to the whole idea. He will either recognize his brotherhood or else feel his disqualification from that identification. He will either be stirred to seek a more committed relationship to the Lord and his people, or else will recoil into resentful hypocrisy or even open rejection. Real Christians are real brothers – and for the reason that they are really saved by the real free grace of God in Jesus Christ.

As believers...don't show favouritism

The inconsistency between faith in Christ and favouritism lies in the nature of the Christian salvation. 'He that prizeth the person of Christ,' observed Thomas Manton, 'prizeth all his relatives.'[1] Manton's use of the idea of blood relatives is apt. Those whom Jesus has saved by the shedding of his own blood of atonement are thereby adopted as children of God. Just as favouritism within an earthly family is a pernicious denial of proper familial bonds, so partiality among believers is a denial of the blood-bought privileges of those brothers and sisters who are subjected to such discrimination. It is, of course, the discriminators, rather than the discriminated against, that are the real losers, for they are in effect denying the gospel! Those who will not love *all* God's children cannot be truly loving their Saviour!

The word translated **'favouritism'** (Greek *prosopolam-phiais*) occurs in only three other New Testament passages (Romans 2:11; Ephesians 6:9; Colossians 3:25), all of which refer to the fact that, in contrast to human behaviour, there is never any favouritism with God, i.e., he never makes judgements on the basis of criteria that are external and superficial and therefore essentially unfair and consistently misleading. This word, observes Curtis Vaughan, 'is always used in the sense of showing favour to persons on account of external advantages, such as position, wealth or power'.[2]

Our glorious Lord Jesus Christ
The explicit mention of the Lord in his exalted glory, as the object of our faith, further reinforces the point. Favouritism always implies a scale of value or merit and therefore puts some down in favour of exalting some others (with whom we silently include ourselves). When this occurs in the church, it suggests that certain people are more valuable in God's eyes than others. Worse still, it suggests a spiritual superiority in the person who plays favourites – he sits in judgement over the relative quality of the members of Christ's body. Salvation in Christ is, however, all of grace and the sharing of the mercy of God is *the* great leveller in this life – levelling up, not down![3] Why? Because no true Christian can, in sober consistency with the free-grace nature of his salvation in Christ, see himself as more important than anyone else. The mention of Christ as **'our glorious Lord Jesus...'** emphasizes that he is the Lord of glory for those whom he has saved by his own blood. To prefer one Christian to another, because he is wealthy, well-dressed, articulate, pleasant or successful, is to forget what Christ has done in dying in place of sinners. He saved the

spiritually dead. He proved our utter poverty and helplessness in spiritual things. Only through faith in him have we any
real riches – the riches of gospel grace for time and eternity!
Manton, citing Martin Luther, recorded that the Roman
Emperor Theodosius said he would rather be *'Christianus
rusticus'* than *'ethnicus Alexander'* ('a Christian clown than a
pagan emperor') because he 'valued his Christianity above his
empire'.[4]

Favouritism in the church (2:2-4)

The scene is obviously a church service. A rich man and a
poor man enter, each clearly distinguishable by his dress.
Perhaps they are both believers in Christ. We are not told.
The point is that both have come as *bona fide* worshippers of
God and are to be welcomed as such. But what happens?
Special deference is shown to the well-dressed man, while the
poorer man is shunted aside and made to feel unwelcome.
What has happened, says James, is that a discrimination aris-
ing from evil thoughts has just reared its ugly head in the fellowship of Christ's church and opened up a wounding breach
where none ought to exist, even in the minds of those present.
    It is perhaps worth noting in passing that James is not deny-
ing the propriety of recognizing proper distinctions of rank
and respect in society. We are to honour kings and those in
authority and we are to respect those whom the Lord has set
over us in holy things (1 Timothy 5:17; Hebrews 13:7). Scripture recognizes the necessity of order and structure in family,
state and church. In condemning the discrimination which he
outlines, James is not, as it were, proposing a society without
appropriate distinctions. The problem he has in mind is, of
course, discrimination based on thoroughly worldly, man-
centred and sinful criteria.

Here is a good seat... (2:3)
The wealthy man was ushered deferentially to a 'good seat'.
The point is not so much the seat itself as the attitude which
singles him out for special treatment. The same attitude crops
up in the modern church in often quite different ways. A

church in Pittsburgh, in the U.S.A., advertised the personal
appearance one Lord's Day of a famous star of the Cleveland
Browns, a leading American football team. A former Miss
America travels the circuit of certain charismatic churches
and her very glamorous portrait is featured for that Sunday in
the newspaper advertisements inviting people to attend these
churches. Come to church, in other words, to hob-nob with
the great and bask in their reflected glory! The use of such
attractions, not excluding the periodic ministrations of the
current corps of celebrity preachers (without whom, some
people seem to believe, effective ministry would vanish from
the face of the earth), cannot easily shake off the taint of
undue respect for persons. Enthusiasm for following celebrity
ministry is rarely matched by loyal and sacrificial service in
local congregations where the going is tough. Carnal discrimination fills too many churches in the twentieth century and
there is no doubt that the churches have been reaping as they
have sown. What Francis Schaeffer has called 'the mindset of
accommodation' in the evangelical churches is eloquent testimony to the fruitlessness of much of the gilt-edged evangelical activism of our day.[5] When worldly attitudes prevail, the
church simply ceases to serve Christ.

There is a wide-ranging challenge in James' epistle for congregations and believers everywhere. Are the well-off in your
church listened to more seriously than the poor? Do they –
the rich – expect to have more influence? Do preachers tread
lightly on the sins of the rich and the clever, while railing
against the excesses of the poor? Do you welcome folks of
other races into your fellowship, without the taint of pater-
nalism? Does your church make a big effort to attract the edu-
cated, while showing little interest in gathering in working
people? Do you get excited about old people coming to the
Lord, or is it 'young families' that consume your intercessions
about congregational growth? Are there hidden 'favouritisms'
in your heart that make you feel that while some people in
your church are the kind you want to see in the assembly,
there are others you would not miss, were they to move on
elsewhere? Jesus prayed for the true unity of the church on
the very eve of his death on the cross. The only faithful
response on our part is to practise the doctrine of being one in
Christ Jesus! (John 17:21).

Judges with evil thoughts (2:4)

Favouritism tells us something about those people who so readily practise its wicked discriminations. They are **'judges with evil thoughts'**, says James. If, in assessing our attitude to someone, we prefer wealth to grace, and fame to humility, as the determining standards, we are no different from a corrupt judge who tries a case on everything but its merits. The correct principle of God-honouring discernment has been set aside in favour of spurious man-centred criteria. In contrast, hearts set on Jesus Christ actively resist the temptation to judge people by the externals and seek all the more to discern the work of God in their lives. 'We do not prize a horse for the gaudry [showiness] of his saddle and trappings,' writes Thomas Manton, 'but for his strength and swiftness...go by a wiser rule in valuing things and persons than outward excellency: do not think that faith best which the ruler professeth, (John 7:48), nor those persons best that glitter most with worldly lustre. Christ cometh often in a disguise to us...in his poorer members.'[6]

Why favouritism is foolish (2:5-7)

A great deal of what we do is a matter of habit. We live on 'auto pilot' for so many of the humdrum activities of life. For this reason, we can easily forget if we switched off the oven before we left the house. Again, we may have no recollection as to how many lights were red or green on the way to a friend's house! Taking our actions for granted is a part of each day's life. But that does not mean these actions are trivial. Sometimes we need to go back and make sure that the oven really is off! And sometimes we need to re-examine our most easily held assumptions and check them against the measure of the Word of God. It may well be that the rich man, the poor man and those who greeted them so differently gave scant thought to what was happening. We tend to act almost subconsciously in terms of our normal expectations: rich and poor alike can get to accept unthinkingly 'the usual treatment'. What we need, however, is not a comfortable conscience with whatever seems to be the way of things, but a clear view of the will of God and the spiritual impetus to do things his way! If we do this, we may well discover that what we thoughtlessly took for granted was marked with condemnation by God,[7] whereas his way is full of the richest blessings!

Think critically of the practice of favouritism! Don't just let it happen! Ask *why* there should be such discrimination. James offers us two basic and practical facts that ought to bring us to re-evaluate the ways in which we respond to human diversity (2:5-7).

Has not God chosen those who are poor? (2:5)

Look at the real Christians in the real churches of Jesus Christ. Who are they? And from where have they come in their coming to faith in Christ? Is it not obvious that the bulk of the people God has saved are **'poor in the eyes of the world'**? (2:5). There is a lowliness about the Lord's people in this world and it is all bound up in the fact that Christ came to preach the gospel to 'the poor' – those who are poor in both temporal and spiritual terms (Luke 4:18; 7:22). Even in the United States – the land we associate with large and wealthy churches and a billion dollar Christian TV industry – the astounding fact is that the average local church consists of just seventy-six men, women and children! The truth of plain observation is that the church in every country and generation is made up largely of ordinary folk. Well, says James, these are the people whom (1) **'God has chosen,'** (2) **'to be rich in faith,'** and (3) **'to inherit the kingdom he promised to those who love him'**! It is therefore an insult to the poor to treat them as second-class citizens in the body of Christ (2:6). The real sin, of course, is not so much insulting the poor as it is insulting God. To despise those to whom he has reached out in gospel love is to question his grace and is ultimately equivalent to despising him!

Is it not the rich who are exploiting you? (2:6)

Even if we consider our own treatment by the poor and the rich, we will soon realize that the latter are the very people who have exploited us! It is the rich who are ready to sue the clothes from off our backs! It is the rich and famous who, more often than not, **'are slandering the noble name of him to**

whom [we] belong' (2:6-7). To make up to the rich, for no better reason than the fact that they are rich, is not only unscriptural but utterly irrational. Therefore, we need to keep everything in God's perspective and deal with men and women simply as fellow-sinners in need of a Saviour; indeed, as equally the kind of people for whom the Lord Jesus Christ died. The gospel is to be declared to *every* creature; and Christian love is to be shown to all and not merely to one class of people. There is certainly no reason to honour those who, as Calvin puts it, 'proudly calumniate the glory of God'.[8]

It ought to go without saying that there is neither virtue in merely being poor nor vice in merely being rich. God does not favour the poor and disfavour the rich *as such*. There is no natural, innate or self-generated disposition in the poor to be open to the gospel. The gospel is, however, addressed to real need and, by the grace of God, it is the weak things of this world that are chosen by him to confound the great and self-satisfied. Not many of the rich and famous are found in the kingdom of God (1 Corinthians 1:26-27). Salvation is by grace alone and saves from rich and poor alike. There will be many poor people who will die in their sins, just as there will be some wonderful trophies of grace saved from among the wealthy. The gospel is the call of God's free grace to *sinners,* irrespective of their personal economics! It follows that the witness of Christians ought to look at men and women as those who, needing Christ in their lives, are to be won with an even-handed winsomeness that reflects the love of God for his fallen world – that world he 'so loved...that he gave his only-begotten Son, that whoever believes in him should not perish, but have eternal life' (John 3:16 NASB).

10.
The royal law

Please read James 2:8-13

'If you really keep the royal law found in Scripture, "Love your neighbour as yourself," you are doing right' (James 2:8).

One Sunday morning after church, a pastor was talking to a visitor, who he did not then know was an employee of a secret service arm of the government. 'May I ask what your work is?' he asked, brightly and innocently. 'Oh,' said the visitor, equally brightly, 'I like it very much!' This unforgettable invitation to talk about something else effectively illustrates that the simplest way to evade an uncomfortable question is to change the subject.

The same holds for conversations in which the claims of God get too close for comfort. When Jesus challenged the woman of Samaria about the fact that she had had five husbands and her present man was a 'live-in boy-friend', she speedily changed the subject to the denominational differences between the Jews and the Samaritans! (John 4:17-20). How much easier it is to 'talk church' than face one's personal immorality! Another stratagem is to play off one part of the Bible against the other, using one part of it to justify a clear contravention of some known teaching of God's Word. There is just the suggestion in James 2:8-13 that the Lord's brother is anticipating such a ploy from some of his readers. He had been speaking of the evil of favouritism in the church – specifically, discrimination against the poor and in favour of the rich, merely because they were, respectively, poor and rich. But it hurts to be told where we have been going wrong, especially when it relates to something we have become so used to as to accept it unthinkingly as the normal thing to do. 'Just a moment, James,' we explain, 'we were loving our neighbour, as Moses said in Leviticus 19:18, and it's just that you can't spend time with everybody...and, well, these were important people in the community. We only wanted to make sure that they knew we recognized them and we did want them to feel at home in our fellowship.'

There is, admittedly, a certain point to this. It is true that we cannot spend time with everybody and we cannot allow ourselves to become consumed with false guilt about things we really could do nothing about. At the same time, it must be recognized honestly that it is a lot easier to persuade ourselves that we are faithful to the Lord (plus-or-minus a few inconsistencies) than to face squarely up to our real sins! And this, I am persuaded, is the very reason why James sets forth the principle that favouritism is plainly and simply wrong! (2:1-4). If we get a clear grasp of that truth, as the bedrock of our attitudes to other people, then we will not be inclined to press the 'royal law' of Leviticus 19:18 into service as an excuse for such worldly discrimination as we do practise towards certain classes of people, whether on the basis of economics, sex, age, race, good looks or whatever! The explanation of the 'royal law' in 2:8-13 is designed, of course, to remove it for ever as an excuse by setting it in its proper context and applying it correctly to our consciences so as to produce consistently God-honouring interpersonal relations in our lives.

What is the 'royal law'? (2:8)

The opening statement is thoroughly positive: **'If you really keep the royal law...you are doing right'** (2:8). This 'law' is from Leviticus 19:18. The whole verse reads, 'Do not seek revenge or bear a grudge against one of your people, but love your neighbour as yourself. I am the Lord.' Jesus republished this in his masterly response to the question of the Pharisee as to which 'is the greatest commandment in the Law'. The Lord said, '"Love the Lord your God with all your heart and with all your soul and with all your mind." This is the first and greatest commandment. And the second is like it: "Love your neighbour as yourself." All the Law and the Prophets hang on

these two commandments' (Matthew 22:37-40). The apostle
Paul makes exactly the same point, with the added explanation: 'Love does no harm to its neighbour. Therefore love is
the fulfilment of the law' (Romans 13:9-10). Elsewhere he
says, 'The entire law is summed up in a single command:
"Love your neighbour as yourself"' (Galatians 5:14). Jesus
also stated this principle another way, when he commanded
his disciples: 'In everything, do to others what you would
have them do to you, for this sums up the Law and the
Prophets' (Matthew 7:12).

This 'royal law' is a New Testament substitute for the entire
moral law of God in the Bible. To love our neighbour as our-
self does not cancel out our obligation to live according to the
comprehensive fulness of God's Word. The whole point,
from Moses to Christ, is that the royal law actually focuses
upon, and confirms, the essential unity of God's moral law.
Furthermore, it demonstrates that, in terms of the gospel of
Christ, that law becomes the warp and woof of Christian
thought and action. We are not 'under law, but under grace'
says Paul (Romans 6:14). That is to say, the law is not, to us,
a way of salvation but has become, in Christ, a way of saved
living for all who believe in the Lord and are saved by his free
grace. As a perfect standard of righteousness, the law underscored the practical impossibility of saving ourselves through
self-generated effort (works-righteousness); we saw in our
own experience the imperfection of our attempts to keep it, in
our own strength. The law, as such, could not save us or
empower us to keep it perfectly. But Christ, through his
perfect keeping of the law, his substitutionary atonement in
bearing the penalty of the law and his free gift of salvation by
grace through faith, has freed us from the necessity and
impossibility of keeping the law as the means of salvation and
has made the law, to us in Christ, a perfect law of liberty
(1:25). He has written the law on our hearts as the pattern for
newness of life in daily living as his disciples! When Jesus
enunciated the royal law for the benefit of the Sadducees, he
was not setting aside the Ten Commandments as if they were
an inferior species of divine revelation which could be rele-
gated to some museum of biblical doctrines (Matthew 22:36-
40). He was rather showing the morally and spiritually transforming import of the whole law by highlighting the practical

core of its teaching. Jesus did not, then, offer this 'royal law' as a vague and ethereal summary of God's commands, which would allow us to ignore the specifics of the law and operate out of some nebulous 'law of love', the content of which could be determined by our inward subjective conviction as to the leading of the Lord. No! What Jesus was saying was that love to God (the first and greatest commandment) and love to others (James' royal law) are the *basis* for holiness in terms of obedience to God's whole Word. Law and love are, of course, inextricably linked. Where there is no love there is no law. Where there is no law there is no love. If we love Christ we will, as he says, keep his commandments (John 14:15). Conversely, obedience is the hard evidence that we know the Lord (1 John 3:14). In a most profound sense, we may indeed call the 'royal law' the 'law of love' because it is the law both loved and lovingly lived – with respect to both God and our neighbours. It is love – the love of God in Christ, received by faith – that unifies the Law in our obedience and translates it into a joyful expression of new life in our risen Saviour. Our willing obedience to God's moral law becomes, then, a celebration of love.

But why is this law called the **'royal law'**? The two basic possibilities are (1) that the law is 'royal' in that it is sovereign or supreme in that it governs the interpretation and application of other specific laws,[1] or (2) that it is royal in that it relates to a king who has given it, that is to Christ as King.[2] The latter view is very attractive, but falters on the simple consideration that all of God's law relates to its sovereign Giver, whereas the point being made in the context is the overarching claim of love in the exercise of discipleship. This law is 'royal' because it expresses a governing principle of personal holiness. It is the spirit in which we observe the letter of the law in daily life.

The royal law presupposes a prior commitment to the first and great commandment: 'Love the Lord your God with all your heart and with all your soul and with all your mind' (Matthew 22:37). And that means first knowing Christ as your personal Saviour. Only true love for the Lord will motivate genuine Christian love for others.

The royal law also involves bringing the same love that motivates actions on your own behalf into every act towards your neighbour. This is true as to both degree and mode. In other words, you will love your neighbour *as much as* you love yourself; and you will act for your neighbour *in the same manner as* you act for yourself. There is no arbitrary limit of love that says, 'I've loved that neighbour enough!' The love of Christ is an abiding love. And our love for others is not to be exceeded by our love for ourselves, the point being that while we do not normally need any coaching in order to love ourselves, we do need to learn how we are to love others! So we are challenged to look away from ourselves to the blessing of others in the name of the Lord Jesus Christ. And we are encouraged to pour our love out upon the world in the name of Christ, for if we **'really keep'** the royal law, we **'are doing right'**.

How to practise the royal law (2:9-13)

This may be summed up in three points: admit sin; accept God's explanation; and act on the Lord's will immediately.

Admit sin (2:9)
James now drives his point home: **'But if you show favouritism, you sin and are convicted by the law as law-breakers'** (2:9) Favouritism is not to be justified on the grounds that you were 'loving your [rich] neighbour' while the other [poor] fellow was just an unfortunate omission due to lack of time or real opportunity! Favouritism may be loving *some* neighbours, but this is not the same as the Christian grace and duty of loving one's neighbours. It is sinful 'love' motivated by selfish and worldly considerations. As such it breaks the royal law! This is not only a bare statement of fact. There is also an inner witness to this truth in the consciences of James' readers. James is not merely saying, 'You are sinning because I say so,' but rather, 'You know all along that you are sinning, because this royal law tells you so in your own conscience. You are silencing the voice of your own conscience and denying the law of the Lord itself!'

It is not at all difficult to see how this can apply to attitudes in churches today. When a young couple with children visit a church, they attract a lot more attention than an elderly widow, a student or someone who is mentally handicapped. The conventional wisdom on church growth is that you need young settled families to grow a church. The tendency is then to see almost everybody who is not part of a young family as less desirable building-blocks for the growing church in principle (i.e., sociological and economic principle divorced from the gospel) and, consequently, to pay less attention to them in practice. This is a great evil and an utter contradiction of the nature of the body of Christ as a complete and complementary gathering of believers with diverse origins, circumstances and, not least, spiritual gifts. Why should the poor, the elderly, the sick and troubled, the handicapped and the unemployed be considered second-class material for the ministry and life of a church of Jesus Christ? In the light of the scriptural pattern for ministry, the current zeal for 'young families' (preferably those who give a lot of money to the church) looks suspiciously like an unholy desire for nice comfortable churches that can enjoy outward success unencumbered by the very people and problems that the Lord himself said were the focus of his own ministry! Admit sin!

Accept God's explanation (2:10-11)
To emphasize that this is no trifling matter, James adds, **'For whoever keeps the whole law and yet stumbles at just one point is guilty of breaking all of it. For he who said, "Do not commit adultery," also said, "Do not murder." If you do not commit adultery but do commit murder, you have become a lawbreaker'** (2:10-11). The point is that 'Partial obedience is actual disobedience.'[3] The law is like a tight-rope – you only need to fall off it once. The truth is, as James adds later, 'We all stumble in many ways' (3:2). And the man who only stumbles once is, as someone once observed, a beast as rare as the unicorn. Now, why does the Lord's brother tell us this – and in such a stark, uncompromising way? Let me suggest two fundamental reasons.

1. The first is to expose the fallacy of *legalism*. Legalism is the attitude, predisposition, religion – call it what you may – which seeks self-justification by means of keeping laws, sometimes with the most meticulous attention to detail. The Jews

were famous for this. Indeed, virtually all of Jesus' confront-
ations with the leadership of the Jews were essentially on this
point. The great condemnation of the Pharisees was to be that
they kept the minutiae of the law but neglected the weightier
matters, such as 'justice, mercy and faithfulness' (Matthew
23:23). Their neglect of these fundamental elements of discipleship to God indicated, of course, that they refused to
accept that their law-keeping could never save them, because
they could never keep the law at all! The legalist isn't looking
for a Saviour who saves by free grace through his own atoning
sacrifice as sin-bearer and perfect law-keeper. The legalist is
working his own way to heaven. He is commending himself to
God. He is earning his eternal corn by the sweat of his own
brow.

The legalist mentality, however, tries to wriggle around the
problem. He ignores the fact of his own helplessness to save
himself, whether by law-keeping or any other ways. Then,
through meticulous observance of outward rituals and observances, he constructs a basis for acceptance with God through
partial obedience. In other words, 'good deeds' are offset
against 'bad deeds', on the assumption that God will save a
sincere trier. He is blinded both to his own lost nature and the
necessity of salvation by grace through faith in Christ.

For all its apparent obsession with moral rectitude,
legalism actually creates whole categories of allowable sins.
Manton calls them ante-dated and post-dated sins.[4] Ante-
dated sin is when we decide to do something wrong now, with
the intention of repenting at a later date and perhaps doing
some good deed by way of making amends. Post-dated sin is
when we feel that we are allowed a sin or two now because we
have been keeping on the straight and narrow in the recent
past, like the small boy caught stealing apples whose defence
was that he hadn't taken any before (compare Ezekiel 33:13).
Only the perfect obedience of the Son of God can save a
sinner.

2. The other side of the question concerns the *Christian use
of the law of God*. The Christian does not trust in the law for
salvation. He trusts in Christ, who alone has kept the law perfectly and borne the penalty of the law for those he is saving,

as their Substitute. In Christ, in saving faith, the law is now a perfect law of liberty. Instead of being an impossible blue-print for a works-righteousness salvation through futile human effort, the law becomes a liberating model and pattern for a holy life that is being steadily transformed by the love of Christ and the indwelling power of the Holy Spirit. The Christian is no longer trying to save himself; he is living out of love to his Lord in accordance with the free grace of the gospel! He is free in Christ to live by the law of the Lord. He is free to delight in the law as his rule of life in discipleship to Christ.

The keeping of the royal law is, as we have already seen, a celebration of love. Christ defines who our neighbour is – the one to whom love is to be shown. When Jesus was asked, 'Who is my neighbour?' (Luke 10:29), he replied with the parable of the Good Samaritan and thereby completely exploded the religio-racial discrimination which the Jews took for granted as righteous! Your neighbour, by the measure of Jesus' words, is *anyone* whom you have opportunity to help! This is a universal truth, notwithstanding the fact that our families and the Lord's people are our neighbours in a special way.[5] Christ also defines the nature of the love which governs our obedience to his law. Jesus told us to 'love one another' as he loved us and added the encouragement, 'By this all men will know that you are my disciples' (John 13:34). His love is sacrificial – the love that took him to the cross. It was this love that led Paul to say, in what Manton calls 'a glorious excess of charity', that he could wish himself 'cursed and cut off from Christ for the sake of my brothers' (Romans 9:3). This is the attitude of heart that ought to greet the stranger, poor or rich, at the church door. This is the standard and the challenge to our faithfulness to Christ, who first loved us in all our unlovableness.

3. Act on the Lord's will, now! (2:12-13)
Open-faced, warm-hearted and eager-spirited discipleship is what the Lord is calling for from every one of us! We are urged to **'speak and act as those who are going to be judged by the law that gives freedom'** (2:12). We must remember three things: first, that the 'law that gives freedom' (better, 'law of

liberty' [AV, NASB]) is not some blank cheque to do as we like, but the divine standard by which we are to live; second, that we ought to think of ourselves as those who are 'going to be judged'; and third, our speaking and our actions are to be ordered according to the law of liberty. The point is that as believers, we are to love the law because we love the Lord. Christians live in the light of the law of liberty – that is to say, in the light of salvation by grace. The idea is that in trusting Christ, in receiving the gospel, the law is written on our heart and we are free. Mercy is our portion; mercy must be our way of life.

The warning is plainly and honestly stated: **'because judgement without mercy will be shown to anyone who has not been merciful'** (2:13). An unmerciful attitude in one who professes to have received mercy in Jesus Christ is a contradiction. An unmerciful pattern of dealings with others, in a professing Christian, is a reversal of God's order and a denial of his love. It incurs the just anger of the God who is holy and cannot look upon sin.

The crowning truth, nevertheless, is that **'Mercy triumphs over judgement!'** (2:13). This is not to say that mercy and judgement are in contradiction of one another in the mind and purpose of God. On the contrary, they are in perfect harmony because of the perfect sacrifice of Jesus Christ. And this is reflected in the way the Christian handles mercy and judgement. Mercy points to the cross. The believer loves his Saviour and therefore, like him, delights in mercy. But he can also look judgement in the face, as he trusts in the mercy of Christ with a holy confidence. The delightful paradox is that the one who lives (1) according to the law of liberty and (2) as one who is being judged is precisely the person who enjoys the practice of godliness and the quiet assurance of salvation! Mercy 'triumphs' in the Christian's life, because the Christian salvation is both mercy received and mercy lived out – and all because of the infinite love and mercy of God in Jesus Christ! Having been so blessed with the unmerited free grace of God, the Christian cannot but recoil from the evil of discrimination in the church, whether on economic, social, racial or any other grounds. Mercy truly received issues in mercy unconditionally shared.

A debtor to mercy alone,
　Of covenant mercy I sing;
Nor fear, with thy righteousness on,
　My person and offering to bring.
The terrors of law and of God
　With me can have nothing to do;
My Saviour's obedience and blood
　Hide all my transgressions from view.

(Augustus Montague Toplady).

11.
Faith without works

Please read James 2:14-20

'What good is it, my brothers, if a man claims to have faith but has no deeds? Can such faith save him?' (James 2:14).

When a choir has to prepare for a special event at short notice – and isn't exactly over-burdened with musical expertise – it sometimes happens that a certain piece just won't work and has to be left out. I vividly recall one such occasion. The choir of Holyrood Abbey Church, Edinburgh, just had not been able to master a particular item. 'No!' said the Rev. James Philip, an accomplished musician as well as a gifted expository preacher, 'we'll just have to drop that!' 'Och,' said a choir member, 'could we no' jist give it a try and go on in faith?' Mr Philip looked at him, then the rest of us, shook his head and, with a twinkle in his eye, sighed: 'But faith without works is dead!'

Few things are more obvious in life – our own life as well as the lives of others – than a disparity between words and deeds, hopes and accomplishments. And nowhere is that kind of gulf more significant than in matters of faith. When James addressed the problem of 'favouritism' in the church assemblies of the first century A.D., he showed it to be no trivial mistake but a fundamental denial of the 'royal law' of Christian social behaviour, which requires that we love our neighbours as ourselves (2:8). What James did, in effect, was to show that faith in the 'royal law' had to be accompanied by a pattern of behaviour consistent with it. It is just not good enough to *say* that you are following the Lord's will when your *deeds* indicate otherwise. There is the clear suggestion here of a unity – a full and necessary consistency – between faith and action.

James' second 'case study' takes up this point explicitly and explores the precise relationship between faith and practice. He first addresses the subject of 'faith by itself' ('faith without works' AV) (2:14-20). Then, in the passage which will be the subject of our next chapter, he goes on to illustrate true faith – the faith that really works (2:21-26).

What use is a 'faith' that has no deeds? (2:14)

The argument is stated in the form of a question: **'What good is it, my brothers, if a man claims to have faith but has no deeds?'** (2:14). The negative way in which this is cast should not be allowed to obscure the thoroughly positive intent of the question. The purpose is to show that genuine faith is never an empty thing. Genuine faith is fruitful. That is the underlying assumption. Saving faith – true faith in Jesus Christ as the only Saviour – therefore inevitably has powerful transforming consequences in the way we think and the way we live. In contrast, fruitless 'faith' loses credibility and invites the question: 'Is this person really a believer?'

If a man claims to have faith

Notice that the text does not say, 'If a man *has* faith'. It says, 'If a man *claims* to have faith'. The focus is on the fact that this person *professes* to believe. In this respect at least, he is indistinguishable from other Christians. All believers profess faith in Jesus Christ with their lips. Confessing faith 'with your mouth' is absolutely basic (Romans 10:10). And unless there is clear and substantial evidence to the contrary, such confession ought to be taken at face value. James does not intend us to be automatically suspicious of every profession of faith. He does challenge us, however, as to the meaningfulness of our own personal public commitment to Christ. Candid self-examination, not the intrusive inquisition of others, is his primary goal. He will not allow us to be 'all talk and no walk' without being called to account before the bar of God's revealed Word!

But has no deeds
If you were to ask many people what 'good deeds' are, they would probably think of the Boy Scouts ('Have you done your good deed for today?') and 'giving to charity'. In the popular mind, good deeds comprise a rather narrow field of one-off, one-at-a-time and once-in-a-blue-moon acts of unusual generosity – special, voluntary kindnesses, quite separate from the normal way one lives one's life. In contrast, the Lord sees 'deeds' in a broader, more 'ordinary' context. They are simply the everyday fruit of a living faith. They encompass the whole of life's activities from the private and the seemingly trivial to the most public and costly and self-sacrificial. This is to say that faith 'produces the goods'. It generates the evidence of God-wrought transformation in the whole life of the believer. 'Where there is faith,' says Thomas Manton, 'there will be love: affection followeth persuasion; and where there is love there will be work; therefore do we often read of "the labour of love" (Heb.6:10; 1 Thess.1:3) and "faith worketh by love". Faith, which is an apprehension of God's love to us, begetteth a return of love to God, and then maketh use of so sweet an affection to carry out all its acts and services of thankfulness...'[1] Faith is not a naked agreement that God exists or certain biblical teachings are true. Neither is faith an inert and inactive feeling that, somehow or other, you are 'saved' and will go to heaven one day. Faith is the believing, loving and obediently acting response of a heart regenerated by the Holy Spirit. To be regenerated (born again) and converted (brought to conscious repentance towards God and faith in the Lord Jesus Christ) is to be the subject of a work of God's grace. This has results. It bears fruit. It cannot but bear fruit.

What good is it, my brothers?
What good is all talk and no walk 'faith'? asks James. Where is the 'profit' (AV) in it? **'Can such faith save him?'** (2:14). Here, the role of works in relation to faith comes into sharper focus. The classic theological dictum is relevant here: *Sola fides justificat, sed non fides quae est sola* – Faith alone justifies, but not that faith that is alone. Good works, as the fruit and evidence of living faith, are inseparable from being in the

state of grace. Works are not the instruments of salvation (as in all forms of works-righteousness) but they are the indispensable evidence of salvation. The focus is upon faith and works together – on action and confession co-ordinately witnessing to the manifold grace of God. 'Present your bodies as living sacrifices, holy and pleasing to God,' says Paul, 'which is your spiritual worship' (Romans 12:1). This is the principle underlying the challenge issued by the Lord's brother in this verse. The answer to his question is obvious: the kind of 'faith' that has no accompanying fruit is useless.

Why faith without works is dead (2:15-19)

Three arguments are now marshalled to support the thesis of the fourteenth verse.

How good are good wishes? (2:15-16)
James turns to a most practical demonstration of his point. If some Christian brother or sister is poor and needs clothing and shelter, it may seem very nice to express a personal interest in his or her welfare and say how much you hope he or she will be able to eat well and keep warm! But **'what good is it,'** asks James, if you do nothing about his or her actual physical needs? (2:16). Again, the answer is obvious. Good wishes without good actions give the lie to the pious words. The thought only counts if something tangible is done to help. 'The belly is not filled with words,' wrote Manton, 'or the back clothed with wishes. This is but like that mad person that thought to pay his debts with the noise of money, and instead of opening his purse, shaked it. The poor will not thank you for good wishes, neither will God for saying you have faith.'[2] Words prove that you know what you ought to do; mere words show that you haven't got the heart for it.[3]

How do you show faith? (2:17-18)
The second line of argument presses closer still to the heart and conscience: **'Faith by itself, if it is not accompanied by action, is dead'** (2:17). It might be helpful to hyphenate 'faith by itself', for this is not *true* faith waiting for works to come

along. It is a species of pseudo-faith – 'faith-by-itself' as distinct from biblical Christ-centred faith. It is the kind of faith which cannot produce fruit, because it simply does not have the root of the matter! It is 'dead' faith and therefore is not real faith at all! Looking back to verses 15 and 16, this is to say that faith without action is as empty as charitable words without practical helpfulness. We return to the truth that 'Faith alone justifies, but not that faith that is alone.' Why is this the case? Because all who have been brought to saving faith in Christ are 'created in Christ Jesus to do good works, which God prepared in advance for us to do' (Ephesians 2:10). 'Faith,' observes the incomparable Manton, 'is the life of our lives, the soul that animates the whole body of obedience...Never think of living *with* Christ, unless you live *in* Christ: and there is none liveth in Christ but "he bringeth forth much fruit."'[4]

An illustration of the force of this is given in the following verse: **'But someone will say, "You have faith, I have deeds"'** (2:18). The 'someone' is evidently a believer who is speaking with a man (the 'you' in the verse) who appears to believe that a bare confession of faith in words is adequate as an expression of faith in Christ. This Mr Someone, who agrees with James, answers, 'You have faith (i.e., 'faith-by-itself', 2:17); I have deeds (i.e., in context, faith issuing in a definite programme of obedience). **Show me your faith without deeds, and I will show you my faith by what I do.**'[5] This is exactly what Jesus was talking about in the Sermon on the Mount, when he charged us: 'Let your light so shine before men, that they may see your *good deeds* and praise your Father in heaven' (Matthew 5:16). In the same vein, Peter advised wives whose husbands were not Christians: 'Be submissive to your husbands, so that, if any of them do not believe the word, they may be won over without words by *the behaviour* of their wives, when they see the purity and reverence of your lives' (1 Peter 3:1-2). Furthermore, it is entirely consonant with this emphasis that the Lord says that the lost will be 'judged according to *what they had done*' (Revelation 20:12). Similarly, the unconverted, hypocritical church members will be sent from the presence of the Lord with the words: 'Away from me, you *evil-doers*' (Matthew 7:23). Why this emphasis on deeds? Because deeds, in the last analysis, are the clinching test of the credibility of whatever faith a person may profess!

Are you better than demons? (2:19)

In one of the most searching observations in Scripture, Mr Someone delivers what is, in fact, God's assessment of 'faith without deeds': **'You believe that there is one God. Good! Even the demons believe that – and shudder'** (2:19). Plenty of people will say they believe in the existence of God. The Hebrew Christians to whom James addressed his letter were well acquainted with that most central text of Old Testament piety, the 'Shema' of Deuteronomy 6:4: 'Hear, O Israel: the Lord our God, the Lord is one.' Every Jew could recite this and more. But suppose it was just that – mere repetition? What meaning could that have? Look at the demons, those ministering spirits of Satan. In their way, the demons assent to an otherwise orthodox creed. They too 'believe in God'. They know for sure – they 'believe' – that God exists.

They believe the truth of the Shema! And their works are utterly barren and dead as well! Their 'faith' in God is faith-without-works. Their 'faith' involves not love but hatred towards the God they know is there. They 'believe' but are reprobate unbelievers! And that is why any so-called faith that is devoid of practical discipleship and the fruits of personal holiness is really no different in principle from the 'faith of demons'!

But wait! There is a difference. The demons **'shudder'**! They actually have a more informed 'faith' than human hypocrites! Men and women can make their easy professions of faith and live their worldly lives as if there were no God at all. Their casual blasphemies about 'the man upstairs' can roll off their tongues with never the slightest tremble at the consequences of offending a sovereign and holy God! Why is it that demons tremble, while sinners can sail on in blissful unconcern? The answer is that the demons are not so blind as people. They know their latter end. They know what the justice of God must mean in the end. They were ejected from God's presence with Satan when he fell. They know who God is, albeit in the hateful reversion of the reprobate mind. They really fear the wrath to come. But careless sinners say they believe in God positively, go on in daily life to live as if he did not exist and yet can dream that they are safe in the everlasting arms! And so it is, as John Calvin sombrely remarks: 'He then who despises an acknowledged God is much worse.' When James says, **'You believe that there is one God. *Good!'*** he speaks with heavy irony, as if to say, 'What an achievement, to "sink below the devils!"'[6]

Are you listening? (2:20)

'You foolish man, do you want evidence that faith without deeds is useless?' (2:20). Yes! It is possible to assent to a lot of truth about God, even to be able to argue about doctrine and define the contours of the Christian life, and to convince yourself that you are saved, when the evidence of your spiritual sterility is staring you and everybody else in the face. Look at the realities! Do you really need more evidence of the fact that 'Faith without deeds is useless'? Listen! Listen! Listen! 'Hear,' says the Lord, 'and your soul will live!'

12.
Faith that gets to work

Please read James 2:21-26

'You see that a person is justified by what he does and not by faith alone' (James 2:24).

All true children of the Protestant Reformation hold very dear the doctrine of 'justification by faith alone'. Justification was, as William Cunningham declared in his foundational studies in historical theology, 'the great fundamental distinguishing doctrine of the Reformation'. There is, he added, 'no subject which possesses more of intrinsic importance than attaches to this one, and there is none with respect to which the Reformers were more thoroughly harmonious in their sentiments'.[1] The central point is, of course, that a person becomes right with God[2] through the instrumentality of faith in Jesus Christ as the only Saviour of sinners. Clearly justification involves a lot more, on God's part, before ever a sinner is saved. There first had to be the free grace of God and the death and resurrection of Christ before there was a gospel to be proclaimed to a lost world. The 'justification by faith alone' doctrine refers not to what God did first but to what we do in the process of being saved. And the point is that it is *faith alone* – which is itself the gift of God (Ephesians 2:7) – and not any intrinsic or self-generated merit or so-called 'good works' on our part – that is instrumental in effecting our salvation.

This is the unmistakable teaching of Scripture. Salvation is, as to our side of the transaction, all of the grace of God, through the instrumentality of faith. It is not of ourselves: 'not by works, so that no one can boast' (Ephesians 2:9). But then we read James 2:24! And it seems, on the face of things, to dent the monolithic certainty of the rest of Scripture on this point of justification: 'You see that a person is justified by what he does and not by faith alone.' It was this verse which led the German Reformer Martin Luther to offer the startling opinion that the epistle of James had no evangelical character *(kein evangelisch Art)* and to make his famous invidious comparison with the epistles of Paul to the effect that it was 'a right strawy epistle' *(ein recht strohern Epistel).* Christendom has not followed Luther in these opinions and they serve as a salutary reminder that even great saints have a blemish or two! Nevertheless it is necessary to show that James is not contradicting the teaching of the rest of the New Testament when it says, as in Romans 3:28, that 'A man is justified by faith apart from observing the law,' and, in Galatians 2:16, that 'A man is not justified by observing the law, but by faith in Jesus Christ.'

The answer is to be found in the purpose of each author. Paul was speaking about the *instrument* of justification – the means by which we may gain acceptance with God. This instrument is, as we have seen, faith in Jesus Christ – *sola fide,* faith alone. James, on the other hand, is discussing our *confidence* of justification in the light of what God says about the nature of living, justifying faith – the faith that alone justifies is never alone as to its evidential fruits in changed behaviour. James comes at faith from the other side: what kind of a faith is it that has no measurable transforming consequences? Real faith works at being faithful. In this sense, all who are truly justified before God are 'justified by what they do and not by faith alone,' i.e., by the 'faith' that 'has no deeds' (2:14), 'faith by itself' (2:17), 'faith without deeds' (2:18). James' precise point is that fruitless 'faith' is not the real thing! How do we know? Because it simply does not give evidence of being the real thing!

There is no contradiction between James and Paul. Paul establishes that 'Faith alone justifies,' while James pins down the practical criteria by which we are enabled, if not indeed compelled, to ask ourselves the question: 'Is the faith I profess with my lips that true saving faith that alone justifies?' Paul answers the legalists who think they can work their way to heaven by their own best efforts, while James speaks to the antinomians and easy-believists who trust in their conviction that they are 'saved' Christians, even though they have put practical godliness of life to one side.

Our passage for study teaches us about the faith that gets to work by means of two illustrations from faithful saints of the past (2:21-25) and concludes with a restatement of the basic principle (2:26).

Abraham (2:21-24)

The first example of faith as a working faith is that of Abraham's obedience to God's command to take the life of his son Isaac on an altar on Mount Moriah, as an offering to God. You will remember that God had earlier promised Abraham a great succession of descendants (a covenant seed in the line of many generations and of many nations, Genesis 17:6-7). And their mother would be the ninety-year-old child-less Sarah! How Abraham had laughed in the face of such a prospect! Yet God was as good as his word. Isaac was born to Sarah and so confounded Abraham's earlier disbelief. Years later, God commanded Abraham to sacrifice that very life that he had so wonderfully given (Genesis 22:2). Abraham still believed what God had earlier told him – that 'in Isaac' his 'seed' would be called (Genesis 21:12). Nevertheless, he obeyed God and went ahead with his plans to sacrifice his own son. He simply trusted God, although there was no way he could either grasp what was in the mind of God or reconcile the original promise with the present course of action.

Abraham considered righteous (2:21)

The reality of Abraham's faith and his standing before the Lord were both proved to be solid by his willing obedience with respect to the proposed sacrifice of Isaac. **'Was not our ancestor Abraham considered righteous for what he did when he offered his son Isaac on the altar?'** (2:21). He was 'considered righteous' (i.e., justified), then, in the specific sense that the validity of his relationship to the Lord was being evidenced in his faithful actions. This is different from the Pauline sense of justification as God's once-for-all declaration of a sinner to be righteous in his sight, upon the occasion of that first exercise of saving faith in Christ. That definitive 'justification' had taken place years before when Abraham had first become a believer. James' focus is upon the productive nature of justifying faith: what Abraham *did* confirmed that he was in that newness of life – the condition of being justified – into which he had been brought through living faith.

His faith was made complete (2:22)
This is further confirmed in 2:22: **'You see that his faith and his actions were working together, and his faith was made complete by what he did.'** 'The meaning,' comments Robert Johnstone, 'is not that works supply anything defective in the grace of faith itself, but that they reveal it in its fulness of wealth and beauty, as by the leaves and fruit a tree is made perfect.'[3] This is another way of saying that Abraham was growing in his faith. Obedience takes faith nearer to its goal. Good works increase faith, while faith expresses itself in more good works. This is the essence of the faith that justifies. James asks us, by implication, 'Is this your faith? Is this your life? Are you growing in personal godliness?'

Scripture was fulfilled (2:23)
The Scripture itself declares that, some thirty years before Isaac ever came into his life, **'Abraham believed God, and it was credited to him as righteousness'** (2:23; Genesis 15:6). Significantly, the passage quoted is the one which Paul uses in Romans 4:3 and Galatians 3:6 to establish the biblical doctrine of *justification by faith alone*. James' argument is this: God justified Abraham three decades before he faced that test of faith with Isaac. He passed the test with Isaac. Therefore the faith he had exercised from the beginning (Genesis 15:6) was the real thing. He was truly right with his God. His faithfulness was the proof. Because of this, Abraham **'was called God's friend'** (2:23; see also Isaiah 41:8; 2 Chronicles 20:7). He experienced an ever-deepening fellowship with the Lord. That is what holy living does in every Christian's life. In the practical obedience of committed discipleship we grow closer to the Lord. We see the fulfilment of all that he promised us in the gospel of Jesus Christ, even when we first heard it and trusted Christ as our Saviour. We see the increase of the fruit of the Spirit in progressive conformity to the pattern of Jesus himself, both in his precepts and his example.

Justifying faith is faith that acts (2:24)

When all these strands are drawn together, the conclusion is inescapable: **'You see that a person is justified by what he does and not by faith alone'** (2:24). Williams' translation conveys the thrust of this verse: 'You see that a man is shown to be upright by his good deeds, and not merely by his faith.'[4] The contrast, as Adamson neatly observes, is 'between faith minus works and works minus faith – not between faith and works...We may say that Abraham was justified by faith (Paul) in that he trusted God and obeyed his voice in respect of his son Isaac; he may be said to be justified by works (James) because his trust and obedience led him to take Isaac – that is, to do something.'[5] His was an operative, working, living faith-in-exercise, not an inert, fruitless, dead faith-by-itself. Faith alone justifies, but not that faith which is alone.

Rahab (2:25)

Just to press home the point as dramatically as possible, James turns from the sublime to the ridiculous: from patriarch to prostitute, from a godly man to a heathen woman! His second and deliciously unlikely example is the Canaanite prostitute Rahab, whose history is recorded in the second chapter of Joshua: **'In the same way, was not even Rahab the prostitute considered righteous for what she did when she gave lodging to the spies and sent them off in a different direction?'** (2:25). 'By faith,' says the writer to the Hebrews, 'the prostitute Rahab, because she welcomed the spies, was not killed with those who were disobedient' (Hebrews 11:31). Furthermore, this heroine of faith was to be an ancestress of none other than the Lord Jesus Christ! (Matthew 1:5). We are not naturally inclined to regard prostitutes as great material for the building of God's kingdom and the extension of the gospel. Rahab stands for ever as a rebuke to our latent self-righteousness and a glorious testimony to the infinite love and free grace of God for all he is saving from their sins.

What is clear from the account in the book of Joshua is that Rahab was a believer before the spies ever arrived at her door (Joshua 2:9-13). She received the spies in peace and facilitated their escape *because* she was a believer in the Lord.

James' point is that she showed the nature of her faith by her works in giving aid to the Lord's people in their mission. She was every bit as faithful as Abraham, albeit in entirely different circumstances. Of course, Abraham was asked to sacrifice his son, while Rahab 'only' hid the spies and covered herself with a relatively safe lie about their path of escape. As tests of faith, however, they must be seen in relation to the relative maturity of the principals involved: Abraham was an experienced believer, while Rahab was a new believer. This serves to underscore the point James is making: all true faith produces works according to the circumstances facing the individual at the time. And these responses all very appropriately express the reality of that person's relationship with the Lord. Rahab was shown to be righteous just as surely as was Abraham. And the proof was the sparing of her life when Jericho fell to the invading Israelites (Joshua 6:17,23).

The conclusion: faith without deeds is dead (2:26)

The conclusion returns us to the original question: 'What good is it, my brothers, if a man claims to have faith but has no deeds?' (2:14). The preliminary answer of 2:17 is now restated with sombre finality: **'As the body without the spirit is dead, so faith without deeds is dead'** (2:26). The likening of faith to the body and works to the spirit is a delightful reversal of the usual associations, emphasizing all the more the seriousness of practical holiness. The 'thought' is not 'everything'! What we actually do is integral to the spiritual dimension of life. True faith is not 'spirit' as opposed to 'letter,' but 'the letter' lived out spiritually, i.e., according to faith. Good works are the life that reveals the nature of the faith we may say we have. No works: no real faith. No faith: no real works.

If we turn James' illustration around and state it positively, we may say that a living faith is like a healthy growing body. Look at little children. Their bodies are bursting with life; their skin is new and smooth; their cuts and scrapes heal so quickly, we almost watch them disappear; their eyes are bright and their minds full of lively inquisitiveness; they see nothing ahead but greater joys and delights than they have known hitherto; they exude a childish but beautiful optimism;

they love life and they look pre-eminently to the future and what it will unfold. This is a picture of vibrant faith that looks to Christ and all that he will do – and, not least, acts out of love for him and in anticipation of his everlasting smile. This is the faith that gets to work.

13.
You want to be a teacher?

Please read James 3:1-2

'Not many of you should presume to be teachers, my brothers, because you know that we who teach will be judged more strictly' (3:1).

'The disease of evil-speaking,' wrote John Calvin,' is more odious than other sins.'[1] The sins of the tongue have already received a mention in James' despatches: 'If anyone considers himself religious and yet does not keep a tight rein on his tongue, he deceives himself and his religion is worthless' (1:26). Christians, said James, should be 'quick to listen' and 'slow to speak' (1:19). We all, without exception, know how destructive the tongue can be. Certainly, all sensitive and serious Christians can recall with shame times when their untamed tongues blighted their walk with God and shattered relationships with other people, even their one-time friends. There is no human faculty with which a person can become more infatuated than the power of speech. Every human sin is mediated, even facilitated, by speech of one sort or another. It may be anger or seduction, sarcasm or flattery, criticism or dissembling – the tongue is the wind that whips the embers into a consuming blaze. The 'crabbity auld wifie' and the 'grouchy auld chiel' of my native Scotland stand in testimony to the potential for life-long enslavement to unhallowed speech, for even when all other faculties are diminished in the process of ageing, an unsanctified tongue can still hold forth in the full flush of its perverted powers. Indeed, the temptations are greater with age, precisely because powers fail and ambitions become no more than personal history. If we are not rooted and grounded in the love of Christ and the joyous expectation of heaven, then life cannot but fade into frustrated disappointment and this will inevitably be vented in a testimony of bitterness. This argues the need for young and old to bring the tongue under the lordship of Christ so that they may become powerful instruments of righteousness in his service. James takes this up as his third 'case study' in the life of faith. As before, we shall divide our discussion of his words, and deal in this chapter with his rebuke of the widespread human 'itch' to teach[2] (3:1-2), leaving his explanation of the power of the tongue to the succeeding study (3:3-12).

Not many teachers (3:1)

James does not begin with a theological formulation or some sociological statistics. He launches into a very practical problem: **'Not many of you should presume to be teachers, my brothers...'** (3:1). 'Teachers' translates the Greek word *didaskaloi,* the singular of which, *didaskalos,* is used of Nicodemus by our Lord when he called him 'a teacher of Israel' (John 3:10 AV). Jesus was raising his eyebrows when he addressed Nicodemus in that way. It was as if he was saying: 'Nicodemus, you claim to be a teacher and yet you have just shown me how ignorant you are!' What was in view was his credibility as a teacher. And this is precisely the focus of James, namely, the ease with which we can regard ourselves as having the right to be critical of others, the right to be heard and heeded by them, the right, in effect, to be regarded as their teachers – while, all the time, we are the ones who need to be taught!

It ought to be recognized clearly that this strong caution in no way detracts from the necessity of the official public teaching ministry of the church. God constantly raises men up for the preaching ministry of the everlasting gospel. Their number is, of course, a relatively small proportion of the total membership. Even here, however, the call for restraint must not go unheeded. Too many men – this is a particular problem in the United States – in effect call themselves to the teaching ministry by enrolling in theological seminaries on their own charges, graduating with a degree and seeking a congregation in the open 'market'. This can be achieved without that man first having shown himself to be mature and responsible in work, family and community, without his demonstrating a mature Christian commitment to a local fellowship, in which he has clearly exhibited the gifts of ministry and eldership, and without his being called and sent by the people of God to prepare for the ministry. 'No one takes this honour upon himself,' records the writer to the Hebrews, 'he must be called by God, just as Aaron was' (Hebrews 5:4).

Neither does James' stricture diminish the place and importance of private exhortation and rebuke in the life of the church. Every Christian is to be able to give a reason for the hope that is in him. Every Christian must foster good personal relations with his brothers and sisters in the fellowship. We are to encourage and admonish one another, but in the context of the Word of God, the love of Christ and an attitude of genuine humility that speaks truth only in love and pointedly esteems the other more highly than himself!

What concerns the Lord's brother is a critical spirit; what someone has called 'the indulgence of the pride of knowledge'. This can rear its ugly head from different angles. The critical spirit can infect and seriously impair whole congregations of Christians. Or it can be expressed in ministerial demagogy: we have all met a pastor or an office-bearer who is always right and must have things his way. And we see it in the church-crawling Christians who only stay long enough in any congregation to discover all the reasons why they can't join but must look for another church. The point is that when anybody has the attitude that 'It's my way, or the byway,' that person is enslaved to the presumption that he or she must know better and is a teacher rather than a listener. Robert Johnstone strikes home to the heart of the problem and is as relevant today as when he wrote: 'I am afraid that a carping and supercilious spirit…is far from uncommon in our congregations. These people come to God's house, not to receive food for the mind and heart, but to judge composition, and orthodoxy and manner of delivery. They act rather as if they were members of a court of examiners, trying a student's qualifications for the ministry, than either as enlightened

Christians or anxious enquirers after salvation, hearing for the good of their souls the words of eternal life from their pastor and God's servant.'[3] Pastors are not the only ones to fall under such scrutiny. Anyone who does anything in the church can be a target. Fault can always be found with the elders, the deacons, the social committee, the fellowship as a whole and this or that member. 'It is an innate condition of the human make-up,' observed John Calvin, 'to make one's reputation by scoring off other folk.'[4] There is, however, a biblical standard against which to measure our attitudes: 'Join with others in following my example, brothers,' said the apostle Paul, 'and take note of those who live according to the pattern we gave you. For, as I have often told you before, and now say again even with tears, many live as enemies of the cross of Christ' (Philippians 3:17-18). Paul obviously did not relish saying hard things and when he did it was with humility, sorrow and a majestic reverence for the Word of God as the rule of everyone's faith and life. 'A good man,' remarks Thomas Manton, 'takes no delight to rake in a dunghill; others' failings cannot serve his mirth and triumph...Censures are full of *passion,* but Christian reproofs of *compassion.'*[5] Too often, the desire to be a teacher in the church arises from a compulsion to assert some superiority over others and to be thought of as a person of knowledge, ability and sagacity. How different is the motivation that comes from the free grace of God in Jesus Christ!

Three practical arguments (3:1-2)

We who teach will be judged more strictly (3:1)
Ours is a day in which, to use a very apt American expression, everyone feels it his inalienable right to 'put in his "two cents" worth'! A self-centred world is obsessed with 'rights' and the voicing of opinions, however absurd or inflammatory, is invariably the simplest way of exercising the 'right' of freedom of expression. Phone-in radio talk-shows give everybody a shot at being an expert for a few minutes – an instructor, if you will, of the whole nation, or at least of all those listening to the radio at the time!

But there is, in fact, a great responsibility in the task of teaching others. It is no slight thing in God's eyes to begin to express opinions on spiritual things. It is not simply a matter of individual 'freedom of expression'; whatever we say affects those who hear it – positively or negatively. However casual or 'unofficial' the remarks, the vital question is: 'Is God being honoured? Is his will being served? Is his truth being exalted? Are the claims of his love being promoted? Is what we say helpful? Is it conducive to the personal growth of others and the advance of God's kingdom? If we need to take care over our personal and public opinions and answer for every idle word (Matthew 12:36), how much more solemn is the task of teaching others in the Lord's name – how much more fearful a presumptuous exercise of that function, when the Lord never called us to it![6]

James, you will notice, includes himself in his exhortation: **'We who teach will be judged more strictly.'** His purpose is not to shut our mouths so that we will say nothing out of fear of being wrong. He rather means to impress upon us that the opportunity to speak carries with it a profound responsibility. We shall have more to answer for – we immediately place ourselves under the adjudication of a more stringent standard. And this we must take seriously, if we are to be faithful disciples of our Lord. It is worth remembering that Jesus reserved his most trenchant denunciations for the Pharisees, those false teachers who 'travel over land and sea to make a single convert', and 'when he becomes one,' succeed in making him 'twice as much a son of hell' as they are themselves! (Matthew 23:15).

We all stumble in many ways (3:2)
Reinforcement for this point is found from what I like to call 'the biblical doctrine of imperfection'. We all stumble. None of us is perfect. This is a fact of life, even though it is not an excuse for going on being imperfect. God commands us to 'be holy, because I am holy' (Ephesians 1:4; 1 Peter 1:16). James' point is simply to underline the dangers which attend a proud use of the tongue. If we truly accept our own frailty, we will be less inclined to dispense gratuitous opinions and censures, both because of a healthy caution about our own potential for

error and a self-righteous spirit and because of a deeper compassion and understanding of the failings of others. People who live in glasshouses shouldn't throw stones. Those who deeply feel their own need to be taught by the Lord do not itch to dispense their pseudo-wisdom to others. 'Reckless words pierce like a sword, but the tongue of the wise brings healing' (Proverbs 12:18). 'There is nothing which serves more to moderate extreme rigour,' remarks Calvin, 'than the knowledge of our own infirmity.'[7]

If anyone is never at fault in what he says... (3:2)
Stumbling in our speech – saying the wrong thing – is the easiest of mistakes. Offending people and, more importantly, sinning against the Lord, rolls off the lips long before the hand stretches out to act offensively. The thrust of this verse appears to be 'We all find it easy to offend with our tongues. Well, let me tell you, anyone who has managed to tame his tongue completely is perfect and must be able to control his whole body perfectly.' This is, of course, a *reductio ad absurdum* argument. No one has ever perfectly tamed his whole body (the easier job), far less controlled his tongue (the more difficult task)! Our untameable tongue is the ever-present reminder of the power of indwelling sin, our helplessness to cure ourselves and our perennial need of the grace of Jesus Christ to cleanse us and enable us to persevere in faithfulness to him. Our need is made obvious by the very weakness of our tongues and we are pointed, perhaps in an oblique way, to our need of Christ and the indwelling power of the Holy Spirit in our daily lives!

At the same time, albeit in a rather veiled manner, we are pointed to the tongue's potential for good. James takes this up more fully in 3:9. Suffice it to say that a tongue claimed for the Lord – and, clearly, teaching that is dedicated to spreading his truth and love throughout the church and the world – must have a power as positive and restorative as a perverted tongue is negative and injurious. The tongue, like time, is there to be redeemed and made happy in captivity to Jesus Christ.

14.
The power of the tongue

Please read James 3:3-12

'With the tongue we praise our Lord and Father, and with it we curse men, who have been made in God's likeness' (James 3:9).

Words, more than anything else in human experience – and more quickly – form impressions that stick. More significant, however, is the damage that can be done by unhallowed and ill-considered words that flow from a spirit of criticism. It is this that James wants us to grasp so that we may bring this most powerful faculty – our tongue – under submission to the Lord Jesus Christ. In 3:2, James unveiled a proposition and an implication. The former was that the tongue is an exceedingly powerful faculty; the latter, that it may be powerful for good or for evil. These notions are now investigated and illustrated in verses 3-12 in such a way as to leave us in no doubt as to the Lord's will for the way we use the tongue. The tongue is to be tamed and be subject to the rule of Christ. Four principal points are made to drive this home to our consciences: we must see, firstly, how the tongue has *power to control our lives* (3:3-5); secondly, we must see the *potential destructive power* of the tongue (3:5-6); thirdly, *the incapacity of man to control* the tongue (3:7-10); and fourthly, that *these things ought not to be* – godliness should characterize all our speech (3:10-12).

The controlling power of the tongue (3:3-5)

Two illustrations serve to demonstrate just how destructive

the human tongue can be: first, the bridle and the horse, and secondly, the rudder and the ship (3:3-4). Then James will state the principle involved (3:5).

The bridle and the horse (3:3)
In the courtyard of the City Chambers in Edinburgh, there stands John Steell's massive bronze of *Alexander and Bucephalus*. Alexander was not yet 'the Great' when he succeeded in taming his horse, the fiery Bucephalus. His father, King Philip of Macedon, had failed to break the animal and was about to send it away, when Alexander protested. The king said the lad could keep the horse if he managed to control it. Alexander noticed that Bucephalus was unsettled by his own shadow, so he turned him to the sun, gathered the reins, carefully mounted the steed and soon had him completely under his control. That shadow had been a 'little' thing, but it was the key to mastery of a large and powerful animal.

James uses the bit in the horse's mouth to make his point that a large and potentially unruly force can be subdued and redirected by a relatively small piece of equipment: **'When we put bits into the mouths of horses to make them obey us, we can turn the whole animal'** (3:3). A car steering-wheel might be the modern equivalent – with power-assisted steering, the slightest touch can turn the whole vehicle. In the computer age, the tiniest electrical current is translated within the computer to a command that can control a flood barrier or a mighty crane. So it is, says James, when the tongue is controlled – the whole body feels the blessings!

The rudder and the ship (3:4)
One day in my boyhood, I went with my pal Stuart to a pond to watch the launch of his newly-built motorized model boat. He set it, started up the motor and sent it on its maiden voyage across the pond. It was fine for the few minutes before the rudder jammed. Then his little RAF Rescue Launch began to show an increasingly urgent need for rescue itself! It circled round and round out in the middle of the water. Then to make things worse, it began to go down at the stern and we had to watch helplessly as it vanished from sight, a floating hatch cover the only reminder that my friend's long labours had

gone to a watery grave! The rudder made all the difference. The boat was sinking, to be sure, but the jammed rudder put it beyond all rescue. Well, says James, '**...take ships as an example. Although they are so large and are driven by strong winds, they are steered by a very small rudder wherever the pilot wants to go.**' James' ship was, of course, a real ship – a sailing ship, buffeted by wind and wave. The control of the rudder was a matter of life or death as the ship held a safe course through heavy weather. As applied to the tongue, the picture means that the tongue may be controlled so as to help the whole man successfully negotiate the external pressures that threaten to drive him off course. With a sound tongue he will, for example, be able to resist the tendency to be 'blown about with every wind of doctrine'. In being able to 'give a reason for the hope that is in him', he may be able to blunt one of Satan's attempts to lure him off the straight and narrow. With a gentle word here and there, he will be enabled to turn away anger. In any event, the tongue has an effect on his life out of all proportion to its size.

The principle of the thing (3:5)

The tongue is the most powerful instrument of the policies and schemes of the human heart. James touches on this when he states that although '**the tongue is a small part of the body...it makes great boasts**'. He is not talking about 'boasting' in the bad sense in which we use the word today. He does not mean to say that the tongue constantly brags about its supposed power. He means rather that the tongue does have real power! The tongue *can* boast great influence and extensive achievements! And, of course, the most obvious proof of this in our experience is the extent to which we have felt the effects of other people's words. Nothing warms our hearts more than sincere and heart-felt expressions of love and esteem. Nothing hurts as much as hard words of bitter criticism and reproach. Words can go deeper than any knife.

The destructive potential of the tongue (3:5-6)

The negative, destructive potential of the human tongue is illustrated by fire and its effects. As with the previous discussion, the illustration precedes the application of the principle involved.

The spark and the forest fire (3:5)

'Playing with fire' is an appropriately menacing figure of speech. Many a family has been burned out of their home because of the careless use of a match. Even if the fire is used under controlled circumstances, things can occasionally go wrong. Some years ago, the U.S. National Parks Service decided on the controlled burning of a small area of woodland in order to provide nest sites for an endangered species of bird. But the fire spread too rapidly, burned thousands of acres and, most tragically, took the life of one of the fire-fighters. **'Consider,'** then, **'what a great forest is set on fire by a small spark'** (3:5).

Words, too, can spread like wildfire. Rumours, the 'grapevine' and the 'bush telegraph' can carry opinions, lies, and sometimes even the truth, as fast, or faster than, the normal news channels. A famous instance of this occurred in South Africa during the Zulu War. Rider Haggard, the author of *King Solomon's Mines,* was in Pretoria when he heard the news of the Zulu defeat of the British at Isandlwhana from his Hottentot washerwoman – a day before the first official despatch arrived from Natal![1]

When the words are slanderous rumours or pernicious errors, the consequences can be devastating. God's Word says of the fool that 'At the beginning his words are folly; at the end they are wicked madness' (Ecclesiastes 10:13). If foolishness is a cancer of the soul, then heresy is a cancer of the church. Speaking of the advance of the heresy of Arianism in the church of the fourth century A.D., Thomas Manton quotes an early commentator as saying, 'Arius, a small Alexandrian spark, enkindled all the world in a flame.'[2] The power of the tongue is never to be underestimated. The pen can indeed be mightier than the sword.

The tongue as fire (3:6)

In America, people talk about 'getting burned' in a personal relationship or a business deal. This covers a lot more than words, of course, but it is an apt description of the way a wicked tongue can wreak its particular brand of havoc. **'The**

tongue also is a fire,' says James (3:6). Fire can look beautiful in its place. Before tarmac roads replaced the granite setts which used to pave our city streets, the two annual 'bonfire nights' – 24 May (Victoria Day) and 5 November (Guy Fawkes night) – chequered British cities and towns with street bonfires. Fireworks added their brilliant pyrotechnics to the general merriment of the crowds that attended these events. But the beauty of fire is the beauty of an awesome terror that can – and frequently did – turn these occasions into scenes of tragedy. It is not for nothing that fire symbolizes the fearsome terrors of a lost eternity (Revelation 21:8) and the righteous wrath of God against sin (Deuteronomy 4:24).

James makes four observations about the inflammatory power of the tongue.

1. The tongue is **'a world of evil among the parts of the body'** (3:6). This reminds us of all he has already said about the capacity of the tongue to engender wickedness. The use of the word 'world' indicates the cosmic scope of human speech to promote evil. 'In the ordinary use of the tongue,' says Johnstone, 'there is an enormous mass of moral evil.'[3] Listen to what people say in ordinary conversation. Listen to children arguing, and hear the blood-curdling threats and savage abuse they can heap upon each other. The world around us is in a state of war – a war in which the tongues chatter like machine-guns and slanders fly like mortar bombs between the entrenched prejudices of hardened hearts. 'The tongue "diffuses error, kindles strife, inflames the passions, stimulates to vice, originates crime. It breaks hearts, embitters families, distracts communities, divides and destroys churches."'[4]

2. The tongue **'corrupts the whole person'** (3:6). In the days when Pittsburgh, Pennsylvania, made more steel than most of Europe, there was so much dirt and grime in the air that a day without wind was called 'a two-shirt day'. Shopkeepers and businessmen had to change at lunch-time just to be presentable. Shop-counters had to be wiped clean repeatedly through the business day. Sometimes the sky could be so darkly polluted that the street-lights had to be switched on in the middle of the day! Dirt like that could get in almost anywhere – it 'corrupted' the whole city! When the tongue is used

as 'an organ of sin',[5] it pollutes the whole personality and degrades and depraves our very humanity, as God intended it to be in the beginning.

3. The tongue **'sets the whole course of his life on fire'** (3:6). The word translated 'course' is a Greek word literally meaning 'wheel' *(trochos)* and carries the notion of the unfolding circle of our existence. It is a vicious circle of galloping self-destructiveness.

4. The tongue **'is itself set on fire by hell'** (3:6). Here is the root of the matter. The fuel for the tongue comes from hell. And Satan stokes the fire. When our lips are unclean, they speak for Satan. That is the significance of Isaiah being touched upon his lips by 'a live coal' from God's altar. His lips were cleansed to fit him for serving the Lord as a prophet. The holy fire made him the very mouthpiece of God. In no way could his tongue be said to be 'set on fire by hell'. He would speak for God. So may we, when our tongue is renewed and redirected by the power of the Holy Spirit, out of a heart-commitment to the Lord Jesus Christ.

We need God's help (3:7-10)

Modern man thinks he can solve his own problems. How many times have you heard a politician declare: 'We created this problem, we can find the solution to it'? Like too many fetching slogans, this is simply a *non sequitur* – it does not follow. And whether it is an expression of undiluted humanist hope in the triumph of secular man or merely a catchy motto to win over the voters, it is still a lie – a lie that will inevitably be exposed by time and experience. Too many man-created problems are irreversible, and obviously not going to be solved by man, for a simplistic statement of that kind to retain any credibility whatsoever. The case of the human tongue is a perfect illustration of the more general problem.

The problem – the untameable tongue (3:7-8)
Man thinks because he has achieved some things, he can achieve anything! For example, he can tame all sorts of animals

(3:7). Why then can **'no man...tame the tongue'**? (3:8).
In the first place, man ought to acknowledge that taming animals was not made possible by the mere ability and intelli-
gence of man. It was a gift of God! God gave man, in Adam,
dominion over the creatures of his created world (Genesis
1:26-28). This was renewed to Noah after the flood (Genesis
9:1-7). Man's achievements are *all* ultimately derived from
God! Man has no cause to boast in his own vaunted self-
sufficiency and ingenuity!

Therefore, in the second place, the reality of man's
untameable tongue and the perennial problem of human
wickedness should leave him without the slightest doubt as to
his need of a Saviour. Why? Because he is helpless in his own
strength, by his own unaided will, to tame his own tongue – it
is **'a restless evil, full of deadly poison'** (3:8). Paul says of
unconverted sinners: 'The poison of vipers is on their lips.'
And the root of it all is that 'There is no fear of God before
their eyes' (Romans 3:13,18). 'Evil men...' says the psalmist,
'...make their tongues as sharp as a serpent's' (Psalm
140:1,3). There is an unmistakable allusion to the fact that
when Satan first tempted Eve in the garden of Eden, he
appeared in the form of a serpent and it was with words that
he achieved his deadly goal.

The proof – the inconsistencies of the tongue (3:9-10)
But are people really that bad? After all, aside from a lapse
here and there, most people are relatively restrained in their
utterances! So where is the proof that James' relentlessly
negative characterization of the human tongue is accurate?
The proof, says James – if proof is really needed – is found in
the inconsistency with which we use our tongue. In other
words, it is precisely those times of unrestrained utterance,
when stress or anger reaches behind the façade of social con-
vention to the deeper dispositions of the heart, that the
viciousness of an unrenewed tongue is revealed. And it is not
just the fact that 'people sometimes swear' or let out
unguarded remarks in the heat of the moment. It is the fact
that *both* good and pious words and bad and impious words
can come from the same lips that proves the deep need of our
soul for cleansing and reformation. **'With the tongue we**

**praise our Lord and Father, and with it we curse men, who
have been made in God's likeness. Out of the same mouth
come praise and cursing'** (3:9-10). The point is that the latter
is the contradiction of the former. When we slander men, we
profane the name of God!

The Christian who can pray to the Lord in exalted language, but who breathes ridicule at everybody who does not
quite meet up to his expectations, has not faced his own
depravity. This was true of Peter when he cursed and swore
and denied the Lord Jesus Christ as he stood in the high
priest's palace yard on that terrible night when Jesus was
arrested. Through this dark experience, Peter learned some
profound truth about himself and his deep need of Christ.
Many a believer needs to be confronted by (or about) his own
radically self-contradictory words and be led to a closer and
consistent walk with Christ.

And to those in the world who find it so easy to pepper their
language with casual invocations of damnation upon all and
sundry, the message of James is totally uncompromising. It is
sin. And it will be a self-fulfilling prophecy, if there is no
repentance towards God and faith in the Lord Jesus Christ.
'On our own streets,' says Robert Johnstone, 'the swearer's
awful prayer is lamentably familiar to our ears – the words in
which, if they have any meaning, he prays for everlasting
destruction on himself or his neighbour.'[6] This is exactly what
Jesus has declared: 'But I tell you that men will have to give
account on the day of judgement for every careless word they
have spoken. For by your words you will be acquitted, and by
your words you will be condemned' (Matthew 12:36-37).

This challenge applies to far more than blasphemous and
foul language. Verbal savagery can be clothed in the cleanest
literary garb and pretend to be justified by employing
honeyed and even pious expressions. It is not difficult to
'damn with faint praise'. The inconsistency of which James
speaks can come out in many different ways, but they all teach
the same basic lesson and point to the same basic need. Some
years ago, a young theological student discovered something
of this in a most unlikely way. The students were gathered in
the dining room for their evening meal, the food was on the
tables and they were assembling at their places in preparation
for him to ask the Lord's blessing on the meal. He arrived at

a canter, rushed to his place and prayed with the most sublime
eloquence as he thanked the Lord for the food. Then he
opened his eyes, found himself looking into a huge dish of the
most sickly-coloured 'beef strogonoff' and loudly and spontaneously blurted out: 'What kind of rubbish is this??!!' This
brought the house down, needless to say. But that student –
and everyone present – immediately saw the contradiction,
however comical in the context, of that juxtaposition of
thankfulness in principle and revulsion in practice. The very
laughter which was a kind of 'Amen' to the tension between
God's provision and the cook's production served all the
more powerfully to demonstrate how easily the same tongue
can pour forth opposite sentiments. It was therefore a salutary lesson about how much the transforming influence of the
Holy Spirit is needed in the hearts and minds of men and
women.

'My brothers, this should not be!' (3:10)

The abnormality of the Christian's praising God and cursing
men is highlighted by an earnest appeal to the conscience:
'My brothers, this should not be' (3:10). Those who love the
Lord cannot allow themselves to speak out of both sides of
their mouth! The good words do not redeem the bad, but the
bad do give the lie to the good. Christ calls us to discipleship
with our tongues!
    Two simple illustrations arranged chiastically (crossed-
over) in the classic Hebrew manner, drive home the point:

(A) **'Can both fresh water and salt water flow from the same
      spring?**
(B) **My brothers, can a fig tree bear olives,**
(B) **or a grapevine bear figs?**
(A) **Neither can a salt spring produce fresh water'** (3:11-12).

    The subtlety of the illustration lies in the comparison of the
plainly obvious (figs don't produce olives) with the not so
obvious (springs that look and sound the same and therefore
promise good things, but, when you taste them are quite different). Don't be fooled! Don't kid yourself! When salt water

gushes from the spring, you know there's something wrong deep down! And the fact is that salt springs *cannot* produce fresh water.

James' illustration takes his readers to the words of our Lord in his ministry on earth and to the very heart of the gospel of saving grace which is able to transform the whole person, untameable tongue and all. Christ is the living water who gives to all who come to him in faith that water which 'will become in him a spring of water welling up to eternal life' (John 4:13). He says, 'If any one is thirsty, let him come to me and drink. Whoever believes in me, as the Scripture has said, streams of living water will flow from within him. By this he meant the Spirit...' (John 7:37-39). Then the great power of the human tongue can be harnessed for the loving service of the Lord who came to save his people from their sins and we will sing with joy,

'With my mouth I will greatly extol the Lord;
   in the great throng I will praise him'

(Psalm 109:30).

15.
Two kinds of wisdom

Please read James 3:13-18

'Who is wise and understanding among you? Let him show it by his good life, by deeds done in the humility that comes from wisdom' (James 3:13).

Is there a wise man in the house? Anybody here with understanding? Which of you is willing to stand up and own up to having spiritual discernment? In James 3:13, the Lord addresses the congregational meeting, the ministers' conference, the professors of the theological college and the general assembly of the pastors and elders of the church! Will there be any takers? Will anyone say, 'Yes, I am wise. I have understanding. What can I do for you?' Some questions carry the answer on their backs. However shocking James' questions may be he knew, and we know, that it would be more shocking still were anyone to be so full of himself as to stand up and answer in the affirmative. For all that, we must not think that James is trying to put us down, to make us depressed that we are so deficient in wisdom, to rub our noses in the lack of understanding and spiritual discernment we so keenly feel as a personal handicap. James knows that we cannot stand up, with hand on heart, and declare ourselves to be wise. The paradox of godly Christian wisdom is that he who has it is the last to feel himself wise, far less project himself as a notable sage. It is axiomatic that those who would brag about the merits and benefits of their wisdom are possessed of a spirit inimical to true wisdom itself.

James' intention is, of course, neither to make us feel depressed about our relative lack of wisdom (i.e., a poor self-image) nor to discourage us from both acquiring and disseminating the wisdom of God. Quite the opposite is the case.

But if we are to grow in God's wisdom, our consciences need to be stirred up and we need to think seriously about the real issue, namely our relationship with the Lord. The 'fear of the Lord,' is, after all, 'the beginning of wisdom' (Proverbs 9:10; 1:7). There is nothing which will do more to open our hearts to our need of Christ, who is the wisdom of God, than a candid awareness of our own essential lack of wisdom and its implications for our relationship with God and, not least, for our eternal destiny.

James first states the basic principle in the form of a question and answer (3:13), goes on to discuss the nature of 'earthly' wisdom, i.e., a lack of true wisdom (3:14-16), and concludes with an explanation of the true wisdom that comes from God – the 'heavenly' wisdom (3:17-18).

The basic principle of true wisdom (3:13)

The Bible is doctrine without being doctrinaire; it is truth which transcends a merely studied correctness; it is often trenchant but it is never tedious; it always searches the thoughts and intentions of the heart; it imparts information in order to effect reformation. James' approach to the subject of true wisdom marvellously exemplifies this universal characteristic of the inspired, infallible and inerrant Word of God. He does not embark upon a systematic exposition of the biblical concept of wisdom or a word-study of the Old Testament usage of *hokma* (the Hebrew word for wisdom), profitable as these exercises always are. He rather goes directly to our hearts and consciences and begins with the one thing that we cannot but know about our own wisdom, namely, that however wise we may be, we have a long, long way to go! Then he goes on to scythe through all the weeds of all our talk and theorizing about wisdom to tell us that if we have any wisdom at all, it must be shown **'by deeds done in the humility that comes from wisdom'**.

Deeds
Why does James focus upon deeds? Normally we think of wisdom in terms of thought and words, all weighty with experience and discernment. We associate it with some ancient sage

sitting under a tree uttering profound sayings and dispensing masterly judgements. We think of wisdom in almost exclusively intellectual terms. It is what happens in the thought-life. Such is the common assumption about wisdom.

But James says, **'Let him show it** [i.e., wisdom] **by his good life, by deeds...'** Far from being entombed in the world of the intellect, true wisdom is firmly attached to performance! But why this tremendous emphasis on good deeds? The answer surely is in the theme of the entire epistle of James: namely, that when someone comes to faith in Jesus Christ, his life is changed radically from the inside out. That change wrought by the Holy Spirit in regeneration of the old nature into a new nature disposed positively to holiness cannot but affect the course and conduct of life. 'The more a Christian has of true wisdom and spiritual knowledge, the more manifestly will his life at all points be governed by his religion.'[1] Mere talk, however orthodox in terms of the letter, however lofty in tone, however apparently well meant, proves absolutely nothing. This is a hard pill for anyone to swallow. But, then, that may be just because we are too used to consoling ourselves over the repeated failure of our deeds matching our words by saying, 'It's the thought that counts.' Until and unless our thoughts and words translate into godly conduct, they remain at best a goal and at worst sheer hypocrisy. So it is with wisdom. No works means there is no wisdom in the first place. And this means you need to re-examine where you stand with the living God.

Humility

This is powerfully illustrated by James' reference to **'the humility** [or meekness] **that comes from wisdom'**. Clearly, he wants us to see that wisdom's basic mode of operation is in humility. Contrast this with the way the world's wisdom operates. Is humility regarded with admiration in this world? Of course it isn't! On the contrary, meekness is as a rule despised as foolishness and weakness. When Joseph Stalin was a junior revolutionary he clashed with the then Social Democratic leadership over their policy of relative meekness towards the Tsarist authorities. Stalin wanted martyrs – others, of course, never himself – hence he provoked the police into beating and killing the demonstrating workers. Legality and meekness

were foolishness to him, as he went on to prove so
murderously in his later career as a dictator.

Yet this is the great point of actual practice at which the
contrast between Christ and the unbelieving world is most
clearly observable! Our Lord did not open his mouth in the
face of the reviling of his murderers. But men and women
fight with the ferocity of cornered rats over the slightest
offence, real or imagined! This is not to say that it is improper
to defend oneself, verbally or physically – the Lord was prepared to take a whip to the money-lenders who profaned the
temple court and he minced no words in pronouncing the
divine sentence of judgement upon the Pharisees. The point
is that Christ at all times was imbued with a spirit of meekness, whereas we find the spirit of wrath comes to us quite
naturally and easily. Christians ought to be marked out by the
attitude and practice of humility and meekness, even when
declaring the most unpalatable truths to this lost world. Christians ought to be ashamed of 'blowing up' and fuming and
complaining whenever things don't go according to plan.
Christians ought to be dying to the unhallowed emotions that
drove them so powerfully before they were converted to
Christ and which continue to blight their witness as believers.

This is a clear pointer to what true wisdom is. It is the
powerful knowledge that equips the Christian for the practice
of godly living. That is precisely what is meant when the Scripture says that Christ is wisdom to his people (1 Corinthians
1:30). 'Wisdom is ethical conduct in harmony with the nature
of God,' observes Earl Kelly.[2] It is not abstract knowledge,
nor 'pure reason', nor high I.Q. It is a grace – defined by God,
given through saving faith in Christ, nurtured by the Holy
Spirit and exhibited in nuts-and-bolts, attention-to-detail
godliness every day in life. Curtis Vaughan succinctly sums up
the practicality of true wisdom as James explains it: 'The true
test of wisdom is works, not words...and meekness is the natural accompaniment of wisdom. Hence, where there is no
meekness, there is no wisdom.'[3]

Earthly 'wisdom' (3:14-16)

What do you see when you reflect honestly on your own

behaviour? What is your wisdom like? What goes on inside
you, when you think you are responding to a particular situation in the wisest way (or the most justified)? Could it be that
less than worthy motives are lurking in your heart? Could it
be that 'deeds done in humility' are neither in your mind nor
in your actions at that moment?

Identifying false wisdom (3:14)
Do you **'harbour bitter envy'**? (3:14). Do you in fact have bitter feelings towards others? Is there unresolved anger and a
resentful spirit in you? Is there some jealousy towards that
person? Do you have a **'selfish ambition'** in your heart?
Perhaps there is an element of rivalry in your attitude to that
other person, such that, in sharing your wisdom with him, you
are in fact rubbing in how clever you are or you are quietly
enjoying putting him down. You are conscious of dispensing
your wisdom.

Can you say that you are guiltless in these matters? Well,
says James, **'do not boast about it or deny the truth'** (3:14).
Realize that all these feelings and attitudes are the works of
the flesh (Galatians 5:20) and are the contradiction of the gospel and of the Lord himself. We are to have the same attitude
as the Lord Jesus Christ (Philippians 2:5-11). This means that
we can readily spot false self-serving 'wisdom' in ourselves
and distinguish it from the real thing. Is our wisdom expressed
in terms of good deeds done in humility of mind? Or is it set
in the context of envy, bitterness and the convolutions of
inter-personal politics where we jockey for position and
advantage over our fellows? You know your motives. And so
does the Lord! Repentance and renewal, not boasting and
denial, are what you need in the depths of your soul!

The origin of false wisdom (3:15)
James tells it as it is, straight from the shoulder: **'Such "wisdom" does not come down from heaven but is earthly,
unspiritual, of the devil.'** It really is from the pit of hell! It is
false wisdom that is about the work of the devil. The three
adjectives admit no fudging of the issue.

This wisdom is **'earthly'** (Greek, *epigeios*) in that it arises
from the mind of the creature without reference to the
Creator. It is the wisdom of self-proclaimed autonomous

man. 'Their mind is on earthly things,' says the apostle Paul (Philippians 3:19).

The word **'unspiritual'** is the Greek *psuchikos,* which is used in 1 Corinthians 2:14: 'The man *without the Spirit* does not accept the things that come from the Spirit of God, for they are foolishness to him, and he cannot understand them, because they are spiritually discerned.'[4]

The third adjective puts the capstone on this edifice of pseudo-wisdom: it is **'of the devil'** (Greek, *daimoniodes*). 'The false wisdom,' says Adamson, 'is not merely neutral, spurious, or inadequate – but positively demonic: see 1 Tim. 4:1.'[5] The point is twofold. The first is that demonic forces are frequently the inspirers and influencers of what is false in the activities of men and women. Sinners do not act alone, even if they think they do. The second point is that all opposition to the true wisdom of God is, in essence and in fact, doing the work of Satan. James uses the strongest language because he knows just how serious and how dangerous false wisdom really is. It is never to be underestimated or trivialized! When Jesus described the Pharisees as belonging to their 'father, the devil' (John 8:44), he was making exactly the same connection. If God is not your heavenly Father through faith in Jesus Christ as the only Saviour from sin, then you remain under the thraldom of Satan – and the gospel holds out to you the new life, which Christ died and rose again to accomplish in all who will trust in him.

The consequences of earthly wisdom (3:16)

Bogus wisdom sooner or later has devastating effects. **'Disorder and every evil practice'** follow in its wake. Broken hearts, broken homes, broken laws, broken covenants, confusion, social strife, war – all the forerunners of a lost eternity are fed and fostered by the kind of 'wisdom' that is animated by a spirit of envy and selfish ambition. This was precisely the problem in the Corinthian church, to which Paul addressed some of his most searching exhortations. The divisiveness which had riven that body into warring factions – those who severally claimed, by their way of it, to follow 'Paul,' 'Apollos,' 'Cephas' and 'Christ' – was laid at the door of their forsaking 'the message of the cross' for 'words of human wisdom!' (1 Corinthians 1:10-31). But, as Paul goes on to say,

'God is not a God of disorder but of peace' (1 Corinthians 14:33). The 'wisdom' which ends in disorder and dissension ought not to be found among the followers of Christ.

Heavenly wisdom (3:17-18)

The wisdom which James wants all his readers to have is of an entirely different stamp. Point by point, albeit in a different order, he sketches out the radical contrast between the heavenly and the earthly wisdom, again in such a practical way that it will be all but impossible to mistake where we stand in relation to the issues that he sets before us.

The origin of true wisdom (3:17)
True wisdom **'comes from heaven'** – it is never self-generated in a man or a woman. Putting it another way, the 'knowledge of the Holy One is understanding' (Proverbs 9:10). James surely echoes the earlier thought in 1:17, where he said that 'Every good and perfect gift is from above, coming down from the Father...' All that is good has a heavenly and divine source.

The characteristics of true wisdom (3:17)
Seven practical characteristics identify the true wisdom: it is **'first of all pure; then peace-loving, considerate, submissive, full of mercy and good fruit, impartial and sincere'**. We are led straight to Christ, for James echoes our Lord's teaching in the 'Beatitudes' (Matthew 5:1-12) and applies it to the qualities of that wisdom which God gives to his people.

1. **'Pure.'** The studied use of the expression *'first of all'* indicates that here we have the primary motive which is at the heart of the wisdom from above and, indeed, of every other Christian grace. 'Blessed are the pure in heart, for they will see God' (Matthew 5:8). 'The truly wise man,' comments Robert Johnstone, 'is he who has conformity of spirit to the "only wise God," who believes what God teaches, loves what God loves, lives as Jesus lives – He who was the express image of the invisible God.'[6] The heavenly wisdom is the perfect righteousness of Christ applied. And when we receive that

wisdom, we know it to be pure, even if we are not ourselves pure. Indeed, the very purity of the wisdom of God is highlighted all the more by our awareness of the dark shadows of indwelling sin. God's wisdom is pure.

2. **'Peace-loving.'** Wisdom is peacable – it 'never starts quarrels, strife, dissension, and turbulence'.[7] As far as is possible, if it depends upon us, we are to 'live at peace with everyone' (Romans 12:18). Jesus says, 'Blessed are the peacemakers, for they will be called sons of God' (Matthew 5:9). In contrast, the troubles in the Corinthian church (1 Corinthians 3:3) and all the strife that occurs between people (James 4:1-3) arise from unhallowed desires of one sort or another – all, ultimately, the contradiction of the wisdom of God.

3. **'Considerate.'** True wisdom never forgets how patient and forbearing the Lord has been to one's own weakness and foolishness. There is a gracious and holy elasticity in the wisdom of the child of God who has himself experienced the gentle longsuffering of the Lord in saving him from the fully deserved consequences of his sins. Godly wisdom does not insist on its rights as if being legally right is the great thing. Consideration goes beyond mere correctness and delights in the 'justice, mercy and faithfulness' which are given by the Holy Spirit (Matthew 23:23). 'Blessed are the meek,' declared our Lord, 'for they will inherit the earth' (Matthew 5:5). True wisdom is characterized by meekness, even the meekness that took Jesus so quietly to the cross to die in our place.

4. **'Submissive.'** A spin-off of meekness is submissiveness, which in this context means being 'easy to be entreated'. This is not equivalent to being what today is called a 'push-over' or 'an easy mark'. The idea is of a heart that is not obstinate, but overflowing with a humble and accepting spirit, like that of which Jesus spoke in the first Beatitude: 'Blessed are the poor in spirit, for theirs is the kingdom of heaven' (Matthew 5:3). This is the temper of humility, which is born of entire dependence upon the Lord and issues in the spirit that does not think more highly of oneself than one ought to think. The

meek person is therefore inclined to esteem others better than himself (Romans 12:3; Philippians 2:3) and does not need to be coerced into kindness and graciousness in his dealings with others.[8]

5. **'Full of mercy.'** Mercy in Scripture is active compassion. It is both attitude and actions. True wisdom is never an ivory-tower theoretical exercise. It looks for ways of doing people good, especially when they are in trouble. 'Blessed are the merciful, for they will be shown mercy' (Matthew 5:7).

6. **'...and good fruit.'** The life of the wise is like gathering the fruit of the summer (Proverbs 10:5) and, like honey from the comb, is sweet to the taste (Proverbs 24:13-14). The grace of the Lord Jesus Christ fills the heart and life – both the inner and outward life – and brings forth fruit that touches the need of a hungry world. 'Blessed are those who hunger and thirst for righteousness, for they will be filled' (Matthew 5:6).

7. **'Impartial'** refers us back to 1:6 and to all that James said about not doubting, but being single-minded in devotion to the Lord. The Greek word (*adiakritos*) occurs only here in the New Testament and is thought by most scholars to refer to our inward disposition towards the Lord and his truth, rather than to the modern focus of 'impartiality', which is usually 'fair-mindedness' or an unbiased outlook.

8. **'Sincere'** indicates a complete lack of hypocrisy. True wisdom is steadfast for the Lord and is completely open and wholly unpretentious about it. This is the faithfulness which stands out in the face of opposition. 'Blessed are those who are persecuted because of righteousness, for theirs is the king-dom of heaven' (Matthew 5:10). The wise man knows where he is going and to whom he belongs!

The consequences of having true wisdom (3:18)
The image of sowing and reaping is often used in Scripture to illustrate the temporal and eternal consequences of both sin and righteousness (e.g., Job 4:8; Matthew 6:26; 13:3-39; 1 Corinthians 15:36-44; Galatians 6:8-9). 'There is an intimate connection,' writes Thomas Manton, 'between our

endeavours and the Lord's recompenses.' Our actions 'are seed; they fall upon the ground, not to be lost, but to grow up again; we may taste the fruits of them long after they be committed; be sure you sow good seed.'[9]

James applies the sowing-reaping model to the temporal aspect of redemption: **'Peacemakers who sow in peace raise a harvest of righteousness.'** He answers 3:16 which showed the evil fruit of 'envy and selfish ambition'. The 'harvest of righteousness' is the harvest that consists in righteousness – that is righteousness itself, growing personal righteousness, progressive sanctification, conformity to the will of God and the image and pattern of Jesus Christ.[10]

'Sing joyfully to the Lord, you righteous;
   it is fitting for the upright to praise him'

(Psalm 33:1).

16.
Why so much strife?

Please read James 4:1-3

'What causes fights and quarrels among you? Don't they come from your desires that battle within you?' (James 4:1).

In concluding his discussion of the wisdom that comes from God, James said that 'Peacemakers who sow in peace raise a harvest of righteousness' (3:18). His point was that true wisdom issues in a calm and peaceable way of dealing with controversial matters. This was not peace at the expense of the truth, but a peaceable insistence upon the claims of God towards the ultimate goal of healing, reconciliation and practical unity. Now, in virtually the same breath, James turns and asks us, **'What causes fights and quarrels among you?'** (4:1). Why are we not the way we ought to be as followers of the Lord Jesus Christ? Why do we have platitudes instead of real peace, fights in place of fellowship, strife instead of sanctification?

Strife in the church is a painful subject, as anyone who has experienced it can testify. One expects these things in the 'world', but it always is a shocking contradiction of the very nature and purpose of the body of Christ. We do not normally expect Christians to be nasty. But you don't have to be around a church too long to run into someone who fills that description. You, reader, may have been one yourself or, God forbid, maybe you still are! Inconsistency, unmortified sinful attitudes and downright hypocrisy are found somewhere in every body of Christians in the real world of sinners, even if they are sinners saved by grace (or say they are). The New Testament epistles and the Old Testament prophets are unintelligible aside from this reality. And the fact that these things ought not to be (3:10) lends all the more pointedness to the earnest exhortations of the biblical writers. It is beyond doubt that James was writing to real situations in which there was strife between professing Christians – situations no different in principle from what we have all seen and, to which, in one way or another, we have all been party in our own day; situations which need to be resolved with brokenness of heart and contrition of spirit, so that the true healing of the gospel may be experienced and evangelistically demonstrated to a world that is in bondage to sinful strife in all its forms.

James examines the *origin* of strife (4:1), the *nature* of strife (4:2) and the *answer* to strife (4:3). It should be noted that his full and final conclusion is not stated until verse 7, when he says, 'Submit yourselves, then, to God.'

The origin of strife – sinful desires (4:1)

What is the genesis of our fights and quarrels? **'Don't they come from your desires that battle within you?** (4:1). We like to think that we are 'taking a stand for principle' when we are engaged in controversy – we are right and 'they' are wrong. Sometimes this may actually be the case. Obviously, someone is in the wrong. Of course, everybody on either side believes that the other chap is to blame – or more to blame. We tend to make our side the ethical bench-mark of the controversy and excuse ourselves of substantial wrongdoing or mixed motives. It is always the other fellow who has to change his ways! Candid self-examination is as rare as hen's teeth. Changing the figure somewhat, it is like the story of the American farmer who heard a thief among his chickens one night. With shot-gun at the ready, he peered into the darkened hen-house and challenged the invisible intruder. 'Who's there?' he said. Back came the hopeful answer: 'There ain't nobody here but us chickens!' The world is like that: 'There ain't nobody here but us innocent people.' Not a sinner in sight, except the other fellow, of course. Well, James isn't interested in debating the 'whys', 'whos' and 'wherefores' of relative responsibility and blame. Most of the time we all have a share of the guilt and all of the time we all need a piece of

honest biblical reflection on our motives. So he starts with the
'desires' that he knows we know 'battle' within us.

By **'desires'** is meant the gratification of the flesh, in the
sense of worldly pleasure. The Greek is the plural of *hedone,*
from which the philosophical word, Hedonism, is derived.
Hedonism is the classical philosophy of pleasure as the
highest good of man. A number of Greek schools held differing forms of this religion – for pleasure-seeking is, was and
ever shall be a religion. Nothing gives good old-fashioned sin
a cloak of legitimacy more than dressing it up as a
'philosophy' and elaborating a high-sounding theoretical
framework upon which to hang its oh-so-earthly attractions.
The root of the matter is simply the pleasures of the 'world'
(as opposed to God) *versus* the way of temporal and eternal
blessing in discipleship to the Lord of all.

These 'desires' are at war within us. Paul says the same
thing to the Roman Christians: 'In my inner being I delight in
God's law; but I see another law at work in the members of
my body, waging war against the law of my mind and making
me a prisoner of the law of sin within my members' (Romans
7:22- 23). These 'desires' are particularly connected with the
body and its natural appetites – the body, that is, as it is
affected by that mysterious but real influence called 'indwelling sin' by the theologians. We want sensual pleasures – to see
things, to do things and, insofar as these appetites are not
controlled, to crave more and more unhallowed gratification.
We cannot fail to understand what James is saying. We have
all experienced this to some degree or other. No one is yet 'a
perfect man, able to keep his whole body in check' (3:2). In
extreme cases of enslavement to a particular besetting sin, we
will often observe, or experience ourselves, the situation
where a man knows what he is doing is wrong and admits it
even with tears, at the same time as he defeatedly protests his
inability to stop doing it. This is the nature of enslavement to
any bad habit, at least where a man has a conscience about his
actions.

These 'desires' are the weeds of the soul. Like the weeds in
your garden, you can pull them out and keep them down all
summer, then leave them untended for a two weeks' holiday
at the sea-side, only to come back to a jungle that has engulfed

your precious vegetables! 'He who allows his sinful propensities to rule uncontrolled,' remarks John Calvin, 'will know no end to his lusts.'[1] It takes Holy Spirit-empowered self-control to produce consistently the peaceable fruit of righteousness in our hearts and lives.

But how do these 'desires' become the genesis of quarrels? The simple answer lies in the fact that *sinful* desires are *selfish* desires. They gnaw away within us in order to give us our own way. With delicious understatement, Robert Johnstone observes that 'The race of Diotrephes, who troubled the churches of Asia because he "loved to have the pre-eminence," is by no means extinct.' Somewhere in every quarrel is this love for ascendancy over others. It may be on one side or the other, but frequently it is on both. You can surely think of many ways in which animosities have developed between people you have known. James is not concerned to discuss specific cases, but he is concerned that we search our hearts about the issue itself and make appropriate application to our own behaviour. If righteousness loses in the battle *within us,* then it will soon break out in battles *outside us* – in the fellowship of God's people. It is inevitable that pride and selfishness in one person will eventually clash with pride and selfishness in another. And it is also true that such sinful commitments will contest the righteous desires of those who are faithfully bearing a testimony for the Lord and his Word.

The nature of strife – wanting our way (4:2)

I was always told, when I was growing up, that if I ever wanted something, I had 'a good Scots tongue in my head'. That is to say, don't expect anybody else to give you something, if you are not prepared to ask for it yourself. Wanting and asking are two sides of one coin. These are brought together by James, but in such a way as to challenge the quality and direction of both our wanting and our asking. Do we want the right things in the right way?

'You want...'
George was the very picture of rugged and unruly childhood.

His tousled mop of curly red hair was matched by an outgoing and confident personality backed by an insistent tongue. He was only three years old but he always knew what he wanted. He had few words, but they all were made to count and foremost among them was the motto of his one-man army: 'A want yin tae!' (the Berwickshire vernacular for 'I want one too!'). Whatever anyone had – especially his brother and sister – George wanted one too! And from that moment, he waged war with mouth and mitt until he either had his way, or was checked by parental discipline or sibling self-defence.

'I want one too!' is the root of man's second deepest problem (the first is: 'I want to be my own god.'). It burns people up to be denied what they want. **'You want something but don't get it. You kill and covet, but you cannot have what you want. You quarrel and fight'** (4:2). 'Starting a quarrel is like breaching a dam,' wrote Solomon, 'so drop the matter before a dispute breaks out' (Proverbs 17:14). 'As charcoal to embers and as wood to fire, so is a quarrelsome man for kindling strife' (Proverbs 26:21). But quenching the 'I want' urge does not come naturally. Escalation is the normal outcome. Quarrels are the international 'arms race' at the local level. David took a fancy to Bathsheba and lust soon turned to adultery, deceit and murder. Jezebel wanted a vineyard, so Naboth and sons were killed. When tempers are hot and restraints melt away, as they always do in such circumstances, then anything is possible – even killing.

The Scripture declares that he who hates his brother *is* a murderer (1 John 3:15). 'Character assassination' is an apt term and the murder it describes no less real for the absence of a literal corpse. Words can kill. People murder in their hearts even if their hands never lift a dagger. Any personal irritation or disagreement can erupt into the murderous attitude of which the apostle John speaks. This is true within the fellowship of the church and you know that Satan is trying his hardest to shatter the body of Christ. And we must admit that he has had plenty of help from us. Too many church Annual Business Meetings are blighted by rancour and discord from some quarter. Bible Study groups and personal conversations so easily become arenas for the taking of sides. The fact that the truth – the Word of God – is the subject at the heart of these interactions means that disagreements can very easily develop into divisiveness. What ought to foster bonds of unity – 'the unity of the Spirit through the bond of peace' (Ephesians 4:3) – is perverted by human sin into an unholy justification for spiritual pride and broken fellowship. The history of the church is not encouraging in this respect. There can be no doubt that Christians bear the heaviest responsibility for forging loving bonds of fellowship with other true believers and not allowing them to be broken by differing convictions on points that do not vitiate a genuine Christian commitment. James' words must challenge every single Christian.

'You do not ask...'
There is something deeper than even broken relationships with our brothers and sisters in Christ. The root of the problem is the neglect of prayer and a broken relationship with the Lord. **'You do not have, because you do not ask God.'** The name of God is not in the Greek text but has been added by the English translators to clarify the verse.[2] James appears to be reminding his readers of our Lord's words in Matthew 7:7: 'Ask and it will be given to you...for everyone who asks receives...'

This is not to say that God will grant any old (sinful) desire you happen to have, just because you check it with him first! James knows when he brings up the subject of neglected prayer that this in itself is bound to suggest a re-examination of the 'desires that battle within'! To bring a petition to God carries with it the necessity of the ethical-spiritual review of the petition itself. Is what I want offensive to God? He has certain standards. How do my 'desires' – that have been eating me up with frustration and anger – measure up against his will? These are the questions that James is raising by implication. And it is clear that James' point is that where there is true and living prayer fellowship with the Lord, people ask for different things and with altogether different motives, because they are committed to the revealed will of God as the rule for their faith and practice.

When our prayers, such as they are, become no more than the handmaid of our desires, they are not real prayers but a kind of lucky charm in words. The strife that bedevils people's lives often flows from unhallowed desires aided and abetted

by prayerlessness, which, in some, is due to a complete lack of
prayer and, in others, is masked by the illusion of an empty
form of prayer that in fact denies the Lord and his revealed
will.

The answer to strife (4:3)

This is confirmed in the next verse: **'When you ask, you do not
receive, because you ask with wrong motives, that you may
spend what you get on your pleasures.'** You will 'notice that
James has moved on from quarrels to the more fundamental
problem of worldliness. Perhaps some people would respond
to James by saying, 'But we did pray – we did ask God to give
us what we wanted!' James anticipates this by saying, in
effect, 'You did not get what you want because you asked
with wrong motives. You did not submit your desires to the
lordship of Christ. The result was that the heavens were brass
to your self-centred petition. As the psalmist has told us, "If
I had cherished sin in my heart, the Lord would not have listened" (Psalm 66:18).' Prayers of that sort, says Calvin,
'wished to make God the minister of their own lusts'.[3] This is
a denial of the holiness of God. And when we put this
together with all that James has said about quarrelling and
fighting, we see that strife and the worldliness which underlies
it always indicate estrangement from God. Manton sums it up
in terms of three practical points about prayer: '1. ...We pray
amiss when our ends and aims are not right in prayer. 2.
...Our ends and aims are wrong when blessings are for the use
and encouragement of our lusts. 3. ...Prayers so framed are
usually successless; we miss when we ask amiss.'[4]

The other – positive – side of this is that in the Christian life,
a constant and faithful prayer life is the great antidote to the
rise of sinful desires and overweening pride. When believers
pray properly – individually and corporately – the windows of
heaven will open and the cancers of self and strife will wither
in the healing breath of the Holy Spirit. 'Holy desires have a
sure answer.'[5] 'He fulfils the desires of those who fear him',
says the psalmist, 'he hears their cry and saves them' (Psalm
145:19). 'You hear, O Lord, the desire of the afflicted; you
encourage them, and you listen to their cry...' (Psalm 10:17).

Here is the 'how to' of putting an end to the strife that presently arises in your inner being – the means of nipping future problems in the bud. It is often said with respect to the affairs of nations that as long as they are still talking they can't be fighting! This is, in a sense, a parable of prayer and its healing effect. As long as we are seriously talking with the Lord – even if we are wrestling in our prayers as surely as Jacob physically wrestled with the Lord at Peniel (Genesis 32:22-32) – we will not be consumed with sinful strife, neither will we be fighting with other people! And the reason for this is simply that it is in the exercise of believing prayer that fellowship with the Lord and the fellowship we share with believers become deeper and more firmly established. The cliché, 'The family that prays together stays together,' encapsulates a profoundly happy truth. In the prayer of a fellowship, lives are opened up, burdens shared and joys and sorrows poured out before the Lord in such a way as to receive the blessing of the Lord, part of which is the warming of our hearts one towards the other. With shared love in Christ comes the victory over envy and that unholy spirit of seeking one's own way at the expense of others. 'Love...does not envy' (1 Corinthians 13:4). 'Submit yourselves, then, to God...' (4:7-10).

17.
Worldliness and its cure

Please read James 4:4-10

'Submit yourselves, then, to God. Resist the devil, and he will flee from you' (James 4:7).

Revival and reformation are really two sides of the one coin. Yet it has become commonplace for churches to seek 're-newal' while apparently seeing no necessity for a return to biblical ethical and moral absolutes. The same churches that wink at, or even condone, the mass-murder of unborn babies, and are ever seeking 'insights' that will allow them to accept homosexual behaviour as an 'alternative life-style', are very concerned about growth and revitalization. For example, the 1988 Synod of one of America's 'main-line' churches, the Episcopal Church, was reported as 'grappling' with the loss of 500,000 members (15% in twenty-five years) and talking about the need for 'evangelism', while issuing a report hailing extra-marital sexual relationships (both pre- and post-marital) as potentially 'life-giving'![1] There was no indication that these two factors – the approval of sin and the withering of the membership – were seen as integrally related. Indeed, the chosen solution to numerical decline in many such churches is to move towards even greater accommodation to the spirit of the age: to 'attract' people back and not to 'turn them off' with old-fashioned and restrictive teachings! The accom-modationist religion of the twentieth century baptizes immorality and still looks for the blessing of God, even as it slides inexorably towards impotence and extinction![2]

James was aware of the destructiveness of worldliness in the church – both for the lives of individuals and the health of the body as a whole. His discussion of strife, principally among professing Christians, clearly had these disastrous effects in view. He showed that quarrels originated in unworthy motives – sinful, selfish desires that battle within (4:1); that they become worse as we continue to indulge our desires and refuse to connect our frustration with our own prayerlessness and breach of communion with God (4:2); and finally, James suggested that the answer lay in the renewal of right motives – in a living personal relationship with God (4:3). Building on this, James goes on in 4:4-10 to expound the theme of the inconsistency and incompatibility of 'worldliness' with true godliness. The general principle that friendship with the world is hatred towards God is expounded in verses 4-6, while the cure for worldliness is then explained in verses 7-10.

The antithesis between God and the world (4:4-6)

The principle is stated in the most uncompromising terms: **'You adulterous people, don't you know that friendship with the world is hatred towards God?** (4:4).

Adulterous people (4:4)
It should first be noted that when the readers are described as **'adulterous people'**, the language is figurative and is not an accusation of sexual immorality. The point is that selfishness and love of the world are to be seen as spiritual adultery. Christians are, by their own profession of faith, collectively the 'bride of Christ'. But by their squabbles and hatreds, they show themselves to be wandering off God's 'straight and narrow' way in practice. This is 'adulterous' because it is a betrayal of professed love for the Lord and covenanted commitment to faithful discipleship. Friendship with the world is sin because it is ultimately the denial of God and of his power to save us from our sins.

Friendship with the world (4:4)
But what is **'friendship with the world'**? The 'world' in this expression is that world which is opposed to the living God and his revealed will as set out in Holy Scripture. 'Worldliness' – that highly unpopular word even among Christians –

describes the attitude and pattern of life which arises from
open rebellion against God. That said, we must not reduce
'friendship with the world' to a short list of outward actions.
Too often, Christians have identified worldliness simplisti-
cally with activities like smoking, drinking, dancing, styles of
dress, hairstyles and the like. Without minimizing the relevance of any categories of behaviour, we must always resist
the externalizing of worldliness, as if there were no deeper,
more profoundly motivational and spiritual considerations.
Throughout his epistle, James makes this point about sin in all
its manifestations. He views worldliness primarily as 'the
spirit of a life, not its outward form'.[3] It is altogether possible
to be quiet and mild-mannered in one's life-style and yet be
inwardly consumed by worldly desires and aspirations. And it
is not impossible to look worldly, by someone's definition of
worldliness, and in fact be a godly person. James challenges
our whole pattern of life; both outward behaviour and inward
aspirations and desires. 'Friendship with the world,' then, is
when these inner desires and motives are in harmony with
those of the world that does not know and does not want to
know God. It is when we seek what the world seeks, when we
want the riches that fade away, when we hunger for the praise
of men that God says is a snare, when we much prefer the
pleasures of 'the old man with his affections and lusts' to the
righteousness of Christ – it is then that we know we are friends
with the world and would rather not be distracted or inter-
fered with by the God of the Bible.

Hatred towards God (4:4)

Friendship with the world is not some 'alternative life-style'
that is all right with God. It is open war with God. James says
with stark simplicity that it is **'hatred towards God'**. The
forceful and uncompromising language is carefully chosen to
overthrow any tendency in our minds to explain away our
compromises with the world as less than serious infringe-
ments of the known will of the Lord. You know how it is: the
first sin is the difficult one; repeated offences come more easily and can eventually be redefined as good or at least relatively inoffensive. James is out to prick those consciences that
need to be pricked. His aim is to put us firmly back on track
after having shown us how we have wandered away from the

Lord. His teaching here is identical to that of Paul when he told the church: 'The carnal mind is enmity with God' (Romans 8:7 AV). This is the doctrine of the antithesis – the utter contradiction between God and his righteousness, on the one hand, and the world, the flesh and the devil on the other; between worldliness and godliness. We need to be in no doubt about this great divide: because we need the clearest conception of what it means to live after the Spirit and not after the flesh, what it means to live for Christ as over against living for self. The Lord is calling us to his side of this antithesis – to true peace, to inextinguishable hope, to inexpressible joy, and all in the salvation won by Jesus Christ.

The choice is yours! (4:4)

This principle – the antithesis between worldliness and godliness – is now driven home with relentless vigour. **'Anyone who chooses to be a friend of the world becomes an enemy of God'** (4:4). Every individual is responsible before God for his chosen path. James is saying, 'Let us begin right now with the real situation in your life! What are you planning to do with God's will – today? How are you responding at this precise moment to the claims that God has made upon your behaviour? How do your commitments square up against what God is saying in his infallible Word? Friendship with the world is a matter of deliberate choice. No one can excuse himself by saying someone else made him do it, whether peer-pressure, upbringing, environment, demons, the devil himself or some fatalistic "predestination"!'[4] We know when we are setting our face in a particular direction, however great the pressures we may feel to be upon us at the time. And we also know that our attitude to God himself is the basis of our choices. 'He who "determines" to be a friend of the world,' observes James Adamson, 'becomes an enemy of God, not because God hates him but because he hates God.'[5]

Grace for the humble (4:5-6)

Taking this further, ask yourself what the Scriptures say: **'Or do you think Scripture says without reason that the spirit he caused to live in us envies intensely? But he gives us more grace. That is why Scripture says: "God opposes the proud but gives grace to the humble"'** (4:5-6).

The thrust is this: 'We know what Scripture says. Scripture never teaches that the Holy Spirit, who indwells every believer, would lead us to "envy intensely"'. This ought to go without saying, because to be given to selfish and worldly desires is clearly a contradiction of all that Scripture teaches about the leading of the Holy Spirit in the life of the Christian. What God gives is *grace*. He gives us 'more grace' than the 'intense envy' that is the driving force of so much worldliness! And that is why Scripture – in this instance, the quotation of Proverbs 3:34 – says that God gives grace to the humble, but opposes the proud! Pride, which is the essence of self-centredness, is in turn the root of practical worldliness. In contrast, humility is a grace flowing from Christ, nurtured by the ongoing exercise of faith in him and issuing in greater rewards of God's favour and love. The apostle Peter quotes the same verse from Proverbs in 1 Peter 5:5 with reference to the order of the church – specifically the relationship between the 'young men' and the elders – and goes on to declare the fundamental principle of practical blessing: 'Humble yourselves, therefore, under God's mighty hand, that he may lift you up in due time.'

The cure: discipleship to the Lord (4:7-10)

James 4:7-10 has been likened to a psalm.[6] It begins and ends with the same thought and, in between, is a selection of practical thoughts relating to the central theme of submission to the Lord.

> **'Submit yourselves, then, to God.**
> **Resist the devil, and he will flee from you.**
> **Come near to God and he will come near to you.**
> **Wash your hands, you sinners,**
> **And purify your hearts, you double-minded.**
> **Grieve, mourn and wail.**
> **Change your laughter to mourning and your joy to gloom.**
> **Humble yourselves before the Lord, and he will lift you up.'**

The basic cure for worldliness is submission to God (4:7). What is meant here is not so much submission in the sense of obedience to this or that command of God (although that goes without saying), but rather the spirit of submissiveness in which we Christians are deeply humbled before the Lord and are profoundly committed to being his disciples. This is the same lowliness of spirit spoken of by our Lord in the Sermon on the Mount: 'Blessed are the poor in spirit, for theirs is the kingdom of heaven,' and earlier by the prophet Isaiah:

'For this is what the High and Lofty One says –
  he who lives for ever, whose name is holy:
"I live in a high and holy place,
  but also with him who is contrite and lowly in spirit,
to revive the spirit of the lowly
  and to revive the heart of the contrite"'

(Isaiah 57:15).

This lowliness of spirit is not some morbid feeling of uselessness or worthlessness, but a profound awareness of the majesty of God, of the glorious sufficiency of the redeeming love of Jesus Christ and a deep sense of readiness to be led by the indwelling Spirit of God in simple obedience to the Word of God.

The practical prescription for this life of triumphant discipleship is set out in a series of nine practical imperatives which we are to work out in our daily lives (4:7-9). These may be arranged in three main groupings, as follows:

A. Commitment to the personal God (4:7-8)
  1. 'Resist the devil...'
  2. 'Come near to God...'

B. Commitment to personal holiness (4:8)
  3. 'Wash your hands...'
  4. 'Purify your hearts...'

C. Commitment to a penitential spirit (4:9)
  5. 'Grieve...'
  6. 'Mourn...'
  7. 'Wail...'
  8. 'Change your laughter to mourning...'
  9. '...and your joy to gloom.'

The only antidotes to pride, self and strife are the Lord, holiness and a meek, repentant attitude. Where these elements of living faith are not being exercised and applied, then the evils of which James has already spoken will inevitably flourish. Here, then, is the Lord's prescription for the peace and joy of the Christian life.

Nearness to God (4:7-8)
First understand that Satan is not omnipotent. Resist him and he will flee! He is mentioned because he is the ultimate source of all pride and worldliness. In Christ, we shall be more than conquerors, said Paul to the Romans (Romans 8:37). In Christ, believers share his triumph over the temptations of the Evil One (Matthew 4:1-11; Luke 4:1-13) and his definitive defeat of Satan's kingdom (John 12:32; Colossians 2:14-15). Christ is King and we are only under Satan's dominion with respect to our sin.[7] Satan has been bound, judged, spoiled and destroyed as the prerequisite for the coming of Christ's kingdom *now* (Matthew 12:29; Hebrews 2:14). Powerful as Satan is – the 'roaring lion' of 1 Peter 5:8 – he is not the sovereign lord of God's creation, still less of God's believing people. If we resist him, he will flee!

Understand also that coming near to God is indispensable for and inseparable from resisting the devil. God is the sole source of the strength by which lives are transformed and holiness is generated and sustained. The Christian life is all movement: *away* from Satan and sin and *towards* God and his righteousness. 'The Lord is near to all who call on him,' says the psalmist, 'to all who call on him in truth' (Psalm 145:18). 'The closer we live to God,' writes Curtis Vaughan, 'the more we know of his comfort, support, and power, and the easier it is to resist the devil.'[8]

Clean hands and heart (4:8)
In the Old Testament, the hands and the heart are frequently connected to show the necessity of a personal holiness that is both outward and inward. Who is the true worshipper of the Lord? 'He who has clean hands and a pure heart' (Psalm 24:4). The imagery of washing in general denotes complete cleansing from spiritual and moral defilement. Baptism signifies the 'washing of regeneration' (Titus 3:5 AV). And the

washing-motif continues to be used of sanctification, as each believer seeks to die to sin and live for Christ (2 Corinthians 7:1; Ephesians 5:26). There can, of course, be no meaningful cleaning up of our act, without the purification of the heart. The Pharisees, who had a rigorous and impressive outward regimen of ritual holiness, were variously described by our Lord as unwashed cups, whitewashed tombs, hypocrites and sons of hell, because they had unconverted hearts (Matthew 23). They had no heart-commitment to the Lord and this made their outward holiness a pretentious parody of true godliness. They did not share the prayer of King David, after he had been confronted with his sin of adultery with Bathsheba:

> 'Cleanse me with hyssop and I shall be clean;
>   wash me, and I shall be whiter than snow...
> Create in me a pure heart, O God,
>   and renew a steadfast spirit within me...'
>
> (Psalm 51:7,10).

Brokenness of spirit (4:9)

Central to the psalmist's restoration to the joy of his salvation was 'a broken spirit; a broken and a contrite heart' (Psalm 51:12,17). When James appeals to world-infected Christians to change their laughter to mourning and their joy to gloom, he is not rejecting *Christian* joy, but showing them the way to its true enjoyment. The paradox of new life in Christ once again shines forth: when we are weak, then we are strong: when we are captive to Christ, then we are free; when we are humble, then God exalts us; and here, by analogy with Psalm 51:12-17, when we are of a penitent spirit, then we are in the condition to experience the true joy – the joy of the Christian salvation, enjoyed in the full assurance of a living faith. James wants us to be happy Christians (1:2; 5:13), but he also wants us to understand that any joy which co-exists with a worldly spirit and practice, and includes the assurance of being right with God, is a dangerous mirage. True joy is at once sound, serious and substantial. It is *sound* because it arises out of the exercise of saving faith that looks to Christ for salvation and knows that salvation experimentally through the convicting power of the Word of God and the repentance and renewal wrought by the Holy Spirit in the heart. It is *serious* in that it is the expression of the awareness both of what Christ has gained for his redeemed and what he has saved sinners from in spite of themselves. Joy is not mere jollity. Christian joy is also *substantial* in that it is the expression of 'an infallible assurance of faith, founded upon the divine truth of the promises of salvation, the inward evidence of those graces unto which the promises are made, the testimony of the Spirit of adoption witnessing with our spirits that we are the children of God: which Spirit is the earnest of our inheritance, whereby we are sealed to the day of redemption'.[9] Christian joy is not a mere subjective feeling, in other words, but an objective reality brought about by the work of the Holy Spirit in the Christian's innermost being – his new nature in Christ.

He will lift you up (4:10)

The fruit of submission to God is that he will surely lift up his faithful believing child. This is the same as the grace he gives to the humble (4:6). James returns us to his original theme. The incomparable Calvin sums up this teaching beautifully when he reminds us that 'The grace of God will then be ready to raise us up, when he sees that our proud spirits are laid aside. We emulate and envy, because we desire to be eminent. This is a way wholly unreasonable, for it is God's peculiar work to raise up the lowly, and especially those who willingly humble themselves. Whosoever, then, seeks a firm elevation, let him be cast down under a sense of his own infirmity, and think humbly of himself. Augustine well observes somewhere, "As a tree must strike deep roots downwards, that it may grow upwards, so everyone who has not his soul fixed deep in humility, exalts himself to his own ruin".'[10]

18.
Judging others

Please read James 4:11-12

'There is only one Lawgiver and Judge, the one who is able to save and destroy. But you – who are you to judge your neighbour?' (James 4:12)

The way we speak about other people is never far from James' thoughts. He repeatedly returns to the problem of the use of the tongue. Frequently, he writes of the godly use of this faculty – in prayer (1:5; 5:13,16), in showing love to others (1:19; 2:8) and in praising God (3:9). He also pinpoints very clearly the principal sins of the tongue – being too ready to teach others (1:19; 3:1), sitting in judgement over others (3:9; 4:11), boasting (4:13), grumbling (5:9) and swearing (5:12). Furthermore, James sees these as revealing deeper, inward, spiritual realities. Our speech is often a good index of the state of the heart, notwithstanding the fact that considerable effort may go into concealing with words what is going on in our minds. In the long term even the most cunning dissemblers and deceivers tend to be seen for what they are. Hypocrisy never wears well, because, ironically perhaps, the hypocrite is poorly adapted to keeping his own secret by the very fact that he has a deep-seated love for his sins! In contrast, true godliness is in its very nature transparent and obvious to all.

In our passage (4:11-12), we appear to have returned to the initial theme of the fourth chapter, which asked us the painful question: 'What causes fights and quarrels among you? (4:1-3). The answer given was that this arose from a self-centred spirit – the spirit of worldliness as opposed to godliness. The cure for this is submission to God, which involves self-abasement and a readiness to die to sin in all its forms (4:4-10). We now revisit the evil of self-centredness, this time in relation to the all too common habit of slandering others and, in effect, sitting in judgement on them. James' purpose is to show us what it means to be humbled before God as it applies to the way we speak of others when they are not there to hear what is said.

Do not slander one another! (4:11)

'Brothers, do not slander one another.' The verb translated 'slander' (Greek *katalaleo*) means 'to speak against' someone. The Septuagint, the third-century B.C. Greek version of the Old Testament, uses this in its rendering of Psalm 78:19 with reference to Israel's complaining against God during their wanderings in Sinai: 'They *spoke against* God, saying, "Can God spread a table in the desert?..."' Related nouns are used in 2 Corinthians 12:20 when Paul expresses his fears that he will find 'slander' among the Corinthian Christians and in Romans 1:30, where 'slanderers' receive dishonourable mention in the apostle's list of the sins of lost men and women.

This slander, it should be noted, refers to more than openly subjecting someone to verbal abuse. It is, in the words of Thomas Manton, 'any speaking which is to the prejudice of another, be it true or false'[1] – what the law calls defamation of character and what we call smearing another's good name, or character-assassination. It is every statement that is made with the purpose of belittling someone, or besmirching his or her reputation, and encompasses everything from out-and-out lies to veiled innuendos, and even includes true statements when these are told only to hurt the person about whom they are made.

Motives
The vital ingredient is, of course, the motive behind what is said. How better to harm someone and cover yourself with the aura of righteous indignation than by telling a truth that embarrasses, humiliates or ruins that other person? Many a

man in public life has been destroyed by this means, years after an indiscretion became a thing of the past. And not a few have been handicapped in career advancement by the persistent tale-bearing of something that should have been buried long ago. Vindictiveness does not need lies to be powerfully effective, when true facts, however misleading, will serve just as well.

Motives vary. Sometimes it is a desire for *revenge* of a perceived injustice. 'I don't get mad – I get even,' reads a sadly popular American bumper-sticker. 'Getting even' is the 'justice' of the individualist who has an innate disregard for the rule of law and is only really satisfied when he has taken it into his own hands. Family feuds have gone on for generations, as have so-called 'traditional rivalries' between whole communities and nations.[2] Some people seem determined to wage war on others. Some nations do so quite literally – the Iran-Iraq war of the 1980s affords a prime and tragic example. Sometimes sheer *maliciousness* – what the Germans call *Schadenfreude,* the enjoyment of other people's distress – moves someone to spread dissension and strife where there was none before. More often, the motive is *self-aggrandizement* – putting other people down so as to appear better in relation to them. It is so easy to score points off others with a supercilious aside, a sarcastic remark or a clever innuendo with a double meaning – all delivering a damaging criticism without much danger of being pinned down and called to account for the implied accusations, and all calculated to build up self and put down others. The motive that produces most slanders may well be no more than *'the mere desire to talk,* even when all innocent materials for talk are lacking'.[3] How often do people get together and end up talking about other people – almost always in a critical vein? Manton, with his characteristic wryness, observes that 'John Baptist's head in a charger is a usual dish at our meals.'[4] How true! And what a searching comment from that great Puritan preacher! It's so easy to roast people *in absentia!* And it can be exciting and entertaining – and even can be justified in terms of sharing of wisdom and discernment! When we are finished, however, what started without 'malice aforethought' can only issue in harmful and self-serving character-assassination. We ought rather to have had 'the moral courage to act on the principle that silence, or innocent dullness, is immeasurably better and nobler than the propagation of what may injure and cannot possibly do good'.[5]

Form and content

The form and content of slander, as already noted, can be anything from out-and-out lies to speaking the truth in carelessness or even hatred. It is vital that Christians discern and depart from every appearance of the evil of slanderous 'evil-speaking'.

It has become fashionable, in the name of *'sharing'*, for Christians to broadcast all sorts of information, some of it very sad and very personal, about themselves and other church members – ostensibly in the interests of a more meaningful fellowship of intercessory prayer. On occasion, these stray from what is proper and helpful for public consumption and become the currency of ear-tickling notoriety. Christians too readily forget that sharing a personal problem in a public meeting of the church is not much different from shouting it from the house-tops. The consequences of public exposure of personal matters need to be very carefully weighed before such matters are shared outside of the confidentiality of pastoral and private counsel and, in general, the wisest rule to follow is that private matters should remain private, whereas public matters should be dealt with in public. Where there is no necessity to publicize a problem, it should be resolved privately. Sad to say, 'prayer requests' are sometimes little more than the gossip columns of church newsletters and magazines. There is, of course, a place for sharing specific matters with the whole fellowship of your church, whether these are problems needing solutions or reasons for praise and thanksgiving. But this in no way denies the propriety – and, indeed, necessity – of maintaining privacy with respect to many aspects of personal life and thought. This is frequently a matter of the finest judgement and spiritual discernment, but that in no way means that making such judgements is to be sidestepped. To avoid 'sharing' becoming a subtle species of slander will take great sensitivity and Spirit-filled wisdom.

Little more need be added to what has already been said

already about outright *falsehoods*. Propagating defamatory lies, half-truths, innuendos, unfounded criticisms and exaggerated opinions all falls under the ban of God's Word. Satan, who is 'the father of lies', has a field day with these particular sins, especially among the Lord's people. An unsanctified Christian tongue is his most effective tool in undermining the church's witness in the world. We must therefore close our mouths and ears to the 'slander' of which James is speaking!

Speaking as brothers and sisters in Christ
It is no accident that James addresses his readers as brothers: **'Brothers, do not slander one another.'** Brothers and sisters in Christ share a common life, purchased by his atoning sacrifice in dying on the cross in their place. Those who have been saved by grace know that slanderous speech is from the pit of hell and can have no place in the life of God's truly believing children.

Who are you to judge your neighbour? (4:11-12)

James now takes us a step further: **'Anyone who speaks against his brother or judges him speaks against the law and judges it.'** Slander is more than bad or ill-meant words. It always involves deeper dimensions. Three points in particular are touched upon: first, slander is a pernicious form of judgement; second, slander is a judgement of the law of God; and third, slander is ultimately to dethrone God and enthrone oneself as the ultimate arbiter of what is right.

Sitting in judgement (4:11)
The basic point is that all slander tends in the end to become a matter of sitting in judgement over another person's heart. This is not to say that it is wrong to hold opinions with respect to the spiritual condition of other people, providing these opinions are firmly based upon the faithful application of Scripture, incontrovertible evidence of practical disobedience to scriptural standards of holiness – and all of this assessed in a generous, loving and compassionate spirit. It is obvious that we cannot avoid forming opinions about each

other. In the nature of the case, all our interpersonal communication, whether verbal or non-verbal, leads us to make
judgements and arrive at conclusions. We form views and
conceive of actions on the basis of the input we are able to
glean in the course of our contacts with others. We inevitably
make judgements about all and sundry – including people –
many times every day of our lives. It is quite obvious that this
is what biblical wisdom is all about. This is why we need to be
led by the Holy Spirit into the truth of God's Word and discern the mind of the Lord with respect to the entire spectrum
of our thoughts and actions.

What then are the **'judgements'** that are so wrong, in
James' view? They are simply those which we have no right to
make: judgements, opinions, evaluations, assessments –
dress them up as prettily and piously as you like – that are
prejudiced against the person of whom they are made! Such
judgements are those not subjected to God's law but made
without regard to the principles of the Word, the obligations
of love towards others and even without reference to the facts
themselves! This is what Jesus meant when he told us, 'Do not
judge, or you too will be judged. For in the same way as you
judge others, you will be judged, and with the measure you
use, it will be measured to you' (Matthew 7:1-2). Jesus does
not deny us the right to settled opinions; he simply insists that
our opinions take into account our accountability to a higher
law – the law of God – and recognize that the standard of our
opinions and judgements is his revealed Word. Furthermore,
James would appear to have in mind the fact that, if we
can have difficulty interpreting men's actions, we certainly
cannot read their hearts! And yet, we rush to all sorts of
judgements about the motives of others and even about their
eternal standing before God![6] Well, says James, before you
write somebody off and imagine God is happier with you than
with him, remember the gravity of what you are thinking and
saying and ask yourself just how justifiable your actions are in
the light of God's Word!

Judging the law of God (4:11)
Furthermore, to judge in this way – slanderously – is to speak
against the law and judge it. **'When you judge the law, you are
not keeping it, but sitting in judgement on it.'** Perhaps we can

illustrate this. Suppose you are of the opinion that eighty miles per hour is the proper speed at which to travel on the motorway and you are determined to drive at that speed, you are not just saying that you think the people that thought up the present speed limit are less wise and less informed than you; you are setting yourself up in judgement over the law, which states that you shall drive no faster than seventy miles an hour on the Queen's highways! It is as simple as that! Law works that way: you either submit to it or set yourself above it!

So it is with God's law. If you don't keep it, you are saying it isn't for you, you are above it and you are not going to let it interfere with your life if you have anything to do with it! You may not feel that that is your attitude, but fact, not feelings, is what James is talking about. Now James may here be thinking specifically of the 'royal law' – 'Love your neighbour as yourself' (2:8). You who have the attitude[7] that justifies speaking against others are in effect denying the 'royal law'. You are not content to love your neighbour as yourself. You are sitting in judgement over him.

This was the problem the apostle Paul deals with in Romans 14. Some Christians were judging their brothers over certain matters of conscience. A man couldn't be a vegetarian without being despised. True, his conviction that it was a sin not to be a vegetarian did indicate that he was weak in faith. But since when were believers to despise those who were weaker in faith than themselves? Others in the Roman church, also weak in faith, had scruples about food and the observance of certain special religious days (associated with Jewish practice). Paul did not say that these 'weaker brethren' were correct. Indeed, he wanted them to be instructed (Romans 14:19-23). But he did not want anyone to make new laws of behaviour not specifically set down in Scripture. Scripture is sufficient. Scripture is the measure. And to go beyond or aside from Scripture is to sit in judgement upon it.

Judging God himself (4:12)

The clinching argument puts opinionated man very firmly in his place: **'There is only one Lawgiver and Judge, the one who is able to save and destroy. But you – who are you to judge your**

neighbour?' The chain is completed: to slander your neighbour is to judge him; to judge him is to judge the law you are breaking in slandering him; and, finally, to judge the law is to judge the God who gave the law and to forget who you are before your Judge! The argument is devastating and unanswerable. Sinners may excuse themselves with grumbling and resentful protestations of their innocence or pass it all off in defiant unbelief, but God's logic is relentless and he will not be denied.

The person who refuses to submit to God's sufficient self-revelation, the Bible, is in effect 'playing God'. This is ultimately the nature of sin – man intent on being his own god! To reject God's will, to make judgements he has not made, is to usurp his position as the only Lawgiver and Judge. This is to say that all human law is, or ought to be, derived from law as it comes from God. Jehoshaphat, King of Judah, recognized this when he told his judges: 'Consider carefully what you do, because you are not judging for man but for the Lord, who is with you whenever you give a verdict' (2 Chronicles 19:6). This is the invariable basis of true justice in human societies. Without it one is left at best with an arbitrary pseudo-justice which does no more than restrain greed, and at worst with 'laws' that tyrannize and exploit the people in the interest of a clique. Manton correctly points out that the sequence of slander, judging law and rejecting God is a fruit of the spirit of Antichrist at work: 'The setting up of another lawgiver is properly antichristian; for then there is one head set against another, and human authority against divine. It is Paul's character of antichrist (2 Thess. 2:4), that "he as God sitteth in the temple of God"; that is, making himself absolute lord of consciences, bringing them to his obedience, working them to his advantage.'[8]

'But you – who are you...?' is God's withering reply. We are reminded of that most majestic of divine monologues, recorded in Job 38-42, in which the Lord teaches us the meaning of humility and submission to the infinite, eternal and unchanging God: 'Where were you when I laid the earth's foundation? Tell me if you understand' (Job 38:4). Question after unanswerable question, God challenges man, who in his arrogance 'darkens' the counsel of his Creator-God 'with words without knowledge' (Job 38:2). This is holy ridicule, not the vicious scorn of sinners. And it demonstrates to rebellious humanity its real position before the living God.

'The One enthroned in heaven laughs;
   the Lord scoffs at them.
Then he rebukes them in his anger
   and terrifies them in his wrath, saying,
"I have installed my King
   on Zion, my holy hill"'

(Psalm 2:4-6).

The second Psalm is an apt commentary on the deeper purpose of James' searching rebukes, which is that men and women would hear and heed the gracious call of Zion's King, who is none other than the Lord Jesus Christ! This is James' purpose: that we should believe in Christ, the crucified, buried and risen Son of God and Saviour of the world, and so glorify God and enjoy him for ever.

19.
Planning for your future

Please read James 4:13-17

'What is your life? You are a mist that appears for a little while and then vanishes. Instead, you ought to say, "If it is the Lord's will, we will live and do this or that"' (James 4:14-15).

We live in a time when prediction of, and planning for, the future are taken for granted as a normal part of life. Statistics, percentage probabilities and computer projections form the prophecy department of secular humanism. We can now know who will win the elections after a mere 10% of the vote is counted, what the weather will be next month[1] and what inflation and the exchange rate of pound, dollar, yen and mark will be in thirty, sixty and ninety days from now. We are saturated with a kind of 'planningism' on every hand. Diaries, desk planners, wall planners, menu planners, Christmas clubs, five-year plans, mortgage payments and computer programmes that 'ping!' when we are supposed to feed the dog all conspire to organize our lives from here to what is optimistically called the 'foreseeable' future. As a society we are decisively orientated towards the future. We are bombarded with advertising that charges us to 'plan the future' and 'get a piece of the [Prudential's] rock' to ensure 'peace of mind' in the Shangri-la of our retirement dreams. Add the rosy predictions of scientists who see man controlling everything from hair-colour to longevity and his own future evolution, and a dash of medical speculation about cures for cancer and AIDS, and you round out a picture of a society seeking desperately for a secure future, planned and predicted to the finest detail.

Planning and prudent preparation for future developments

and contingencies is certainly wise. But modern society surely protests too much about many of its plans and predictions. The confident words mask as great, if not greater, uncertainties and fears as have been felt at any time in human history. Men who do not trust God for the rain which alone will give them a good harvest cling all the more fiercely to the charts of the weather-man. Men want to be like God, knowing the end from the beginning, and in their conceit will take comfort from their own speculations about things to come and imagine that they can ignore the God who is absolutely sovereign in his overarching providential plan for human history. Godless man ignores the fundamental fact of his own condition and experience with respect to the future course of events in his life: 'You do not know what a day may bring forth' (Proverbs 27:1).

James addresses this problem of empty confidence about the future in the final section of his fourth chapter (4:13-17). The chapter as a whole contrasts the spirit of worldliness with that of true submission to the Lord. The root of worldliness is pride – the arrogance to be one's own god. Nowhere is this more starkly illustrated than in this matter of planning the future. James first describes the error – planning without providence (4:13); then offers a caution – life is short and uncertain (4:14); and finally gives an exhortation – to practical dependence upon the Lord for all our future days (4:15-17).

Planning without providence (4:13)

'Now listen, you who say, "Today or tomorrow we will go to this or that city, spend a year there, carry on business and make money."' This clearly refers to businessmen in James' own day, although the application is just as clearly to all planning in every age. It goes without saying that planning as such is not the problem. *Attitudes* are the point, in particular the attitude by which we make dispositions for the future in complete assurance that everything will go according to plan and work out in the way we want. The problem arises when the providence of God – and therefore the will of God – is left out of all consideration; it is when men give their own plans the place that actually belongs to divine providence, and so lay aside both any element of dependence on the Lord and a realistic assessment of their own limitations. Scripture warns us of the folly of such an attitude with an almost brutal simplicity: 'To man belong the plans of the heart, but from the Lord comes the reply of the tongue' (Proverbs 16:1). Where, for example, is Napoleon's 'Continental System' or Adolf Hitler's '1,000 year Reich'? History is littered with sometimes only the wreckage, and often no more than the faintest memories, of the greatest of human planning. 'Man proposes,' runs the old but true cliché, 'but God disposes!' The proverbial maxim echoes in the emptiness of our carnal dreaming: 'Do not boast about tomorrow...!' (Proverbs 27:1).

Christians, in contrast, have a high view of God's providence. They know that God is sovereign over the events of human history and that just as surely as the wind and waves obeyed Jesus on the Sea of Galilee so long ago, so they still obey him today as he exercises his authority as Mediator-King.[2] Christians also have the comfort of the covenant promises of God for their lives in time and eternity and the assurance that God is the One who answers believing prayer. Christians, nevertheless, are capable of subverting the blessings of their own faith. They too can be presumptuous about the future and promise themselves things that God has never promised them. Sometimes it is simple worldliness, like the businessmen of James 4:13. But on occasion it can be a more subtle kind of carelessness that presumes upon God himself in a most unfortunate way.

People can do strange things when they are in love. A young Christian fellow fell in love with a girl he had come to know in the college they both attended. He wanted to marry her and although he had no real encouragement in that direction from her, he became increasingly persuaded that she was the Lord's choice for him to marry. Plucking up his courage one day, he confided to her that the Lord had told him they were to be married. She was taken aback and could only say to him that the Lord had not told her that this was to be the case and that, as things stood, they were very definitely not going to be married! The 'romance' was over and they never married. Christians, too, can presume too much about their future plans. It is possible to baptize our inward convictions with the certainty of divine decree when in fact we are fooling ourselves. The young man, in his passion for the girl, jumped to the wrong conclusion about the Lord's will.

Jeremiah's stricture about the potential for deceit (including self-deceit) in the human heart still stands for believers and unbelievers alike: 'Who can know it?' (Jeremiah 17:9). We need a holy caution about our own heart and a godly tentativeness about what may or may not be the Lord's will, where it is not explicitly stated in the black and white of the revealed Word of God!

Churches, not just individuals, can also make the mistake of equating their most fervent aspirations with the secret will of God.[3] Some years ago, in the first flush of her newly-formed existence, a thoroughly evangelical denomination in America declared her collective conviction that the Lord was leading her to establish local churches in every county seat in the country within five years! This was her goal. When the time came, however, far from churches having been planted in every county, there were still whole states without any representation of that denomination! Now, zeal for the gospel and the goal of church-planting are highly commendable and to be warmly encouraged in Christians and churches. It is also true that nothing is impossible with the Lord. But it is possible, in the Lord's work, to be presumptuous and to indulge the rash assurance that what we sincerely conceive to be God's will, or to be appropriate goals for the church, will certainly come to pass according to our plan. But God may have other plans, perhaps more humble than our initial aspirations, perhaps more spectacular, but always in pursuit of his perfect will for the advance of his kingdom. Before we boast about what we are going to do in the future – or what we are sure the Lord is going to do – we need to humble ourselves and recognize that we are not privy to his will for the specifics of our tomorrows, but are called to faithful discipleship that labours diligently in the gospel day by day in the full assurance that the Lord is working out his plan and purpose according to his perfect wisdom.

Life is short and uncertain (4:14)

'Why, you do not even know what will happen tomorrow. What is your life? You are a mist that appears for a little while and then vanishes' (4:14). It is all too easy for us to feed ourselves today on the earnestly anticipated successes of a tomorrow we cannot see. Even the world knows it is a mistake to count one's chickens before they are hatched. Christians ought also to know that confidence in the Lord is not a blank cheque by which we sign ourselves whatever future blessings *we* may happen to want, however sincere our desire may seem to us to be. God sometimes says 'No' or 'Not yet' to quite unexceptionable requests from his disciples. It seems to me that James' businessmen, who were professing Christians, were already enjoying next year's profits in their minds. In reality this was an illusory joy, but it is the sort of thing that appeals to us anyway. The only certainty, of course, was that there was a lot of work to do, if their dreams were to become reality. The hope of success was, no doubt, a reasonable one – we have no reason to believe that these men didn't know their business. But 'hope' without dependence on the Lord is not hope, but presumption; it is not the hope that is justified in expecting blessing, but presumption that says to God, 'I can do it on my own, without you!' and therefore is heading for a fall.

Yet here were these men boasting about a whole *year,* when they really couldn't say what was going to happen *the next day!* The bottom line is in the answer to the question: 'What is your life?' The answer? 'It is a mist...' We are 'here today and gone tomorrow'. Like the flowers, leaves in the wind, the wind itself and a fleeting shadow, we have a short passage in this world, and we do not know where we will be tomorrow (Isaiah 40:6-7; Job 13:25; 7:7; 14:2). 'For my days vanish like smoke,' says the psalmist, 'my bones burn like glowing embers' (Psalm 102:3). Life is short and uncertain. Our times are in God's hand, not in our own. Even when we make proper provision for the future, the only life that is truly in our own hand is the one we are living today. The true focus of our life and our service to the Lord is not tomorrow or the next day or heaven itself, but rather this very day – today – the day he has made and given us. This is not to diminish the significance of our future plans or our eternal destiny, but to put in proper perspective human pretensions to control personal destiny into the future. The rich fool in the parable focused his life on the future enjoyment for 'many years' of the wealth he was presently amassing in the bigger barns he was building for their storage. His plans did not, however, coincide with those of the Lord who, you will remember, called him into eternity with the solemn judgement: 'You fool! This very night, your life will be demanded from you.' 'This is how it will be,' comments Jesus, 'with anyone who stores up things for himself but is not rich towards God' (Luke 12:20-21).

For the Christian, the unknowable uncertainties of life are laid at the foot of God's throne. God has said that his grace is sufficient for us. He has told us to pray each day for our 'daily bread' and has promised us to sustain his people and answer their prayers. He has told us not to worry about tomorrow, as to what we will eat, drink or wear, because he knows our needs. Rather, we are to 'seek first his kingdom and his righteousness, and all these things will be given to [us] as well' (Matthew 6:25-34). The Bible says a great deal about how we are to work and provide for ourselves and our families. Yet this is always in the context of the fact that we cannot control our destiny and are dependent upon the Lord for each day's life, as for eternity itself.

'Instead, you ought to...'(4:15-17)

The positive response to planning the future is now outlined by James in terms of three essential steps by which a proper dependence upon the Lord is exercised.

Holy tentativeness (4:15)

One of the great fallacies of the triumphalistic teaching that has deeply infected the evangelical, especially charismatic, churches today, is the notion that Christians ought to be filled with the most massive confidence about everything in life. 'I just *know* that the Lord wants me to do this...' is common language nowadays for everything from sweeping the kitchen to

choosing a husband. People talk – whether they mean it or not
– as if God had given them special revelations about all sorts
of details in life. Guidance – specifically, the leading of the
Holy Spirit – has become rooted more in feelings of inward,
subjective persuasion than in the clear word-revelation of the
Scriptures. Experience is then regarded as revelatory, even
though it is not resting on the full and sufficient revelation of
God's Word. Not to be possessed of such assurance and not to
feel free to use the language of triumphalistic confidence
about one's day-by-day decisions, however mundane these
may be, is widely regarded as a mark of weak or wavering
faith.

Scripture, however, enjoins a holy tentativeness with
respect to our pronouncements about the future. This is not
to encourage doubt, but to recognize the fact that our confidence does not rest on *our* sure knowledge and control of the
future, but upon *God,* who is in control and knows the end
from the beginning. The right attitude says, **'If it is the Lord's
will, we will live and do this or that.'** Truly godly language
reflects the revealed truth of God's Word – indeed *God's* language is the pattern, form and content of all godly utterance.
The point concerns what we think, our attitude, more than
what we say every time we open our mouths. James was not
instituting a law that requires a pious-sounding, 'God willing,'
whenever we decide to go for a pizza! The apostle Paul sometimes said, 'if the Lord will' (1 Corinthians 16:7) and sometimes did not (Romans 15:24). The motive is all-important,
the outward form only meaningful to make the point when
most appropriate, as, for example, when Paul wanted to
emphasize to the arrogant troublers of the Corinthian church
that when he came to sort them out, it would be with the sanc-
tion and the power of the Lord (see 1 Corinthians 4:19). In
any event, saying 'God willing' or writing, 'D.V.' *(Deo vol-
ente* = God willing), is never to be a pious filler, but rather a
solemn recognition that our future rests in the hand of the
Lord's gracious providence and is being unfolded day by day
in terms of the mediatorial rule of the Lord Jesus Christ, in
whom alone is placed all our confidence.

Unaffected humility (4:16)
Sternly, James denounces all boasting: **'As it is, you boast and**

brag. All such boasting is evil.' It is 'evil' – i.e., more than a slight error of judgement – because it is tantamount to robbing God of his sovereignty. It is also dangerous, because it may involve a course of action that has an altogether different outcome from that envisaged. The way of humility and of confiding faith towards the Lord is the way of safety as well as the path of worship and discipleship.

Willing obedience (4:17)
Finally, obedience to the known will of God is the exclusive path of personal holiness. **'Anyone...who knows the good he ought to do and doesn't do it, sins'** (4:16). James is speaking to Christians. 'You know what God's Word says about the future and the providence of God – and what it doesn't. Don't be like the world, which ignores the truth that we are ignorant of tomorrow, which rejects the fact that only God knows what a day will bring forth and which will not admit to being powerless to control one's personal destiny! Trust in the Lord! Look to your risen Saviour, Jesus Christ, for he rules over the future for his people and loves them with an everlasting love. Give him the pre-eminence in your planning. Search the Scriptures for the principles which alone can guide you to blessing in Christ. Listen to God as he speaks in the Scriptures. And obey him, for this is his way, that you should walk in it all your days.'

Does the Lord Jesus encourage a limited and maybe slightly doleful attitude to our planning for the future? Does he mean us to be unsure about all the decisions we come to – perennially doubting that we're doing the right thing? Far from it! He calls us, as it were, to look to the right hand of God where he reigns as Head over all things for the church, to confess his lordship over our lives, both what we can see and what we cannot, and so to enter into the liberty of the gospel, which relieves the child of God from the world's impossible obsession with self-generated security and autonomy from God. Christian! Jesus has set his believing people *free* from the law of sin and death – free from the fears of nuclear holocausts, free from the fear of loneliness and destitution, free for a future which he is working out, which cannot fade away, which is full of his glory and the greater part of which is yet to be revealed!

20.
Listen, you rich people!

Please read James 5:1-6

'Now listen, you rich people, weep and wail because of the misery that is coming upon you' (James 5:1).

With all the holy fire of an Old Testament prophet, James pronounces the dire warning of God's impending wrath against 'the wicked rich'.[1] At the same time, as with all the warnings of Scripture, there is an unspoken call to repentance for all who have ears to hear. And to every Christian there is a challenge about our own stewardship of the gifts that God has given us, so that we might avoid the paths of the 'rich people' of this text. The 'love of money' is still 'a root of all kinds of evil' and with wealth come temptations of a particularly difficult nature. Nowhere does the Bible condemn wealth in itself, but it everywhere warns against its abuse. Scripture is clear that wealth is to be put to work for God, not sunk into the trappings of an ever-increasing 'standard of living' or squirrelled away in Swiss bank accounts against some future 'rainy day'. It seems to me impossible to read the Scriptures without concluding that they enjoin a modest standard of living allied to maximum liberality in support of the Lord's work and the relief of the needy (see 2 Corinthians 8:1-15). It is clearly possible, within the framework of biblical ethics, to work for wealth and to maintain and expand one's wealth. But, as our passage makes clear, wealth is easily abused and made an instrument of oppression.

James 5:1-6 falls into two parts: first, the punishment and, second, the crime. In verses 1-3, James declares the judgement of God upon the wicked rich, in the process showing the ultimate worthlessness of all wealth that is accumulated and used for selfish purposes. Then, in verses 4-6, he details three characteristic sins of this avaricious and acquisitive class of people.

The judgement of the rich (5:1-3)

James wrote to Hebrew Christians and it is generally assumed among commentators that he had in mind here the wealthy class among the Jews. This is said to be supported by (1) the use of the Old Testament term, 'the Lord of Sabaoth' ('the Lord Almighty,' 5:4 NIV); (2) the reference to their having murdered 'the just [one]' ('innocent men,' 5:5 NIV),[2] which some take to be a reference to the death of the Lord Jesus Christ (cf. Acts 3:14); and (3) the similarity between the judgement here pronounced and that which came upon Jerusalem in A.D. 70.

There would, however, appear to be a wider applicability to the moneyed classes of all human societies, who throughout history reject the Lord and worship Mammon. Just as Jesus proclaimed judgement upon the unbelieving ecclesiastical establishment in Matthew 23, with its implications for their descendants in all time to follow, so James directs these words to a different, though sometimes overlapping, class of people both in his own day and in ours.

Weeping and wailing (5:1)
The judgement is stark and chilling: **'Weep and wail because of the misery that is coming upon you'** (5:1). The words rendered 'weep' and 'wail' – the Greek *ololuzo* and *alalazo* – are wonderful examples of onomatopoeia. The sound of each word imitates the action it describes, so that we can hear the ululating rhythms of traditional Middle East mourning cries. This serves to intensify the sense of dereliction – indeed, of damnation – that the rich ought to feel in prospect of the just judgement of God. There is a ring of finality to this awful pronouncement. It tolls the knell of Mammon's false promises and man's self-deceived materialistic faith. The 'misery' has been taken by some to refer to the destruction of Jerusalem in A.D. 70, which sealed for ever the close of the Old Testament

period. There is no compelling reason to limit this judgement
to a specific temporal cataclysm, even one of indubitably
epoch-making significance. The natural reading of the text
speaks of the inexorable extension of the justice of God into
the lives of men and women, in life, death and eternity. And
its relevance, both as a rebuke to the depredations of the rich
and as an encouragement to oppressed believers, can hardly
be said to have diminished with the passing of the centuries.[3]

The prevailing ambiguity of many Christians today towards
the acquisition of wealth – perhaps particularly the so-called
'prosperity gospel', which teaches that wealth and success are
marks of faithfulness to the Lord – finds a timely corrective in
James' words. The TV evangelist scandals of 1987-8 in the
USA exposed something of the need for judgement to begin
at the house of God. How doubly sad that these unrepentant
voluptuaries of electronic evangelism show no more
enthusiasm for cleansing themselves of their excesses than
have the popes and the Roman church of their pretensions to
temporal grandeur and spiritual demagoguery! Those who
say they love Christ ought rather to be like him! The Lord
calls us to liberated contentment with his provision of our
'daily' bread (i.e., for one day at a time) and his sufficient
supply of all our needs.

Rotting wealth (5:2)
The wicked rich will lose their wealth: **'Your wealth has rotted
and moths have eaten your clothes.'** Foodstuffs, clothes and,
in 5:3, precious metals – all commodities that can be hoarded
– are mentioned. We are reminded of Isaiah when he
denounced those who added house to house (Isaiah 5:8) and
of Amos when he condemned the indulgence of luxuries
(Amos 6:1-7). All of these will pass away and their temporary
benefits will evaporate before the wrath of God. If gold is
your all in this life, you will certainly go before the judgement
seat with nothing except your sins and the terrible prospect of
endless retribution. That even gold will 'corrode' emphasizes
its ultimate uselessness as a substitute for a saving relationship to Christ. Earthly treasures are in a state of irreversible
decay from the moment of their genesis. With the whole
created universe, they are 'waxing old as a garment'. The
utter folly of living for such transient objects is the measure of

the desperation of the godless, who would rather massage their sensualist lusts and perish than turn to the Lord and enter into life eternal here and now and for ever!

> 'Better the little that the righteous have
>   than the wealth of many wicked;
> for the power of the wicked will be broken,
>   but the Lord upholds the righteous'
>
> (Psalm 37:16-17).

Hoarding in the last days (5:3)

The corrosion of wealth is, in turn, a testimony to the sinfulness of the piling up of wealth. Hoards, by definition, are unused accumulations of wealth. Their rotting is testimony to their being kept from fruitful use. It is as if these materials of wealth know better than their hoarders the purpose for which God made them. In such a vein, the prophet Habakkuk says of palaces built with the fruits of oppressive materialism, 'The stones of the wall will cry out, and the beams of the woodwork will echo it' (Habakkuk 2:11). The cracking of the one and the creaking of the other presage the fall of a building erected on human misery to satisfy a lust for self-aggrandizement! The decay of opulence testifies to the motives which gave it birth. And, like the blood of righteous Abel crying from the ground, the victims of economic oppression call out to heaven for justice.

Most ominously, the wealth of the faithless rich will **'eat [their] flesh like fire'**. It is, as Manton puts it, 'not only witness, but executioner', because, 'the matter of our sin shall in hell become the matter of our punishment'.[4] The decay of these earth-bound objects of unhallowed desire is but a foretaste of the eternal corruption of the reprobate in hell! From their vantage-point in perdition, the lost will be endlessly burned up by their reflection on the things which they were so obsessed with in this world. The loss of their gods of gold, silver and luxurious excess will be the everlasting reminder of their guilt and the fuel of unceasing, but unrepentant, remorse!

Indeed, such is the awful state of the reprobate rich – those who never repent and turn to the Lord – that they will still be hoarding wealth **'in the last days'** (5:3). One view is that 'the

last days' refer specifically and exclusively to the last days of
Jerusalem in A.D. 70.[5] There is certainly no question that
Jewish Christians would recognize the judgement of God in
that great cataclysm. The destruction of Jerusalem cannot,
however, be regarded as a satisfying explanation of all that
the Scriptures ascribe to 'the last days'. The destruction of the
temple in A.D. 70 was the definitive judgement on the apostate Old Testament church, but its greater significance resides
in the fact that it irrevocably sealed the fact that the 'last days'
had come in the person and work of Christ – 'had *come*,' I
emphasize – not 'had ended'! The 'last days' properly encompass the 'final age' of the Messiah – the period from the first
coming of Christ until his Second Coming at the end of
history.[6] In Christ, the kingdom of God has come. It is an
accomplished reality, even though there is a sense in which it
is both 'now' and 'not yet'. Christ rules 'now' according to this
perfect purpose, but the total accomplishment of that purpose is 'not yet' – and will only come to pass when he returns
to judge the world and deliver up the kingdom to his God and
Father. In that light, it is wholly inappropriate to be storing up
treasures on the earth, for that betrays a self-centred, self-
deceived and self-destructing spiritual condition which has set
its face against the claims of Jesus Christ and has rejected the
realities of the kingdom which has come in power through his
death and resurrection (Matthew 6:19-21).

Another implication of the biblical concept of 'the last
days' is the relative shortness of the time remaining and the
urgent necessity for our response to God's call. The time is
short, Paul tells us, because, 'this world in its present form is
passing away' (1 Corinthians 7:29-31). The fact that you and
I can open an encyclopedia and point to two thousand years
of human history since these words were written in no way
contradicts or invalidates the apostle's assertion. In God's
terms, time is in its very nature 'short' – it is a fleeting twinkle
against the vastness of uncreated eternity. But what is of more
practical significance for us is that *our time is passing away
very quickly*. Whichever comes first – our death or the Lord's
return – we haven't got long in this world! It isn't (as the
Americans say so pithily), 'worth a hill of beans' to argue
about how soon the Lord has to come for Paul to be telling the
truth. Everything from beauty parlours to cemeteries tells us

that we all have a meeting with our eternal destiny in a few years' time at the most! But like the Sodomites – ancient and modern – many of us will get up on the last day of our lives with our hearts intent on another day of sinning. 'Oh, what folly!' James seems to cry, 'Don't you see the need of your own souls? Why then do you go on living in disregard of the living God?'

The sins of the rich (5:4-6)

Apart from repentance, the sinner has only two alternatives: he can either sin boldly or he can redefine his sin as good. It is a testimony to the fact that men made in the image of God have a built-in conscience that most sinners prefer the latter path – they like to have a pious rationale for what they know deep down is simply sin. They want 'their cake' (peace of mind and a good conscience) and they want to 'eat it' (freedom to sin as they please). That is why the Bible hammers away at the same old human sins we love so much and keeps on knocking the same old threadbare excuses that we habitually employ to justify ourselves. God's denunciations of sin home in on the centre of our defences – that which the Bible calls 'the heart'. This is what James now does with the remainder of his discussion of the vagaries of the rich. Having already focused on their implicit selfishness – indeed, Mammon-worship – he now details three principal manifestations of economic oppression: robbing workers of their wages (5:4); living lives of luxurious self-indulgence (5:5); and the murdering of 'the just [one]' (5:6).

Robbing the worker of his wages (5:4)
The law of God requires the fair and honest compensation of employees. The wages of a hired man were not to be kept from him even for one night! (Leviticus 19:13). Special consideration was due to the employee who was known to be poor: 'Do not take advantage of a hired man who is poor and needy...Pay him his wages each day before sunset, because he is poor and is counting on it. Otherwise he may cry to the Lord against you, and you will be guilty of sin' (Deuteronomy 24:14-15; see also Jeremiah 22:13; Malachi 3:5). Compassion

and compensation are inextricably interwoven in God's justice for the worker. The assumption is that when someone has put in a day's work, that day's pay is his by right. It cannot properly be withheld, for to do so is to seize it for one's own use – it is a species of robbery. 'What can be more base,' asks John Calvin, 'than that they, who supply us with bread by their labour should be pined through want? And yet this monstrous thing is common; for there are many of such a tyrannical disposition, that they think that the rest of mankind live only for their benefit alone.'[7]

There will be a reckoning, and the judgement is the Lord's. The stolen wages, as well as the oppressed employees, cry out to the Lord. They take to believing prayer, not to the barricades or the picket line. And their appeal reaches **'the ears of the Lord of Sabaoth'** (5:4 NASB). This reference to God as 'the Lord of hosts' emphasizes that he is the absolutely sovereign and omnipotent God who will vindicate and bless his suffering and oppressed people.[8] Because he is 'the Shepherd of Israel', the Lord may be appealed to with confidence as the 'Lord Almighty' who will powerfully deliver his own flock from their enemies (Psalm 80:1,4,7,14,19).

Luxurious living (5:5)
In the richest of nations there are people trapped in poverty and in the poorest of nations there are those who wallow in luxury and self-indulgence. We have no reason to expect anything else until and unless hearts are changed, as men and women, both rich and poor, come to Christ in faith in numbers that prove decisive for the collective life of whole societies. In our century, Marxism promised the solution to such injustices, only to produce an equitable distribution of recession, repression and depression for the masses and an inequitable apportionment of wealth and power to the new Communist élite, who through state monopolism are even better placed than were the old capitalists to loot the national economy to their own ends. The pigs (revolutionaries) on George Orwell's *Animal Farm* have turned into men (=former tyrants). Godless men, from *laissez-faire* capitalists to totalitarian Marxists, will gouge other people in their power, one way or the other.[9] They will still be giving themselves to self-indulgence in the Great Day. James says they

'have fattened [them]selves in the day of slaughter,' i.e., in the face of the Day of Judgement. Unless they repent, they will perish!

Murdering the innocent (5:6)
Furthermore, they have **'condemned and put to death the innocent man'** (5:6 NASB). NIV wrongly translates this as a plural, although it correctly realizes that 'the innocent', or, better, 'the just' is a personification of all of God's people who perish unjustly at the hands of rich oppressors. It would be forcing the text to identify 'the innocent' with Christ, but we cannot but reflect on the fact that our Lord was the only truly holy and righteous one who gave himself into the hands of wicked men to die for his people (Acts 3:14; 7:52; 22:14). Some may question the strength of James' words: are the rich truly the *murderers* of those they oppress? The answer surely is 'Yes!' And it makes no difference whether they starve them, or do not provide safe working conditions, or simply despise them as so much material for exploitation. If, as Jesus says, he who hates his brother is a murderer, then he who goes out of his way to wreck a man's life or does nothing to prevent his ruination certainly has murder in his heart. James does not overstate the case! And God will not spare the guilty!

The ultimate questions posed by James are 'Where is your treasure? Where is your heart?' Unholy attachment to riches has always been a most powerful snare for men and women, even professing Christians. Ambrose of Milan (c. A.D. 339-397) once sold his church's gold and silver to purchase the release of some prisoners. For this he was severely criticized within the church. He responded to this censure with what John Calvin called his 'wonderful excuse': 'He who sent out the apostles without gold also gathered churches without gold. The church has gold not to keep but to pay out, and to relieve distress. What need to keep what helps not? Or are we ignorant of how much gold and silver the Assyrians carted off from the temple of the Lord? (2 Kings 18:15-16). Would it not be better for the priest to melt it to sustain the poor, if other aid is lacking, than for a sacrilegious enemy to bear it away? Will not the Lord say, "Why have you allowed so many needy to die of hunger? Surely you had gold with which to minister sustenance? Why were so many prisoners carried off and not ransomed? Why were so many killed by the enemy? It were better for you to preserve vessels of living men than of metal." To these you cannot give reply, for what would you say? "I was afraid lest the temple of God lack ornament"? He would reply, "The sacraments do not require gold, nor do these things please with gold that are not bought with gold. The ornament of the sacraments is the ransom of the prisoners."[10]

This is the spirit in which to view, receive, enjoy and administer the economic blessings of the Lord. Jesus says, 'Do not store up for yourselves treasures on earth, where moth and rust destroy, and where thieves break in and steal. But store up for yourselves treasures in heaven, where moth and rust do not destroy, and where thieves do not break in and steal. For where your treasure is, there your heart will be also' (Matthew 6:19-21). You choose: will it be Christ or 'the misery that is coming...'?

Part 3
How to live until the Lord's coming

21.
Waiting patiently for the Lord

Please read James 5:7-11

'Be patient, then, brothers, until the Lord's coming' (James 5:7).

A remarkable transformation now heralds the closing of the epistle of James. After the most uncompromising treatment of seven principal subjects – we have called them 'case-studies of faith in action' (2:1-5:6) – James returns in these last paragraphs (5:7-20) to take up the general theme which he began to address in the first chapter. The tone changes from the thunderous cadences of righteous indignation which attended his earlier denunciations of sin and now takes on the quietness of loving pastoral encouragement. In a four-part conclusion, he draws together some of the main strands of his teaching and exhorts the Lord's people to live faithfully for Christ as those who live in the light and expectation of his return at the end of the age. He calls for *patience* as they await the Lord's coming again (5:7-11); enjoins reverent *prayer and praise* in the midst of life's ups and downs (5:12-13); urges a living *fellowship* of bearing one another's burdens (5:14-18); and, finally, encourages diligent *ministry* to the end that sinners, within and without the church, might be reclaimed from spiritual death (5:19-20). We will devote a chapter to each of these in turn.

The future – the goal of patience (5:7)

James appeals to believers to live their lives in patience: **'Be patient, then, brothers, until the Lord's coming'** (5:7). At one and the same time, this responds to the preceding denunciation of the wicked rich and returns us to the positive themes of the first chapter. At the beginning, James enjoined patient perseverance under trials (1:2-4). In taking this up now, he sets it in juxtaposition to the rich oppressors' destiny of eternal misery (5:1-6). Whereas they should fear the coming of the Lord because it means God's judgement, the Lord's believing people – those who have suffered at the hands of the oppressors – should welcome that great event, because for them it will be their final deliverance by their Saviour. The Christian says, 'Amen. Come, Lord Jesus' (Revelation 22:20), while the world of unbelief goes on its way, careless and contemptuous of the wrath to come.

Looking forward to the reward
The core of James' appeal is, of course, the expectation of the coming of the Lord. Patience does not hang in mid-air, as if it were some abstract virtue that can sustain itself merely by being the right thing to do. All of God's graces – all exercises in being righteous before God and men – have a definite goal in view. Righteousness not only has the prospect of a reward at the end of the road, but, in a fallen world of conflicting temptations and pressures, is partly sustained by that promise of a prize. When Moses is summed up as one of the great heroes of faith in the epistle to the Hebrews, his eye to the ultimate rewards of faithfulness receives particular mention and commendation: 'He regarded disgrace for the sake of Christ as of greater value than the treasures of Egypt, because he was looking ahead to his reward' (Hebrews 11:26). It is this future that is the goal of godly patience – the future coming of the Lord calls us to the life of ongoing faithfulness.

Living out of the future
The apostolic writings are full of the vibrant anticipation of the Second Coming. If the cross is the pivot upon which all of history turns, the consummation is the goal for which Jesus went to the cross and therefore becomes the future reference point for believers as they face the days to come. The New Testament church was taught to live out of the future – in joyful anticipation of the glory yet to be revealed. This reality conditions Christian experience, for, as Paul tells the Ephesians,

'God raised us up with Christ and seated us with him in the heavenly realms in Christ Jesus' (Ephesians 2:6). To the Romans, the apostle declared that we are to count ourselves 'dead to sin, but alive to God in Christ Jesus' (Romans 6:3) – not because indwelling sin is less of a problem for us, or because we do not have to struggle with temptation, but because we are – truly, now, in this life 'new creation[s]' in Christ (2 Corinthians 5:17). This is to say that as we live out of that future which Christ has won for us, so we will experience victory even now in this present world. Thus we are able to exult: 'When Christ, who is your life, appears, then [we] also will appear with him in glory' (Colossians 3:4). As we have already noted in our preceding study,[1] the fact that two millennia have passed since these words were penned in no way lessens their import for the life of faith: 'The Lord is not slow in keeping his promise, as some understand slowness. He is patient with you, not wanting anyone to perish, but everyone to come to repentance' (2 Peter 3:9). What James is saying is that Christian patience is rooted in a deep and ever-fresh anticipation of the Lord's coming. All else falls into place in the light of that future which will open up in all its completeness when Jesus returns bodily to this earth.

The past – examples of patience (5:7-11)

If we are in a sense to live out of the future – that is, to press forwards to our goal – we are not left without the encouragements of the past to impel us on our path. This is the practical usefulness of past history – to learn from it and to act accordingly. The past can be made to work for the future. To encourage us, James gives three examples of patience in action: the farmer, the prophets and the patriarch, Job.

The farmer (5:7-9)
'The farmer waits for the rains and the growth of his crops (5:7). He learns patience through his perennial experience of helplessness to control the annual cycle of weather and his trust that the harvest will mature in due time. Christians, then, ought also to **'be patient and stand firm'**. Why? Because **'the Lord's coming is near'** (5:8). The word 'near' does not *set*

a date but does emphasize a practical reality. God's '"soon's" and "quickly's" are not to be interpreted by our impatient reckonings,' observes Curtis Vaughan. 'With Him one day is as a thousand years and a thousand years as one day. And in the measure that our faith is strong, we are enabled to see things as God sees them. Paul, for example, looking at the afflictions of the Christian life from the eternal perspective, could say that they were "but for a moment" (2 Corinthians 4:17,18).'[2] What is relevant to us is not the year A.D. when Jesus comes, but whether we are ready to meet him *today!* Meanwhile, we must resist the temptation to impatience and complaining – which, of course, inevitably spills over onto others and fosters a climate of discontent and unrest among Christians. The reminder that **'the Judge is standing at the door'** (5:9) picks up the eschatological motif, this time from the other side. If you are not actually exercising faithfulness, you are less than ready to meet the Lord. But he is near – at the door! Do you want to meet him as the Judge he will be to the wicked?

The prophets (5:10)
'As an example of patience in the face of suffering, take the prophets' (5:10). The prophets had long been a byword for steadfast witness under unjust persecution. Jesus told his disciples to 'rejoice and be glad', when they faced insults and persecutions, 'because great is your reward in heaven, for in the same way they persecuted the prophets who were before you' (Matthew 5:12). On the other side of the equation, it was a mark of the unbelief of the Pharisees and their ilk that they were 'the descendants of those who murdered the prophets' (Matthew 23:31; Acts 7:52). No particular prophets are mentioned, for this is the inevitable experience of *all* God's messengers in an unbelieving world which works hard to 'suppress the truth by [its] wickedness' (Romans 1:18). This is what often happened in the past to those who **'spoke in the name of the Lord'**. And the point in mentioning this fact is precisely that it was *because* they spoke in the name of the Lord! All sorts of people suffer bad things in the world and bear up under their troubles. But that says nothing about the reasons for their woes and does not identify them as examples of godly patience. The prophets, however, were sent by God

with the Word of God as their message! They are therefore an appropriate example for our encouragement! They were, as John Calvin comments, 'accepted and approved by God. If, then, it had been useful for them to have been free of miseries, doubtless God would have kept them free. But it was otherwise. It hence follows that afflictions are salutary [beneficial] to the faithful. He, therefore, bids them to be taken as an example of suffering affliction. But patience also must be added, which is a real evidence of our obedience. Hence he has joined them both together.'[3]

Christians, therefore, can draw real comfort from the prophets' example, especially when troubles come our way and we are tempted to doubt the Lord's love towards us. Young Christians more than others are sometimes inclined to think that becoming a believer in Christ will banish most of their problems, or at least in some way make them easy to overcome. The reality is that we 'all share a common destiny – the righteous and the wicked, the good and the bad' (Ecclesiastes 9:2). Even without persecution for preaching God's righteousness in a hostile world, Christians will experience the same sorts of trials as non-Christians. The difference will be in what we make of them by God's grace! And godly persevering patience is the touchstone, while deepening fellowship with the Lord and a rising joy in his salvation will be the fruit of affliction for those who are trusting in Christ day by day.

The patriarch Job (5:11)
'As you know, we consider blessed those who have persevered' (5:11). 'Men who have endured,' says James Adamson, 'win the Christian envy of us all.'[4] Of all the Lord's suffering people spoken of in Scripture, there is no one to match Job in this department. The patience of Job was clearly proverbial in ancient times. Here was a man who, though wealthier than most of us, lived a normal life. Then one day, calamity upon calamity stripped away the comforts, joys and achievements with which the Lord had blessed him and for which he had worked very hard. Unlike the prophets, who must have anticipated that opposition, even persecution, would be an almost inevitable by-product of the work of preaching the truth of God, Job was not in an occupation that could be

expected to draw fire – he was a regular successful farmer and
a godly man who loved the Lord. Yet he did draw fire – the
fire of hell, the vengeful malevolence of Satan! Job was then
put to the severest of tests. His whole 'life' – family, house,
goods, health, peace of mind – everything was devastated by
tragedy and loss. Many a man would have completely cracked
with only a fraction of Job's calamities. Certainly Job was not
stoical and fatalistic. Sometimes he lashed out at all around
him. He complained to God. His mind was often wracked
with terrible agonies. He asked all the questions we would ask
in similar circumstances – and a lot more. But the central
strand is his proverbial patience. He persevered and we can
still see in the pages of the Scripture **'what the Lord finally
brought about'**. Job discovered that the Lord indeed always
has the last word. What Satan began, God ended. The result
was that 'the Lord blessed the latter part of Job's life more
than the first' (Job 42:12). Job learned in these difficulties
what the psalmist later would express with respect to his own
experience: 'It was good for me to be afflicted so that I might
learn your decrees' (Psalm 119:71). This is precisely what
James wants us to gain from our life-experience in a world
which will inevitably throw up trials and tribulations that will
test the mettle of our faith.

The present – the Lord and our patience (5:11)

'Be patient until the Lord's coming!' the Lord tells us through
James. We know what we ought to do, but we also feel our
weaknesses and fear our future failure. James' last word
answers that doubt with a word about the One who alone can
sustain us: **'The Lord is full of compassion and mercy'** (5:11).
This is quite naturally connected with the preceding comment
about Job, but I am inclined to think it a concluding statement
for the whole of verses 7 to 11. The structure of the passage
may then be viewed as follows:

I.   Principal exhortation (what we are to do in the future):
       'Be patient until the Lord's coming' (5:7).
II.   Supporting examples (what has been achieved by others
       in the past): the farmer; the prophets and Job (5:7-11).
III.   Concluding encouragement (what the Lord is to us in the

present): 'The Lord is full of compassion and mercy' (5:11).

At every point, we are to look away from ourselves for the resources to exercise godly patience and perseverance. The world always looks inwards for strength, for man is the measure of all things. The Christian always looks outwards – to the Lord who is full of compassion and mercy. Even the examples of the Lord's faithful people in the past are an invitation to see what the Lord wrought in and through them. Neither Job nor the prophets prevailed because of their personal inner strength – the biblical record honestly sets out their frailties and shows their victories to be in spite of themselves precisely because they are attributable to the grace of God. There is no triumphalistic individualism in either the Bible's record of the achievements of the Lord's people, or in the Lord's prescription for the way we are to live the Christian life. We need to know that the Lord is with us in the middle of our trials. The natural question is to ask, 'Is the Lord against me? And the answer for the true believer must be 'No! He is with me and has only permitted this to happen in order that I might grow in grace and the knowledge of my Saviour.' Jesus told us that we would have troubles in the world, but was at pains to assure us that we need not fear, because he has overcome the world! The common assumption that the fact that God is good and a God of love means that nothing bad should ever happen to us is, at best, sheer starry-eyed sentimentalism and, at worst, a deliberately contrived straw man which provides an excuse to reject the claims of God. Nowhere in Scripture does the Lord promise a rose garden, even to his most faithful disciples. Job is a case in point. The fact that all the apostles, except John (as far as we know), died martyr deaths is wholly consistent with the revelation of God's Word on the possibilities for tough times in the Christian life. The answer is that the Lord 'is full of compassion and mercy'. 'Do but wait a little while,' enjoins Manton, 'and you shall see that the Lord is very pitiful and tender. God's children...when providence hath had its course...can easily see that though the outside and bark of it was rough and harsh, yet it was lined with pity and mercy.'[5] The Christian affirms the fact of Christ's everlasting love for his own and claims the promises of his Saviour! Christ is risen! Christ is coming! He is coming for everyone for whom he died on Calvary's cross! He has said, 'Yes, I am coming soon.' And in the patient exultation of every redeemed soul, the answer ascends to glory: 'Amen. Come, Lord Jesus' (Revelation 22:20).

22.
Praising the Lord

Please read James 5:12-13

'Is any one of you in trouble? He should pray. Is anyone happy? Let him sing songs of praise' (James 5:13).

The culmination of the first chapter of the epistle was James' three-part definition of the 'religion that God our Father accepts as pure and faultless'. This consisted in (1) keeping a tight rein on the tongue (1:26); (2) helping widows and orphans in their distress (1:27); and (3) keeping oneself unpolluted by the world (1:27). These are major contours of the practical godliness of those who love the Lord. Knowing and loving Christ is not a matter of external 'religion' but of deep inner commitment issuing in practical discipleship according to the teaching of the Word of God.[1]

When we turn to the last verses of the epistle (5:12-20), we see these same thoughts emerging, albeit in a somewhat different way. Our present passage (5:12-13) focuses on the godly control of the tongue and the proper approach to the Lord in prayer. The remainder of the chapter touches upon concern for others with respect to sickness (5:14-15), forgiveness of sins (5:16-18) and conversion to Christ (5:19-20). The general theme of keeping oneself unpolluted by the world clearly pervades the entire passage. We have been brought back to the heart of the matter of our Christian commitment.

'Let your "yes" be yes!' (5:12)

James reiterates the teaching of the Lord Jesus Christ in the Sermon on the Mount: **'Above all, my brothers, do not swear**

**– not by heaven or by earth or by anything else. Let your "Yes"
be yes, and your "No," no, or you will be condemned'** (5:12;
Matthew 5:34). Human speech is punctuated by a plethora of
oaths that range from thoughtless 'fillers' to loud-mouthed
expletives to out-and-out blasphemies. We hear this kind of
thing every day of our lives and the worst of it is to hear the
names of our heavenly Father-God and the Lord Jesus Christ
incessantly blasphemed. James Adamson, noting that James'
says 'Above all...,' sadly observes, 'The oath is the com-
monest and most serious moral fault in speech and James is
hardly to be blamed for ranking it *pro panton* [the Greek for
'above all'], above all errors of the tongue, e.g., boasting,
grumbling and backbiting.'[2]

James does not imply that solemn oaths and vows may not
be appropriate at certain times and for particular purposes. It
is proper, for example, for someone testifying before a court,
to 'solemnly swear to tell the truth, the whole truth and
nothing but the truth, so help me God'. Such an oath serves
to emphasize the seriousness of both the case itself and the
consequences of perjury. On the other hand, to meander
through the mundane trivialities of a day's life and lace them
liberally with extraneous oaths and blasphemous expletives is
to demean the very concept of a solemn promise and to offend
against the sanctity of truth and even the honour of God!

The Jews of James' day were extremely scrupulous about
the misuse of the names of God, but they had evidently
invented what today are called 'minced oaths' – oaths that
were modified just enough to remove any literal blasphemy.[3]
They swore 'by heaven' and 'by earth', and perhaps all sorts
of objects between the two, but avoided direct invocation of
God's name. The same is done today by many Christians.
They will not use the name of Christ as an oath, but you will
hear the odd 'heck' (hell), 'darn' (damn), 'gee whiz' (Jesus),
'cripes' (Christ) and slightly more remote minced oaths such
as 'for heaven's sake,' 'for goodness' sake,' and 'by Jove' – all
studied, letter-of-the-law sidestepping of any direct invocation of God himself. They become so much a part of our
language that we are often quite unconscious of them. It is not
uncommon for new Christians to have great trouble cleaning
up their speech, especially if they were in the habit of using
such language – and worse – before they became believers.

Some Christians even think it is quibbling to make a point of such matters – ignoring the fact it was Jesus who made the point and, furthermore, confirmed its seriousness by warning of judgement from God in the case of deliberate flouting of his will! His concern is twofold, I believe.

The first is that irreverence and blasphemy are not merely defined in terms of the precise sounding of the name of God: there is also such a thing as a blasphemous or irreverent attitude which finds expression in the loose and careless handling of the things of God. And the focus of the problem lies in the mistaken notion that one can take any oath at all without invoking the name of God. Taking an oath is, by its very nature, a calling of someone else to witness your oath so that if you don't keep it, you will be called to account for not doing so and the appropriate penalty exacted. No one but God is qualified to witness an oath for he alone is the Judge and searcher of the thoughts and intentions of our hearts; he alone is the holy vindicator of his own perfect justice. It is actually an affront to God to suggest by any oath that 'Jove', or 'heaven' or 'goodness,' far less 'heck' or 'darn', are witnesses and guarantors of the undertaking you have made. It is, in effect, mocking God to ascribe to parts of his creation what is exclusively attributable to God alone. The fact that we do not take the problem very seriously is not proof that Jesus was quibbling about words or that we are making a mountain out of a molehill. But it does prove that we are woefully ignorant of the holiness of God and what it means for us to think and speak about him as well as to love and worship him for who he is in himself and what he has done for sinners like us. True reverence for God is never served by careless minds and loose tongues, but only through a realization akin to that which God gave Moses at the burning bush: 'Take off your sandals, for the place where you are standing is holy ground' (Exodus 3:5). He is 'the high and lofty One' who inhabits eternity and 'whose name is holy: "I live in a high and holy place, but also with him who is contrite and lowly in spirit and to revive the heart of the contrite...creating praise on the lips of the mourners in Israel' (Isaiah 57:15-19).

The second concern is that we realize that taking oaths about all and sundry activities is neither an indication of our personal seriousness and reliability, nor a means of securing

the blessing of God. Quite the opposite is in fact the case. The
man who feels he has to precede all his statements with an
emphatic 'quite honestly' may well be a man with a long-
standing experience of not being believed, perhaps with good
reason.

The words 'I promise you' are too frequently a prelude to
their own breach. 'Swearing is necessary only in a society
where truth is not reverenced.'[4] As to the blessing of God, the
reality is that if we call God as our witness, he will take us at
our word and we will answer for it to him, however casual,
idle or unintentional we may claim our oath or blasphemy to
have been. Far from gaining any blessing, we will fall under
his just judgement for so lightly presuming upon him
(Matthew 12:34-37).

The emphasis on your 'Yes' being yes and your 'No' being
no is not the Lord's attempt to make your language colourless
and bland. It is rather designed to produce a genuine richness
of thought and expression that rests upon and grows out of
truth and a heart-felt reverence for the Lord, for only in this
way will what we say have transparent integrity, be a real
blessing and point men and women to the Saviour who is the
Way, the Truth and the Life. 'The Christian does not need to
swear, for his word is his bond.'[5] The Christian has been
freed, in Christ his Saviour, to speak clearly, precisely, truth-
fully, cleanly, gently, sensitively, seriously and with godly
integrity and holy joy.

Prayer – for times of trouble (5:13)

How then are we to respond positively to the vicissitudes of
life? **'Is any one of you in trouble?'** James answers: **'He should
pray.'** The contrast is with the unbelieving world. Worldly
people do many things when they are in trouble, but true,
believing prayer is not one of them. Some will curse and com-
plain and brood angrily that such things should happen to
them. Others will say nothing at all and try to pass over their
troubles with a stiff upper lip and stoical endurance. Still
others will perhaps plunge into a crash-diving spiral of depression, even to the point of 'nervous breakdown'. Many,
like the pagan sailors on Jonah's ship, will 'each [cry] out to

his own god' (Jonah 1:5). They 'pray' into the void of their gnawing terror and spiritual emptiness, hoping that someone will hear them but having neither conviction nor assurance that there is anyone there at all (cf. Hebrews 11:6).

Difficulties and anxieties ought to be answered with believing prayer that casts all its cares upon the Lord. When we have a burden, it is surely better 'to pray for a strong back, rather than to curse the load'.[6] 'Yes,' someone says, 'I know all that, but when I am troubled, I get so depressed that I just don't seem able to pray. I start to pray, but the very thoughts and sentences dissolve in mental turmoil and bitterness, fear and frustrations crowd out any meaningful prayer.' The answer to such a problem is already in the sense of James' words: 'He should pray' might be better rendered, 'He should keep on praying.' Giving up in defeat is no solution. That is what Satan wants – he aims to abort all your prayers and, like the clever tactician that he is, cut the believer's lines of communication with the only source of his fighting strength! Keep on praying! Cry out for peace from Christ. Take the promises of Scripture and do not rest until they are yours. Pray into the small hours – the Lord did in Gethsemane. Pray yourself to sleep – remember David's anguished prayer: 'I am worn out from groaning; all night long I flood my bed with weeping and drench my couch with tears' (Psalm 6:6). It was surely of such prayer that David says elsewhere: 'Weeping may remain for a night, but rejoicing comes in the morning' (Psalm 30:5). If even the Holy Spirit intercedes for us with 'groans that words cannot express' (Romans 8:26), a little groaning will certainly not hurt us or hinder the blessing of God! We are perhaps too used to tearless prayers. A great many prayers sometimes seem to be little more than exercises in sentence construction – words without soul. Perhaps the way we think we ought to pray when we are alone with the Lord is overly influenced by the models of public prayer to which we are exposed week by week in church gatherings. Public prayer tends to have a formal style and a general content just because it is public. It is often characterized by a studied eloquence – there is surely such a thing as a gift for leading the people of God in prayer – but all too frequently it can be blighted by an utter absence of Spirit-filled spontaneity and urgency, descending to the emptiest repetition of a form of words. The Lord's people

'cried out to the Lord in their trouble' (Psalm 107:6). The
Lord is no more impressed with the 'tongues of men and of
angels' (eloquence, 1 Corinthians 13:1) in prayer than he is in
preaching. He is looking for hearts that love him and trust him
and blurt out their petitions with all the normality and sincer-
ity of unaffected devotion – especially if their sense of need is
so great that it issues in 'groans that words cannot express'.
Lack of words cannot hinder real prayer – nor does it limit the
Lord's answers to prayer!

It should be added that prayer is appropriate in all circumstances, happy or otherwise. In the arena of suffering and
the cauldron of temptation, however, it certainly finds its
natural habitat. Prayer flows out naturally from a believing
heart when assailed by troubles and because it is a rich
channel for the healing grace of God to the soul of his people,
that prayer never stops in a mode of mournful pleading, but
rises to the transforming joy of salvation, which in turn brings
forth the sacrifices of praise and thanksgiving to the God and
Father of our Lord Jesus Christ.

Praise – for times of joy (5:13)

The Christian life, contrary to the mythology and the secret
desire of the non-Christian world, is a happy life – a life of
deep and abiding joy in the Lord, even when disturbed by
trials and tribulations. Christians are often **'happy'** – they
experience a wide range of joys, from times of light-hearted
fun to joys of a profoundly spiritual nature. In all of these, the
sense of the goodness of God is never absent. There is a difference between the joy of communion with God and the
pleasure of sharing a game of 'Scrabble' with Christian
friends, but the mode of expressing that joy is essentially the
same. It is a matter of realizing the joy to be a gift of God and
therefore very naturally returning that joy to him in terms of
praise for his great goodness.

'Is anyone happy?' asks James, **'Let him sing songs of
praise.'** It ought to be the most natural thing in the world for
Christians who are enjoying themselves to want to express
that in singing praises to God. Yes, he is saying that when
things are going well and you are happy, you should be thinking

of the Lord and praising him! This is not the most startling statement in the Word of God, but it does cut across the thinking of all unbelievers and challenges the present practice of many professing Christians. People in general, not excluding many who call themselves Christians, do not feel a great need of God when things are going well. That is, of course, the way of sinners – until we are afflicted, we go astray and the claims of Jesus Christ don't cross our minds. As a rule, the Christian faith is largely thought of and used as a crutch for hard times. Churches will be crowded out when bombs are falling, but peace and prosperity are not seen as equally calling for our attention to the claims of God. When the world is suffering, it *may* turn to God out of fear and uncertainty (and, indeed, that has been the means of many becoming believers in Christ); but when it is happy it doesn't celebrate God's goodness; it has a party – a 'good time' – and celebrates itself, often to openly sinful excess! James' point is just this: joy and happiness are every bit as much a cause of coming to the Lord as are sorrows and troubles. The difference is that when we are happy, we have something for which to praise him. We ought to celebrate before the Lord! Just as Scripture commands us to 'pray continually', so also it teaches us to 'extol the Lord at all times' – his praise is to be always...'on [our] lips' (1 Thessalonians 5:17; Psalm 34:1).

The characteristic medium of Christian celebration is the sung praise of God. **'Let him sing songs of praise'** interprets a single Greek word, *psalleto,* an active imperative of the verb meaning 'to sing praises'.[7] 'Let him sing psalms' (AV) ties in *psalleto* (the verb) with *psalmoi* (the related noun form) and draws attention to the use of the 'Book of Praises' (Hebrew: *Sepher Tehillim* – the title of the book of Psalms) in the praise and piety of Israel. Adamson notes that 'For the Jew singing psalms characterized, and was required of, the righteous man.'[8] The content of the praise is not explicitly specified in the text, which is probably better rendered, 'Let him sing praises!'(NASB) We are reminded of Paul's words in Colossians 3:16: 'Let the word of Christ dwell in you richly as you teach and admonish one another with all wisdom and as you sing psalms, hymns and spiritual songs with gratitude in your hearts to God.'[9] James' point is that when Christians are happy, they want to praise the Lord! Even their expressions

of happiness have the effect of letting 'the word of Christ' –
the inspired, infallible and inerrant revealed truth of God,
which all centres in good news in Jesus Christ – 'dwell in
[them] richly'! The contrast is with the world's celebrations:
with the carousings that litter the streets with drunks on
Friday and Saturday nights, the teenage joy-riders that roar
through sleeping neighbourhoods roaring obscenities and
disturbing the peace and the more ordinary and thoroughly
inoffensive light and jolly conversation in millions of gatherings, small and large, private and public, in homes and elsewhere up and down the land. And these, from the outrageous
to the genteel, have more in common with one another than
any of them do with a group of Christians who, just because
they feel happy, spontaneously decide to sing praises to the
Lord. The Lord and his goodness to us are what cause joy to
swell up in the Christian's heart. To sing his praises is only the
natural response of 'the spiritual man' who has by grace
through faith been given 'the mind of Christ' (1 Corinthians
2:14-16).

Spirit-filled and Spirit-led praise and prayer are integral to
the Christian life. It is impossible to be a true child of God and
not desire to praise him. The world finds this all but incom-
prehensible, but it is the life-blood of believers. It is the
shame of churches when their praise is less than full-throated
and enthusiastic. We Christians, of all the people in this
world, have the most reason to be vibrant worshippers of our
God. People who know us and enter our assemblies and our
homes ought to be witnessing the joy of the Lord in our
praise. Too many in our churches listen to the organ instead
of singing and thirst for wonderful performances of 'special
music' instead of prizing above all the congregational praise
of the Lord's people. James gives us a timeless corrective to
the recurrent tendency for worship to become a spectator
sport instead of the organic effusion of covenant joy in our
risen Saviour. Happy Christians will love to praise God
together with holy gusto! Troubled Christians will grasp the
privilege of prayer to seek the healing and comfort of the
Lord! And the Lord will pour his grace into our hearts with
joyous alacrity as we seek his face in all the circumstances of
our life before him in the world!

23.
Sharing your burdens

Please read James 5:14-18

'Therefore confess your sins to each other and pray for each other so that you may be healed. The prayer of a righteous man is powerful and effective' (James 5:16).

'Fellowship' is one of the most misunderstood and misapplied words in the language of modern piety. It has by and large been hijacked from its biblical roots – more on that in a moment – and associated with a narrow range of Christian social activities, usually involving food and casual conversation and sometimes describing little more than participation in party games. The problem, let me hasten to add, is not that Christian social activities cannot be regarded as an expression of Christian fellowship – our sharing of a broad spectrum of activities ought to flow out of our oneness of fellowship in Christ – but, as Jerry Bridges points out, 'It is just that they are not true fellowship. They may, if entered into for the right purpose, contribute to fellowship, but in and of themselves they are not fellowship.'[1] True fellowship is a deeper and richer element in Christian experience. Beginning with Acts 2:42, which distinguishes 'the apostles' teaching...fellowship...breaking of bread...and prayer' as the fundamental components of apostolic church body-life, Bridges goes on to show that biblical fellowship (Greek *koinonia*) 'is a relationship, not an activity'.[2] As such, it consists in four distinct aspects:

   1. A common life in Christ as a spiritually organic *community* with shared union and communion with the Lord and unity in the truths of the Word of God;[3]
   2. *Partnership* in the goal of glorifying God and promoting the gospel of Christ in the conversion of the lost and the building up of the church;[4]

3. Practical sharing of *communion with others* in spiritual things to the end of bearing one another's burdens and encouraging one another in the faith;[5] and

4. *Sharing material possessions* and thus expressing the most comprehensive unity of Christ's body in meeting practical needs in everyday life.'[6]

James does not develop a systematic theology of fellowship, but focuses on one of its leading evidences – caring for others out of love for Christ (1:27). In 5:14-18, James extends the application of this motif to the place of corporate intercessory prayer within the fellowship. He shows us how those who truly share biblical fellowship *(koinonia)* ought to care for the integrated spiritual and physical welfare of one another. First of all, we are shown what the church is to do when someone in the fellowship is ill (5:14-15). Secondly, the idea of healing is extended beyond the physical to encompass the spiritual health of believers and we are called to respond to needs with confession and prayer (5:16). Finally, we are reminded of the power of prayer as an instrument of fellowship and, by way of encouragement, we are pointed to the example of Elijah (5:16-18).

Praying for the sick (5:14-15)

'Is any one of you sick? He should call for the elders of the church to pray over him and anoint him with oil in the name of the Lord' (5:14). This passage has been interpreted in all sorts of diverse ways. The Roman Catholics make it teach their pseudo-sacrament of 'extreme unction', in which the application of oil to parts of the body of someone who is dying is supposed to prepare him for death – the opposite outcome from that envisaged by James in the passage! The Catholic Douay version of James 5:14 has the sick person sending for 'the priests of the church' – a remarkably inventive 'translation' of the Greek *prebuterous* (elders)! The charismatics, of course, find support here for their 'miracle services' for healings. Calvin and other Reformed commentators see it as referring to a time in the early church when the gift of healing was still manifest.

More satisfactory than all of these, however, is the

straightforward approach which sees this as a statement of what ought to be done in the church in every age when dealing with sickness, with the understanding that the anointing with oil is symbolic of God's influence and was used because it was particularly meaningful to Jewish Christians and is not to be viewed as a necessary 'rite' in later times.[7] Notice five points in particular.

Calling for the elders (5:14)
The sick person is to be open about sharing his or her needs and to call for the 'elders of the church'. You ought not to be secretive about your illnesses. You ought not to go off to the hospital without telling the church people about it. You are not to keep it quiet so as 'not to bother anyone'. Fellowship exists to bother about you. You should call for the prayers of the church, specifically through the elders. Let others help bear your burden. Let God's people pray for you. Let God bless you in the context of sharing your life with your brothers and sisters in Christ.

Prayer by the elders (5:14)
The elders of the church should gather and pray for the sick person.[8] This rarely happens today, even in cases of serious illnesses, yet it ought to be a feature of every congregation's body-life. One night a few weeks before the time of writing, I went with two of our elders to pray with a young man who had been afflicted with sleeplessness for some time. At night he was wracked by nightmares, with intense fears and a sense of the presence of evil. Each elder prayed in turn for his deliverance. The Lord soon answered our prayers, for apart from one slightly disturbed night three days later, that young Christian has been delivered from that particular affliction. God's elders are not called to be 'miracle' workers. We have no 'gift of healing'. God has simply commanded us to pray. He is the hearer of prayer and the healer of the hurts of his people. We pray: God acts.

Anointing with oil
The sick person may be anointed with oil. Some hold the view that the oil was used for its presumed medicinal value and argue that, because of the advances in medical science since,

the practice of anointing was a cultural practice which should not be insisted upon today. Oil was certainly used in the ancient world as a medicine (cf. Psalm 55:21; Luke 10:34). There is, however, no indication of any medicinal use in James 5:14, particularly when the contextual emphasis on effectual prayer and the power of the Lord is given its full weight. James is not talking about calling the physician and taking the prescribed medicine: he is describing how the ministry of intercessory prayer is to be exercised in the case of believers who are ill. This does not suggest that the oil should be regarded as obsolete medicine.

The fundamental significance of oil and anointing in Scripture was its use as a symbol of the grace of God (e.g. Psalm 133:2). This was no doubt the reason why oil was used in connection with miraculous healings recorded in the New Testament. In every instance, the oil is clearly used as a symbol which encourages faith and not as some kind of magic potion (Mark 6:13). In this light, anointing the sick with oil today can only have relevance as a symbol of the grace of God, which alone is the source and power of the healing for which prayer is offered. The anointing cannot be regarded as either essential or effectual in itself.[9]

Healing (5:15)
The promise of healing is annexed to **'the prayer offered in faith'** (5:15). This seems an unconditional promise, as if all such prayers will always be answered with healing. But clearly this must have the same limitations as another broad statement in Scripture, namely, that of our Lord in Mark 11:24: 'Whatever you ask for in prayer, believe that you have received it, and it will be yours.' The point is that it depends upon the sovereign decision of God as to whether the thing asked for will be given. For that reason, the emphasis is placed on our responsibility for fervent prayer and an earnest looking to the promises of God – not on instant and automatic healing. 'The prayer offered in faith' is simply 'the prayer which has its roots in faith'.[10] It is not some special class of miracle-working prayer that acts like magic. The fact is that God does not always heal those for whom his people pray in faith. A prime example is that of Paul leaving Trophimus 'sick in Miletus' (2 Timothy 4:20). Our inward faith-conviction is

not the determining factor – the efficient cause of its own answer. God is sovereign. He answers prayer. And he reserves the right to say 'No' or 'Later' sometimes.[11] His will is what we are to pray will be done (cf. 4:15).

The healing in view may not be the cure of an exclusively physical ailment. The word rendered 'make...well' is the basic New Testament word for 'save' [Greek, *sosei*]. It is used with reference to deliverance from danger (Matthew 8:25), demons (Luke 8:36), disease (Matthew 9:21), sickness *plus* sin (Luke 17:19) and salvation in the spiritual sense (Luke 18:26).[12] The indications in the context support the thought that spiritual and physical elements are compounded in the sickness/healing that James is discussing. This ties in with the normal Christian experience of sickness, for it is invariably linked to spiritual factors – depression, frustration, guilt, sin – from which we need deliverance by the power of God and in which we seek the comfort of his everlasting love. This spiritual dimension seems also to be implied by the assurance that **'the Lord will raise him up'** (5:15).

Forgiveness of sin (5:15)
'If he has sinned, he will be forgiven' (5:15). The net is cast wider than healing, physical or spiritual. We are led to the threshold of heaven to hear the voice of God declaring forgiveness of sin. Two points ought to be borne in mind. There is no implication here that we ought to conclude that our illnesses are the direct result of some unforgiven sin. The line of thought is simply: 'If you know you have sinned, then let this be a time of spiritual healing also. Let illness be a period of wide-ranging reflection on your relationship to the Lord and make it a time of special drawing near to God for his blessing. Let the elders be called; let the need be shared; let there be prayer to cover every real need.' The challenge of James' words for our churches is that we begin to exercise living fellowship in this as in other aspects of our life experience, and so reap the blessings of the promises of God.

Confession and prayer in the fellowship (5:16)

The Lord's brother now goes deeper still: **'Therefore confess**

your sins to each other and pray for each other so that you may be healed' (5:16). The elders are no longer in view. The sick pass from sight. James speaks to us one by one and as fellowships of God's people. He talks about something that is of the essence of true fellowship – of what today is often (and too often, tritely) called 'sharing'.

Confess your sins to each other
This is often taken to refer to the resolution of difficulties that may have arisen between members of the fellowship. Offences certainly should be dealt with. Christians should be reconciled to one another in truth and love. And just as the sick should call for the elders, so also should the offended. Pastoral oversight also includes the healing of rifts and arguments (see Matthew 18:15-20). The overall thrust of 5:14-18 strongly suggests, however, that James has in view something other than the settling of problems in the church. He is thinking rather of shared burdens and mutual support as we face the realities of life in the world together – as a *fellowship,* with positive *fellow*-feeling. Positive discipleship rather than restorative discipline is in view. How we can help each other grow in grace? How can we minister to a brother whose conscience is troubled over some personal sin and feels the need of help from a sound and understanding Christian friend? Here James encourages that person to confide in someone in the fellowship rather than moulder away in isolated introspection.

Such a procedure offers profound blessings, but is also fraught with some dangers of which we ought to be aware. James is not urging public meetings for the parading of sins that should be treated with discreet sensitivity and the minimum of fuss and publicity. He has in mind a restrained, private and confidential sharing between members of the fellowship, unstructured and yet directed by the constraints of the Word of God and the Holy Spirit.

We need to choose our confidants carefully and avoid the religious gossip who stands ready to pick up and pass on the confidences you share. 'Confessing sins one to another' does not require many counsellors, but it does require loving, wise and trustworthy ones. Godly compassion and circumspection in a brother or sister in the Lord are the *sine qua non* of blessing in this ministry of mutual support.

Pray for one another

The other and indispensable side of this sharing process is prayer for one another. We must do this for the broader range of shared concerns – such matters as might properly be shared with the fellowship as a whole – and also for the more private and personal matters in which we have shared a quiet ministry. It is, therefore, absolutely necessary to pray for mutual help with confessed sin. This is true whether it concerns publicly confessed sin or that which is confessed between confidants. Counsel and comfort are often a great help to people in need, but the most important way to help someone else is actually to pray for them earnestly and frequently. The close conjunction of prayer and confession in relation to healing suggests that the 'healing' is broad enough to encompass forgiveness of sins. 'There is a strong suggestion here,' says Donald Allister, 'that more healing (in this broad sense) would be available if it were asked for.'[13]

Our prayers – from the Lord's Prayer to the deepest cries of our own hearts – ought always to have a bit of the plural in them. Individual prayers are still to be prayers for 'all the saints'. Intercession – prayer for others – is the sweetest form of prayer. We join our individual concerns to those of the body of Christ, never more poignantly than in sharing our hurts. As our great High Priest, Jesus Christ is the heavenly intercessor for his people (Hebrews 7:25). As those who exercise the priesthood of all believers, we cannot but pray for others when we pray for ourselves. This is why so much of the recorded prayer in the Bible is in the first person plural. It is why it is so appropriate to say, '*We* would pray, O Lord,...' in leading public prayer in church and in groups. All public prayer is the corporate prayer of the covenant community as it reaches out to the Lord. The one who leads in prayer is not the mediator or intercessor for the group as a whole: he is the mouthpiece of the whole body – the orderly expression of their collective devotion to the Lord and desire for blessing.

Effectual prayer (5:16-18)

'The prayer of a righteous man is powerful and effective'
(5:16). Varying renditions of this text abound, all of them
turning on the meaning of the last word, 'effective'
(energoumene).[14] All of them, one way or another, indicate
the truth that God is pleased to answer believing prayer with
his blessings. The two characteristics of such prayer are the
godliness of the one who prays and the effectual nature of
faithful praying, as it goes forth to the Lord.

Elijah is the perfect example of what James is talking about
(5:17-18). He **'prayed earnestly'** – literally 'prayed with
prayer' – and the Lord answered with mighty demonstrations
of his sovereign power: first drought and then rain (1 Kings
17:1; 18:1). Remarkable as this was, it was the ministry of **'a
man just like us'**. Elijah was no superhuman: he was a normal
human being, like the rest of us, in every respect – the same
flesh and bone, passions and moods, frailties and susceptibilities. But he 'prayed with prayer'. He earnestly persevered
in crying to God. And God answered his prayers. Prayers
'rightly managed cannot want effect', remarks Manton. 'This
is the means which God hath consecrated for receiving the
highest blessings. Prayer is the key by which those mighty
ones of God could lock heaven, and open it at their pleasure...
It is wonderful to consider what the Scripture ascribeth
to faith and prayer: prayer sueth out blessings in the court of
grace, and faith receiveth them...Well, then, pray with this
encouragement, God hath said in an open place, that is,
solemnly avowed before all the world, that none shall seek his
face in vain (Isa. 45:19).'[15]

We began with the place of confession and prayer in the life
of the fellowship of God's people and end with a ringing affir-
mation of the power of true prayer. The Lord who could open
and shut the heavens for Elijah has promised to do great
things for us today when we call upon him in prayer. 'Therefore, since we have a great high priest who has gone through
the heavens, Jesus the Son of God, let us hold firmly to the
faith we profess. For we do not have a high priest who is
unable to sympathize with our weaknesses, but we have one
who has been tempted in every way, just as we are – yet was
without sin. Let us then approach the throne of grace with

confidence, so that we may receive mercy and find grace to help us in our time of need' (Hebrews 4:14-16). The fellowship of Christian churches is the arena in which the sharing of our common life – specifically our confessing sins one to another and praying for one another – receives the richest blessings of the Lord and causes us to grow spiritually, 'until we all reach unity in the faith and in the knowledge of the Son of God and become mature, attaining to the whole measure of the fulness of Christ' (Ephesians 4:13).

24.
Winning others for Christ

Please read James 5:19-20

'My brothers, if one of you should wander from the truth and someone should bring him back, remember this: Whoever turns a sinner from the error of his way will save him from death and cover a multitude of sins' (James 5:19-20).

'My heart's desire and prayer to God for the Israelites,' declared the apostle Paul, 'is that they may be saved' (Romans 10:11). And to the Gentiles he said, 'I resolved to know nothing while I was with you except Jesus Christ and him crucified' (1 Corinthians 2:2). It can come as no surprise, then, that James' final word on the subject of loving one another and desiring the best for one another is an encouragement to be reclaiming those who have either wandered from the truth or have hitherto been strangers to the grace of God. You will immediately discern the progression of James' line of thought. He began with the need of physical healing (5:14-15), went on to our need of spiritual growth (5:16-18), and now comes to the need of reclaiming those who 'wander from the truth' (5:19-20). All of these are set in the context of ministry in a congregation – the fellowship of the church with its faithful and caring elders and membership. No one member is an island: no one is to go it alone in the Christian life. When someone is sick, let the elders be called to pray with that person; where there is need for confession of sin, let the members share their burdens one with another and pray for one another; and when someone turns away from the Lord, let the fellowship minister to that person to bring him or her back within the fold.

Christians caring about Christians (5:19)

The ministry of every Christian begins with the other members of your local fellowship. From there it moves out to the other circles of fellowship (Christians in other churches) and friendship and neighbourliness (the unconverted). James' primary emphasis is upon spiritual care for your most immediate brothers and sisters in Christ: **'My brothers,**[1] **if one of you should wander from the truth**...' (5:19). This is clearly not an exhortation to evangelize the neighbourhood, biblical as that duty undoubtedly is. It is a word about ministry among Christians. So the first question with which James confronts us is this: 'Christian, do you realize that you have a ministry to your fellow-members at church?'

The precise focus of our spiritual ministry to one another is the truth and our response to it. We are to preserve each other from error. We are not to leave the job to somebody else. John Calvin offers a very challenging, and intriguing, point in this regard. We must beware, he says, 'lest souls perish through our sloth, whose salvation God puts in a manner in our hands. Not that we can bestow salvation on them; but that God by our ministry delivers and saves those who seem otherwise to be nigh destruction.'[2] In other words, God gives us the responsibility to minister to our brothers and sisters in the faith in such a way that he may use us to keep them from eternal shipwreck. This is serious work and it is given to every believer to do, as they have opportunity. It is Christians ministering to backsliding Christians, with love, with grace and with the truth as it is in Jesus, that there might be reclamation from the path of destruction. Let us remember that the 'lost sheep' and the 'prodigal son' in Jesus' parables were not unevangelized heathens, but wandering children of God – members of the community of faith who began to turn away from their professed faith in Christ and their covenant relationship to God.

Christians caring about truth (5:19)

The measure of our concern for others is their relationship with 'truth'. We have a mandate to discern error as it arises and apply to it the remedies of the gospel. The word 'truth' is also found in James 3:14, which states, 'If you harbour bitter envy and selfish ambition in your hearts, do not boast about it or deny the truth.' This 'truth' is the body of true doctrine – the revealed, inscripturated Word of God. Thus Paul distinguishes by implication this truth from false substitutes, when he says, 'We cannot do anything against the truth, but only for the truth.' This is 'the word of truth'. To become a Christian is 'to come into the knowledge of the truth'. It is God's Word as over against the word of Antichrist.[3] The truth from which the backslider wanders is the Holy Scripture and, in terms of the personal relationships of living faith, from the Lord Jesus Christ, the living Word, who is 'the way, the truth and the life'.

More than doctrinal error
Wandering from the truth is not a simple matter of doctrinal error. To be sure, it is always rooted in the practical rejection of some truth of the Scriptures. Apostasy, to give it its proper name, is deeper than intellectual error, for it is the putting into practice of a deliberate rebellion against the 'light' which is truth. Most Christian backsliding is 'sinning against light' – the denial in practice of what we have professed to believe, theoretically. Almost any habit injurious to our health can serve as an illustration of this phenomenon. For example, it is indisputable that cigarette smoking contributes to, even causes, heart disease and lung cancer. People know this but cling to the habit anyway. No one smokes, however, because he is committed to getting lung cancer or aims to die of a heart attack! No! The reason for persisting in the habit lies in deeper layers of habituation, bondage and dependence: so the smoker sets aside the health warnings. The problem is not merely intellectual – a matter of ignorance *versus* knowledge – it lies deeper than the mind, in more basic controlling desires, commitments and enslavements.

The danger with James' readers – the Christian Jews of the Diaspora – was the temptation to return to Judaistic legalism and ceremonies. The ties of nation and family, of sentiment and tradition, all constitute a siren call for Hebrew Christians and their modern equivalent, the Messianic Jews. For Jewish Christians, the fact that the Old Testament patterns for worship and life had been God's mandate made it all the more difficult to come to the place of seeing certain parts of it fall away because Messiah had come. This was the significance of the Council of Jerusalem, in which James had taken such a prominent part in easing the transition while handling Jewish susceptibilities with sensitivity and balance (Acts 15:13-21).[4]

We ought not to be as confused over the traditions and habits of the 'world'. These were never sanctioned by God, as once were Jewish dietary rules and temple rituals. Their appeal is no less powerful for that; sin is always appealing when disguised as temptation. This is the hook by which we are led to wander from the truth – the intellectual rationalization follows rather than precedes the first apostate move away from the Lord. The pattern is most frequently: temptation, lust, sin, *then* intellectual justification by change of mind on the relevant doctrine. But sometimes it can be more brazen still: the sin having been embraced, the backslidden Christian still affirms the truth as stated in God's Word, but says, 'God will forgive me, because he loves me and wants me to be happy.' As you reflect on this, you will see the essential perversity in the line of argument: it is saying that God's love (issuing in forgiveness and happiness for deliberately knowingly sinful me) may be set over against his holy and just law. In contrast to this kind of self-serving, sin-excusing, God-dishonouring scheming, the gospel is good news because in the atoning death of Jesus Christ, divine love and justice – always in perfect harmony – provided the means of salvation for sinners, the evidence of which in us is faith, repentance and holy living in Christ. To justify one's sins, or, worse, to sin knowingly and claim forgiveness anyway is, in effect, to deny the nature of the gospel and the saving change which Christ has wrought by grace, through faith, in our innermost being. Sin is more than mere 'bad deeds' or simple ignorance. Wandering from the truth, in Christians, is more than intellectual error. It is from the heart that the issues of life proceed! (Proverbs 4:23 AV).

Am I my brother's keeper?
Perhaps you ask, 'This is all true, but do I really have to stand guard over the failings of fellow-Christians? Is it really my business? I don't want to get into arguments. You know what

people can be like, especially if you butt into their private affairs.'

James certainly did not mean Christians to be fault-finding busybodies who spend their days ferreting around in the church for other people's problems! We have already noted in these studies the importance of the distinction between the private and the public with respect to the voluntary sharing of both confession of sin and burdens for intercessory prayer. How much more care must be exercised in the way in which we watch for and respond to situations in which our brothers and sisters wander from Christ! James clearly has in mind cases of serious, open sin – the kind of problems that call for church discipline. And in this case, I believe, he is talking about church discipline, not at the more advanced and formal level of 'official action' by the elders, but at the level of personal and private intervention to 'nip in the bud' a situation which, if left, will erupt into a shipwrecked faith and public scandal. James' concern is that we *all* stand ready to seek to draw back into the fellowship a brother or sister who seems to be drifting away. We are not to stand by when we see someone in trouble. Why are we our brother's keeper? Several compelling reasons suggest themselves for our consideration.

1. This is commanded in God's Word. Even a neighbour's animals are to be helped if lost or in trouble! (Deuteronomy 22:1). How much more should we be concerned for a wayward professing Christian, whose path is heading for destruction, and maybe, for all we know (because we cannot read the heart), for a lost eternity! That is the force of James' injunction! It is facile to say, 'Once a Christian, always a Christian,' and thus twist the precious doctrine of 'the perseverance of the saints' into a justification for non-intervention. Christians – true, regenerated, converted, believers in Christ – certainly will persevere in the faith. Jesus says they will 'never perish' and cannot be plucked out of his hand. You cannot be more absolute than that! But your calling to intervene in the lives of other people is precisely one of God's means for gathering in those who will 'never perish'! The famous dictum to the effect that the triumph of evil requires only that good men do nothing finds a genuine expression in this question of reclaiming the backslider. God has not said that anyone who merely *professes* faith is *ipso facto* saved and incapable of being lost.

We are all called to 'make our calling and election sure'. Our sins contradict our professions of faith and, to the end that we might know the inward assurance of the 'spirit of adoption', whereby we cry "Abba" – Father' (Romans 8:16 AV) and live holy, consistent lives, we need the ministry of encouragement and exhortation of our fellow-Christians. Looking at it from the other side – that of the desire to put out the effort to reach the wayward Old Testament people of God for Christ – Paul could wish himself 'cursed and cut off from Christ' for the sake of his 'brothers' (Romans 9:3). This is the stuff of which sacrificial love is made and it indicates the crucial role of believers in the ministry of the gospel.

2. We who know what it means to be saved by grace, to be filled with the Holy Spirit and therefore how desperate it is to be without him, can only desire that our brothers and sisters enjoy this same assurance of walking in the truth, this same joy of salvation in Christ. The apostle Paul could say, 'Follow my example, as I follow the example of Christ' (1 Corinthians 11:1). He was saying, in the deepest humility, that following Christ is the most wonderful life in the world. Therefore, he was able to lead from the front and say, 'Be like me, because I am imitating Jesus and that is the only way to go!' If you know Jesus, you must want others to know him too! And, of course, the basis of this is that Jesus wants to be like Jesus! Why? Because, he knows what a joy it is to be perfectly holy, to be united to his Father-God in perfect unity and to share love that is without spot or blemish. Because Christian experience is our *summum bonum* – our highest good – it is what we desire for others. And we cannot stand by and see those who have been our brothers and sisters in Christ, according to their own confession of faith, wander from the truth and take the road to hell!

Three blessings of faithfulness (5:20)

An air of expectancy pervades the final verse of James' epistle: **'Remember this: Whoever turns a sinner away from the error of his way will save him from death and cover over a multitude of sins'** (5:20). If there is success in your ministry then real benefits will flow from that for all parties involved.

Saved from death

The issue is as serious as this: wandering from the truth is the
way of death. It is always true, as we have noted already, that
we cannot read the hearts of men and women. It is true that
the Lord knows those who are his. We only read people's
actions and these are what define the contours of the potential
problem and determine our specific responsibility to them
under the gospel. To stay on a path that wanders from the
Lord and to stay on it until death, without repentance and
renewal, is very definitely to invite eternal loss. Irrespective
of the standing of such a person in terms of the secret purpose
and knowledge of God, there can certainly be no assurance
for any of us that that person is saved. Neither can there be
any easy assumption by that person, while he lives and still
wanders from God, that he is right with God because he happens to believe some truth and indulges generous views of
God's attitude to his wilful rebelliousness. To reclaim a backslider may well be saving him from death, every bit as much
as the conversion of any sinner from his sin.

The Greek word used here to describe the turning away of
a sinner from his error(5:20) is the general New Testament
word for 'conversion' *(epistrepho)*. Thus Christ said of the
reclamation which Peter would experience after his denial of
Christ: 'And when you have turned back [i.e., are converted],
strengthen your brothers' (Luke 22:32; see also Romans
11:14; 1 Corinthians 7:16; 1 Timothy 4:16). It is used both of
the first conversion to Christ (Acts 3:19) and of subsequent
'conversions' from backslidings: in other words, any significant turning-point in our spiritual lives in which the redeeming power of the gospel is experienced. The Christian life may
be punctuated by a number of such episodes of wandering
away from truth and 'conversion' again back to Christ's
'straight and narrow way'. And as long as there are times of
wandering and spiritual laxness in our lives, there will be, by
God's grace, revivals of true faith in our souls. And because
coming to Christ, whether for the first time or in terms of
renewal and restoration, is in our experience like the blind
seeing or life returning to a numb and paralysed limb, it
always takes the character of salvation from death – redemption from spiritual deadness in the heart.

A multitude of sins covered

We hear an echo of Proverbs 10:12: 'Hatred stirs up dissension, but love covers over all wrongs.' 'Love buries sins,' says John Calvin. The idea of the covering over of sin is one of the great redemptive themes of Scripture and redemptive history itself. The very structure of the ark of the covenant, which you will recall was the centrepiece of the tabernacle and temple of the Old Testament people of God, represented among other things the covering of the sins of Israel by atoning blood sacrifice (Exodus 25:10-22). This was basically a box with a lid, which was called the mercy seat. Over the ark hovered the glory-cloud – the theophanic manifestation of God's presence with his people. Within the Ark were the symbols of God's covenant with man – the reminders of man's sin and need of redemption – the tables of the law from Sinai, the manna from the wilderness and Aaron's rod that blossomed. The mercy seat lay between these proofs of man's sin and the God who is holy and cannot look upon sin. Thus, when the blood of the sacrifice for sin was sprinkled on the mercy seat, it signified atonement for sin. God looked down towards the symbols of man's sin, but saw only the blood. The blood on the mercy seat covered sin, God's perfect justice was satisfied and his people redeemed. This was, of course, only a picture of the actual atonement which the Lord Jesus Christ effected in his death on the cross as the substitute for the sins of all who would believe – past, present and future. The Old Testament sacrifices pointed to the blood of Christ which, as Scripture says, cleanses from all sin. Now it is this rich theology of covering which is associated with the winning of others to Christ, for the obvious reason that it is the same blood-bought salvation which alike saves the pagan and the backslidden Christian. The love that ministers the gospel of saving grace to sinners is a love that covers a multitude of sins – their sins, not ours – because it is the love of Christ. When the response to the gospel is repentance and faith, the receiving of the love of Christ does indeed cover their sins, in that for the true believer, the real convert, God sees the blood of Christ – the sin is nowhere to be seen, for it is washed away by the atonement wrought by our Saviour in his death and resurrection. This is grace! This is the glory of the cross of our

Lord Jesus Christ. This is the reason that Paul could cry with such exalted passion: 'May I never boast except in the cross of our Lord Jesus Christ' (Galatians 6:14).

A happy remembrance of faithful ministry
The first words of the last verse say: **'remember this...'** Surely there is a hint of joy in this for those who reach out in love to seek to win others to Christ? Why should we remember that reaching out may lead to salvation and the covering of sins for those we are privileged to bring to Christ? Because there is a well of Christian joy to be tapped for our own walk with the Lord. How could we not be vastly encouraged in our own discipleship when we see our faithfulness used by the Lord to save others? No one needs to be told to be satisfied with his successes. It is the most natural thing in the world to draw satisfaction from our achievements. It is also right! It is the reward of diligence. How much more then will we rejoice in the salvation of lost human beings? How much more will we exult in the advance of the kingdom of our Lord and Saviour Jesus Christ? If God himself rejoices before his angels in heaven over one soul added to the kingdom, shall we not jump for joy as we see one after another converted to Christ and persevering in the faith in the course of our own ministry in the place that God has placed us?

This is practical Christianity: loving God, loving his truth, loving his people and loving the lost and wayward enough to reach out to them with the good news concerning the Lord Jesus Christ, who died that we who believe in him might not perish, but have everlasting life.

References

Preface
1. T. Manton, *The Epistle of James,* p. 8.

Introduction
1. R. C. H. Lenski, *The Interpretation of the Epistle to the Hebrews and the Epistle of James* (Augsburg, 1966), pp. 514-6, in his critique of Luther's position, points out that he held an even more outrageous opinion, in that he held the epistle of James to have been a third- or fourth-hand production, written long after the time of the apostles and put together in a disjointed manner! Lenski, himself a Lutheran, points out that the Lutheran Church never adopted Luther's views on James and goes on strongly to affirm both its canonicity and its Christ-centred evangelical content.
2. George L. Lawlor, *The Epistle of Jude – a translation and exposition* (Presbyterian & Reformed, 1972), p. 2.
3. James B. Adamson, *The Epistle of James* (Eerdmans, 1976 [NICOT]), p. 18.

Chapter 1
1. H. Alford, *The Greek Testament,* Vol. IV, p. 275.
2. J. Calvin, *The Commentaries on the Catholic Epistles* (Baker, 1979) Vol. XXII, p. 279. (Unless otherwise stated quotations from Calvin are from this work.)
3. As above.
4 R. Johnstone, *James* (Banner of Truth, 1977[1871]), p. 31.
5. This ceiling is in a well-known tourist attraction, 'Gladstone's Land' on the Lawnmarket in the heart of Edinburgh's Old Town.
6. Calvin, p. 280.
7. Johnstone, p. 34.

Chapter 2
1. Calvin, p. 281.
2. As above, p.282.
3. Johnstone, p. 37.
4. Calvin, p. 283.
5. J. B. Adamson, *The Epistle of James* (Eerdmans, 1976), p. 57.
6. Manton, p. 57.
7. As above, p. 58.

Chapter 3
1. George Grant, *The Dispossessed: Homelessness in America* (Dominion Press, 1986), pp. 157-162.
2. J. B. Adamson, p. 62, correctly resists the idea that this humility of circumstances should be spiritualized in the Christian grace of humility. The focus is on socio-economic humbleness.
3. As above, p. 61.
4. Calvin, pp. 285-286.
5. Johnstone, pp. 55-56.
6. C.Vaughan, *James: Bible Study Commentary* (Zondervan, 1969), p. 27.
7. Johnstone, p. 58.
8. Adamson, pp. 67-68. Compare 1 Corinthians 9:25.
9. Manton, *James,* p. 81.

Chapter 4
1. Adamson, p. 68.
2. Calvin, p. 289.
3. Romans 7:8 appears to teach the very opposite relationship between temptation and sin: 'But sin, seizing the opportunity afforded by the commandment, produced in me every kind of covetous desire.' The problem is the translation, which would be better rendered, 'But sin, taking a start...wrought...every evil desire.' The thought is not that sinful acts precede evil desires, but that sin, as a principle, began – took its start – by producing evil desires. Paul does not say he got to the length of actually committing sinful acts. He was speaking about the genesis of sin as it creates a tension in the believer's life between the new nature in Christ and the lingering habits of the old man (even though he is dead, Romans 6:6). See W. G. T. Shedd, *Commentary on Romans* (Zondervan, 1967[1879]), p. 182, for the exegesis. Also Manton, p. 99.
4. Manton, p. 100.
5. As above, p. 98.

Chapter 5

1. Manton, p. 114.
2. *Westminster Confession of Faith,* IV, II (Free Presbyterian Church of Scotland, 1976).
3. Manton, p. 114. Compare Galatians 1:6; Ephesians 4:14 with 2 Timothy 3:14.
4. I have discussed this subject more extensively in connection with the 'repentance' of God in the matter of his declared intention to destroy Nineveh (Jonah 3:10). See Gordon J. Keddie, *Preacher on the Run: the message of Jonah* (Evangelical Press, 1986), pp. 95-103.
5. Calvin, p. 292.
6. John Murray, *Redemption Accomplished and Applied* (Banner of Truth, 1961), pp. 95-105.
7. Johnstone, p. 91.

Chapter 6

1. For the exposition of James 1:22-25 see chapter 7 in this book; for 1:26-27, see chapter 8.
2. Cornelius Van Til (1895-1987) taught Christian Apologetics at Westminster Theological Seminary from its inception in 1929 until his retirement in 1975. He wrote many books on the defence of the Christian faith, and his fundamental contribution to Christian thought was the development of Christian Presuppositionalism, as in his classic work, *The Defense of the Faith* (Presbyterian and Reformed Publ. Co., 1955). For all the difficulty of much of his writings, he was a wonderfully simple preacher and a most humble and approachable Christian. His class-room style was very lively and full of fun.
3. Johnstone, p. 99.
4. E. Kelly, *James – A Primer for Christian Living* (Craig Press, 1969), p. 68. I have substituted the English 'silencer' for the original American 'muffler'.
5. Manton, p. 139.
6. As above, p. 148.
7. Johnstone, p. 108.

Chapter 7

1. Manton, p. 153.
2. Johnstone, p. 112.
3. Lenski, p. 555.
4. Manton, p. 159.

5. The NIV rendering of James is perhaps the poorest and most paraphrastic section of that otherwise helpful and reliable translation. The translator(s) of James seem to have made a virtue of surrendering accuracy in the interests of a lack of style. Neither accuracy nor style is served by turning 'the perfect law of liberty' into 'the perfect law that gives freedom' or reducing 'neither variableness nor shadow of turning' (1:17 AV) to 'who does not change like shifting shadows'. Another example is in 1:21 where AV (an accurate rendering of the Greek) 'able to save your souls' comes out as the bland paraphrase 'which can save you'. Keep your eye on the AV, NASB or even the RSV as you study through James in the NIV.

6. Johnstone, p. 118.
7. Vaughan, p. 41.

Chapter 8
1. Calvin, p. 298.
2. Manton, p. 173.
3. George Grant, *The Dispossessed* (Dominion Press, 1986) gives a harrowing account of homelessness in the modern world and challenges the church to a distinctively biblical response.
4. Johnstone, p. 138.
5. Manton, p. 177.

Chapter 9
1. Manton, p. 185.
2. Vaughan, p. 45.
3. It is worth noting, in passing, that whereas the gospel of Christ is the true 'leveller' of men and women, the common humanist notion is that death is the great leveller. It is true, as the poet Thomas Gray observed, that 'The paths of glory lead but to the grave.' Earthly distinctions *are* removed by death. Death brings all men before the judgement seat of God. That is a levelling of a sort. But it is immediately followed, on the one hand, by a second and eternal death for the unbelieving and, on the other hand, by a happy exaltation to reconciled fellowship with God for the redeemed in Christ. Death is an enemy, not a leveller. The gospel elevates to heaven, while death and judgement raze human autonomy to the level of lost eternity!
4. Manton, p. 185.

5. Francis A. Schaeffer, *The Great Evangelical Disaster* (Crossway Books, 1984), p. 141.
6. Manton, p. 192.
7. Johnstone, p. 151.
8. Calvin, p. 304.

Chapter 10
1. Johnstone, p. 158.
2. Adamson, pp. 114-115.
3. Vaughan, p. 52.
4. Manton, pp. 215-216.
5. See 1 Timothy 5:8; Galatians 6:10; Luke 14:12-14.

Chapter 11
1. Manton. p. 233.
2. As above, p. 235.
3. As above, p. 236.
4. As above.
5. Mr Someone's speech probably goes through to the end of verse 20 and is not limited to the sentence indicated by the quotation marks in the NIV.
6. Calvin, p. 313.

Chapter 12
1. W. Cunningham, *Historical Theology* (Banner of Truth, 1960[1862]), vol. II, p. 1.
2. 'Justification is an act of God's free grace, wherein he pardoneth all our sins, and accepteth us as righteous in his sight, only for the righteousness of Christ imputed to us, and received by faith alone' *(Shorter Catechism 33)*. For a helpful explanation of 'justification' in relation to the whole process of salvation (the *ordo salutis*), see John Murray, *Redemption Accomplished and Applied* pp. 117-131.
3. Johnstone, p. 201.
4. Quoted by Vaughan, p. 63.
5. Adamson, pp. 132-3.

Chapter 13
1. Calvin, p. 319.
2. Manton, p. 271. He says, 'This itch must be killed.'
3. Johnstone, p. 213.
4. J. Calvin, *Harmony of the Gospels* (Torrance edition), Vol. III, p. 288.
5. Manton, p. 273.

6. See Ezekiel 33:1-10 for the responsibility of God's messengers.
7. Calvin, *Commentary on Catholic Epistles,* p. 319.

Chapter 14
1. J. Morris, *Heaven's Command* (Penguin Books, 1981), p. 434. Isandlwhana, the first battle of the Zulu War, took place on 22 January 1879.
2. Manton, p. 285. Arianism denied the eternal Sonship of Jesus Christ as the Logos. Christ was 'begotten' in a special way, Arius said, and therefore was created rather than eternal and divine in nature. The Jehovah's Witnesses are modern Arians in their doctrine of the person of Christ. Unitarianism goes even further and sees Jesus as merely a good man.
3. Johnstone, p. 240.
4. J. Adam, *Exposition of the Epistle of James* (Edinburgh: T. & T. Clark, 1867), p. 234 (as quoted by Johnstone, p. 240).
5. Vaughan, p. 70.
6. Johnstone, p. 252.

Chapter 15
1. Johnstone, p. 259.
2. Kelly, p. 174.
3. Vaughan, p. 75.
4. It will be immediately obvious, even to readers who know no Greek, that 'without the Spirit' is another of the NIV's 'dynamic equivalence' renderings in which interpretation obliterates strict translation. The AV rendering 'natural' (man) is a genuine attempt at the translation of the almost untranslatable *psuchikos,* which has reference to being 'of the flesh' as distinct from *pneumatikais* – of the Spirit. See Adamson, p. 152, for an interesting discussion of the difficulties of this word. Adamson's preference for the rendering 'sub-human' is highly doubtful, since being 'of the flesh' (worldly) is nowhere in Scripture equated with being merely 'animal' or 'sub-human'. Men made in God's image, however sinful, are never treated like sub-humans by God – either in time or (even a lost) eternity!
5. Adamson, p. 152.
6. Johnstone, p. 270.
7. Lenski, p. 618.
8. J. Brown, *Discourses and Sayings of our Lord* (Banner of Truth, 1967[1852 ed.]), vol. 1, p. 116-8.
9. Manton, pp. 322-3.

10. This interpretation sees the expression 'harvest of righteousness' as a subjective genitive, as opposed to an objective genitive, in which case the sense would be 'the harvest that flows from righteousness'. See J. Adamson, pp. 156-7 for a clear discussion of the exegesis.

Chapter 16
1. Calvin, p. 329.
2. As I have already suggested more than once in these studies, I believe the loose approach of NIV to the text of Scripture (so-called 'dynamic equivalence') is fraught with dangers. It may seem helpful to add the name of God, as in 4:3, because that is clearly in accord with the thrust of the passage. But what is eroded is the integrity of the text itself, which was deemed sufficiently clear by the Holy Spirit to omit the name of God and leave it to our minds, led by him into the truth, to see the obvious intent. These little 'additions and corrections' – so reminiscent of official tidiness in keeping minutes of committee meetings – in the end seem to suggest that translators see a certain inadequacy in the text as given by God and feel a need to spoon-feed particular interpretations to us readers, as if in this department also, the Holy Spirit will not do the work he has promised through the means he has provided. *Caveat emptor* – Bible translations are not immune from the unhelpful helpfulness of sincere meddling with the inspired text!
3. Calvin, p. 330.
4. Manton, p. 338.
5. As above, p. 342.

Chapter 17
1. 'Episcopalians are grappling with declining membership,' Associated Press (George W. Cornell): *Centre Daily Times,* 3 July 1988.
2. For a searching exposition of 'accommodation' among the erstwhile 'conservatives' and 'evangelicals' see Francis Schaeffer's last and most powerful book, *The Great Evangelical Disaster* (1984).
3. Johnstone, p. 299.
4. The absolute sovereignty of God is clearly taught in Scripture. God does foreordain whatsoever comes to pass. The Bible teaches the doctrine of predestination. But Scripture never portrays God's sovereignty in fatalist terms as a force which removes the responsible free agency of human beings as they

answer to God's claims. Everyone in hell *chose* the road that
led him there, even if a natural predisposition to sin (i.e., his
nature as a lost sinner) impelled him inexorably along that
path. And everyone who is saved by Jesus Christ *chose* to turn
to him in faith, notwithstanding the fact that God is sovereign
in salvation and that no one comes to Christ unless God draws
him by his freely gracious intervention (John 6:44). All these
acts of will are exercised, however, under the umbrella of
God's overarching sovereignty. He does his will in the armies
of heaven and among the inhabitants of the earth, while we
inhabitants of the earth do our wills – freely by our way of it,
yet always in terms of the ultimacy of the will of the sovereign
God. The mystery attending the integration of God's absolute
predestination and man's responsibility and experimental free
agency must always defy a simplistic logical resolution just
because it is a doctrine which takes us beyond the capacities of
the finite mind and gives us a glimpse of the infinite eternal
mind of God. Man cannot, by searching, find out God – we
know him only as he chooses to reveal himself to us and on the
border of that revelation we can only bow in reverent wonder
before that which we cannot fully understand. Now we know
'in part' (1 Corinthians 13:10).

5. Adamson, p. 170.
6. Johnstone, pp. 313-4.
7. F. S. Leahy, *Satan Cast Out – A Study in Biblical Demonology*
    (Banner of Truth, 1975), pp. 22ff.
8. Vaughan, p. 90.
9. *Westminster Confession of Faith*, XVIII, 2.
10. Calvin, p. 336.

Chapter 18
1. Manton, pp. 379-380.
2. There can be a lighter side to ancient rivalries that has a
    healing, even enriching effect. We Scots secretly, even
    openly, enjoy all the ethnic jokes about our alleged thriftiness.
    And we are not above good-humoured jibes at our southern
    neighbours: 'We're not biased,' runs one Scottish crack about
    the prospects for the English football team, 'we dinna care
    who beats England!'
3. Johnstone, p. 328 (his emphasis).
4. Manton, p. 380.
5. Johnstone, p. 328.
6. It is worth pointing out that when the church, through her
    elders, decides who should or should not be received as

members, baptized, admitted to the Lord's Supper, rebuked or excommunicated, as the case may be, these decisions are made wholly on the basis of observable outward actions (confessions of faith, words, deeds) and not at all on the basis of some mystical ability to read the thoughts and intentions of the heart. Only God reads the heart. Church discipline does not pronounce on whether or not a person is of the elect of God: it pronounces on the contemporary consistency of a person's words and deeds (doctrine and life) with the pattern set down in Scripture. It says, 'If you live this way, you cannot be recognized as a Christian, whatever the state of your heart (which we cannot see into, although God surely does).' Even the most discerning Christians only look on the outward side of men and women.

7. The 'in' phrase used today to describe this is a 'judgemental attitude'. It tends to be associated with anyone with strong, rather conservative views, especially as they relate to insistence upon biblically sound theology, separation from the world and non-co-operation in evangelism with those who employ doubtfully scriptural methods of attraction and persuasion and who assign follow-up duties to modernist and Catholic churches. For all that it is in vogue and not altogether inapplicable, I have not used the adjective 'judgemental' in these studies so as to avoid association with these emotive issues and maintain the focus on the precise subject of James' exhortation.

8. Manton, p. 385.

Chapter 19

1. Admittedly this means little in Britain where there are only two basic possibilities anyway (showers with sunny periods or sun with periodic showers!), but in the USA, from where this sun-soaked Scot now writes, we have a precise percentage figure each day in increments of 10%, where applicable, for showers, rain, thunderstorms, snow, etc.!

2. To say that the risen Christ rules as Mediator-King is to say that he rules, as per Matthew 28:28, in terms of his successful mediation between God the Father and the elect, whom he saves through his substitutionary, atoning death. He gained the victory and part of the fruit of that victory is his mediatorial kingship. He rules for those he is saving to be his people. This is one aspect of the threefold office of Christ – as Mediator he is Prophet (the *Word* made flesh, John 1:14),

Priest (the *Lamb* that was slain, Revelation 5:6) and King
(who is *Head* over everything for the church, Ephesians 1:22).
3. The *Westminster Confession of Faith,* XXXI, 4, includes a
healthy corrective to the notion that collective church
decisions are usually wise discernments of the will of God:
'Synods and councils...may err, and many have erred;
therefore they are not to be made the rule of faith or practice,
but to be used as an help in both.'

Chapter 20
1. Johnstone, p. 346.
2. The Greek is *ton dikaion* – 'the just' – a singular, not plural as
in NIV.
3. Adamson, p. 184, suggests a parallel between James 5:1-6
with Psalm 58, in which the Lord's people see and rejoice in
the condemnation of the wicked because by this they know
that God rewards the righteous and that 'there is a God who
judges the earth' (Psalm 58:11). There will be no mourning in
heaven for the lost in hell.
4. Manton, p. 406.
5. D. Chilton, *Paradise Restored* (Dominion Press, 1987), pp.
115ff. The insistence that 'the last days' refer to the time
between the birth of Christ and the destruction of the temple
in Jerusalem (4 B.C. – 70 A.D.) is a central pillar of the
preterist view of the Book of Revelation, which sees it as
largely referring to the period prior to A.D. 70.
6. P. E. Hughes, *A Commentary on the Epistle to the Hebrews*
(Eerdmans, 1977), p. 37 (especially footnote 5).
7. Calvin, p. 345.
8. 'Lord of Sabaoth' – 'sabaoth' means 'hosts' in the sense of
'armies' and is used in Scripture with reference to the angels (1
Kings 22:19; Psalm 103:21; Luke 2:13) and also Israel's armies
(1 Samuel 17:45) and the stars (Isaiah 40:26).
9. I would not wish to give the impression that Scripture is
indifferent to economic systems. The Bible favours a free
market economy, in which people enjoy freedom to work,
earn a living, own property and trade freely. This is a broadly
'capitalist' model. For it to be a blessing, however, it must
operate in the context of grace and covenant faithfulness.
Where the love of God and the law of God are rejected, the
system will break down – as we have seen repeatedly since
Bible times. On the other hand, the Marxist view of the state
is evil from the heart. It denies God and man as his image-
bearer and refuses man the freedoms which God has given for
responsible and fruitful vice-gerentship on the earth. The

'post-Christian' West (including pagan Japan) is economically
successful to the degree that it is able to simulate the biblical
pattern for economic blessing. It is living on the residual
spiritual and moral capital of the faithfulness of earlier
generations. The socialist-Marxist economies are in the throes
of facing their utter failure. They are discovering, although
they do not see it in these terms, that a flatly anti-Christian
system is doomed to self-destruct as it goes along.
10. Ambrose, *On the Duties of the Clergy,* II, xviii, 137ff., cited by
J. Calvin, *Institutes,* IV, iv, 8.

Chapter 21
1. See chapter 10, pp. 185-7. Colossians 3 and 2 Peter 3 place
the whole subject in the proper perspective and demonstrate
the utter fallacy of the imposition of our sense of 'sooner' and
'later' upon God's perfect timetable.
2. Vaughan, p. 109. Those who see the 'coming of the Lord' as
referring to the destruction of Jerusalem have no need to see
the nearness of the event as involving a wait of any more than
a few years. But then, they have a problem with the sheer
scope and finality of the scriptural references to the Second
Coming, for it is quite clear that they cannot be contracted
into some presumably invisible 'return' of the Lord in A.D.
70.
3. Calvin, p. 351.
4. Adamson, p. 192.
5. Manton, p. 434.

Chapter 22
1. See chapter 8, pp. 84-5.
2. Adamson, p. 194.
3. We talk about 'not mincing words', i.e., making no
concessions to polite inoffensiveness. 'Mincing steps' were the
short, neat steps supposedly characteristic of both the walking
and dancing of the ladies of cultured society. Mincing an oath,
like mincing cheap cuts of meat, is chopping up the coarse bits
to make the whole thing more palatable. It is essentially a
cosmetic operation.
4. Adamson, p. 195.
5. As above.
6. Kelly, p. 233.
7. The third person singular active imperative of *psallein*. This
verb is also found in 1 Corinthians 14:15 and Ephesians 5:19.
Originally, *psallein* referred to instrumental accompaniment

and in the course of time encompassed singing with the accompaniment and eventually could refer to singing *a capella* (See Adamson, p. 197).

8. Adamson, p. 197.

9. There is an interesting connection between Paul's choice of words in Colossians 3:16 and Ephesians 5:19 and the Old Testament's 'Book of Praises' (what we call 'The Psalms'). The words 'psalms' *(psalmoi)*, 'hymns' *(humnoi)* and 'songs' *(odai)* appear in the titles of the Septuagint (the third-century B.C. Greek Old Testament) version of the 150 psalms. This was the Bible version with which the Hellenistic Jews of the ancient world would be familiar – so the very mention of these words must have connected in their minds with the divinely inspired songs of their heritage from 'the sweet singer of Israel'.

Chapter 23

1. J. Bridges, *True Fellowship* (Navpress, 1985), p. 15. This is a splendid practical treatment of the subject well worth careful study.

2. As above, pp. 16-23.

3. 1 Corinthians 12:13; 1 Thessalonians 2:11; 1 Peter 2:5; 1 John 1:3.

4. Philemon 17; Galatians 2:9; Philippians 1:5.

5. Ephesians 4:11-13; 1 Thessalonians 4:1; 1 Timothy 3:2; 5:17; 2 Timothy 4:2.

6. Acts 2:44-45; Romans 12:13; 2 Corinthians 8:13-14; 9:13; Hebrews 13:16.

7. D. S. Allister, *Sickness and Healing in the Church* (Latimer House, 1981) 46 pp., is a most helpful survey of the principal biblical passages dealing with the subject.

8. 'Elder' translates the New Testament Greek *presbuteros,* from which we have the English words 'presbyter, presbytery and presbyterian(ism)' (in ecclesiology) and 'presbyopia' (long-sightedness). 'Elder,' 'pastor.' and 'bishop' are overlapping, interchangeable terms in the New Testament (Acts 20:17,28; Titus 1:5,7). Elders have responsibility for spiritual leadership and pastoral oversight in the congregation (Acts 11:30; 14:23; 15:4; 21:18). Within the one office of elder there is a distinction of *function only* – between elders who are set apart to labour in the word and doctrine (often employed full-time and customarily known as 'ministers') and those who shepherd the flock in other ways (1 Timothy 5:17).

9. The cessation or continuance of (charismatic) gifts of healing in the church today is irrelevant to the question of anointing with oil in connection with prayer for healing. In either case, the oil is symbolic of what we are praying that God, not man, will do. James 5:14 is not a 'charismatic' issue.
10. Vaughan, p. 118.
11. See Revelation 6:10-11 for an instance of the latter.
12. Allister, p. 37.
13. As above, p. 38.
14. The main question concerns whether *energoumene* is in the passive or the middle voice: i.e., is it passive, as in NIV ('effective') or middle, as in ASV ('in its working') and RSV ('in its effects')? See J. Adamson, pp. 205-210, for a detailed treatment of the exegetical issues involved. Adamson argues persuasively for the middle voice interpretation which, if correct, places the emphasis upon an active, energetic, believing prayer, which is attended by effectiveness in its very exercise. This motif is also represented in AV ('effectual fervent prayer').
15. Manton, p. 465.

Chapter 24
1. The word 'brothers' is an epicene (i.e., genderless) usage of a word normally reserved for males. According to the bogus exegetical arguments of so-called 'biblical feminism', this is 'sexist' language prejudicial to the dignity of women.
2. Calvin, p. 361.
3. 2 Corinthians 13:8; Ephesians 1:13; Colossians 1:5; 1 Timothy 2:4; 2 Timothy 3:7; 2 Thessalonians 2:10-12.
4. F. F. Bruce, *The Acts of the Apostles – the Greek Text with Introduction and Commentary* (Eerdmans, 1970), p. 296.